OFFICERS, NOBLES
AND REVOLUTIONARIES

OFFICERS, NOBLES
AND REVOLUTIONARIES

ESSAYS ON EIGHTEENTH-CENTURY FRANCE

WILLIAM DOYLE

THE HAMBLEDON PRESS
LONDON AND RIO GRANDE

Published by Hambledon Press 1995
102 Gloucester Avenue, London NW1 8HX (UK)
P.O. Box 162, Rio Grande, Ohio 45674 (USA)

ISBN 1 85285 121 X

A description of this book is available from
the British Library and from the Library of Congress

Typeset by York House Typographic Ltd

Printed on acid-free paper and bound in Great
Britain by Cambridge University Press

Contents

Acknowledgements

The essays reprinted below are reproduced by the kind permission of the original publishers

1   *French Historical Studies,* 6 (1970), pp. 415–58.

2   *Past and Present,* 57 (1972), pp. 97–122.

3   *Annales du Midi,* 80 (1968), pp. 65–77.

4   *Sociétés et groupes sociaux en Aquitaine et en Angleterre,* ed. P. Butel (Fédération Historique du Sud-Ouest, 1979), pp. 201–14.

5   *Historical Journal,* 27 (1984), pp. 831–59.

6   *Australian Journal of French Studies,* 29 (1992), pp. 230–40.

7   *Studies on Voltaire and the Eighteenth Century,* 191 (1981), pp. 866–72.

8   *The Impact of the French Revolution on European Consciousness,* eds H.T. Mason and W. Doyle (Alan Sutton, Gloucester, 1989), pp. 1–10.

9   *French Historical Studies,* 16 (1990), pp. 743–48.

10 *Terminer la Révolution,* eds F. Furet et M. Ozouf (Presses universitaires de Grenoble, 1990), pp. 25–41.

11 *Revolution and Counter-Revolution,* ed. E.E. Rice (Basil Blackwell, Oxford 1990), pp. 95–108.

12 Author's copyright.

13 *Proceedings of the Annual Meeting of the Western Society for French History,* 17 (1990), pp. 1–9.

Introduction

The twenty-five years over which this selection of articles and essays were published were ones of intense and lively debate in the history of the French Revolution and its antecedents. When the first was published, the great controversy over the social interpretation of the Revolution begun by Alfred Cobban's inaugural lecture of 1954 was approaching its climax in the English-speaking world, and beginning to find echoes in France, too. The last ones appeared as historians took stock of the controversy and sought to identify new directions for research in the 'post-revisionist' atmosphere engendered by international commemoration of the Revolution's two hundredth anniversary.

Cobban was dead by the time I began to publish, and I never met him; but like most research students in the field in the 1960s I felt obliged to address the challenging agenda which he had set. Although the pieces here on the history of Bordeaux and of the parlements grew out of doctoral work, subsequently published as a monograph,[1] the problems they confronted were ones identified by Cobban, or at least epitomised by his approach. Those who, in the heat of debate, sometimes stigmatised me as a 'Cobbanite' perhaps failed to notice that most of the essays reprinted here rejected the ideas of a historian better at provoking discussion than resolving it. Pitiless in criticising the 'orthodox' left-wing interpretation, Cobban was happy to accept some of the traditional right-wing orthodoxies almost without question. He saw little wrong with the notion that strong, decisive and enlightened monarchy could have saved the *ancien régime*, but that its attempts to do so were frustrated

---

[1] *The Parlement of Bordeaux and the End of the Old Regime, 1771-1790* (London, 1974).

by the selfish obstruction of a benighted and increasingly reactionary nobility. My early researches left me unconvinced by such claims, and, in the essays on the parlements and the alleged 'aristocratic reaction',[2] I set out the grounds for my scepticism. They seem to me worth reprinting because they have broadly stood the test of time. While the interpretation of Terray in the article on the parlements met with prompt and perhaps justifiable criticism for being over-simplistic,[3] the arguments about Maupeou's motivations seem to have won general acceptance, and those about the weakness of the parlements after 1774 at least a suspicious tolerance. A somewhat modified version of them was certainly included, by invitation, in an authoritative international collective survey of the political culture of the *ancien régime* published for the bicentenary.[4] Most scholars also now seem to accept that there was no aristocratic reaction, at least in the political, ideological and social senses. Shortly after this essay appeared, impressive independent research confirmed its suggestions about the alleged social reaction.[5] Its most radical claims, however, concerning the so-called 'feudal' reaction, raised questions so large that they remain unresolved. While the most important recent survey of the peasantry in the Revolution refuses to abandon the notion,[6] the arguments which I advanced have never been frontally tested, and so remain on the table.

The most controversial of all Cobban's suggestions provoked another group of these essays. The idea that the French Revolution was fundamentally the work of a rising, capitalist bourgeoisie was, he argued, a myth. It was, on the contrary, brought about by the frustrations of a declining, non-capitalist bourgeoisie dominated by office-holders. The main evidence for their decline was, he believed, a decline in office prices. But he cited no serious evidence for that contention. Having discovered and used a remarkable Bordeaux source for the price of ennobling offices,[7] I decided to tap it further to explore whether any general decline did take place in that booming commercial city.[8] Finding it did not, I turned to other sources to try to establish a

---

[2] Chapters 1 and 2, pp. 1-48, 49-74.

[3] See J.F. Bosher, 'The French Crisis of 1770', *History*, 57 (1972), p. 19.

[4] 'The Parlements' in K.M. Baker (ed.) *The French Revolution and the Creation of Modern Political Culture*, i, *The Political Culture of the Old Regime* (Oxford, 1987), pp. 157-67.

[5] D.D. Bien, 'La réaction aristocratique avant 1789: l'exemple de l'armée', *Annales, ESC*, 29 (1974), pp. 23-48, 505-34.

[6] P.M. Jones, *The Peasantry in the French Revolution* (Cambridge, 1988), pp. 42-59.

[7] Chapter 3, pp. 75-86.

[8] Chapter 4, pp. 87-104.

general picture on a kingdom-wide scale.[9] The result offered no support for the idea of a declining bourgeoisie; but the enquiry revealed how little was known about venality of office in general in the eighteenth century. This has been the object of most of my researches since 1980, and will be the subject of a monograph to appear shortly after this collection.[10] A preliminary report on one aspect of venality, meanwhile, explores how contemporaries thought about this central institution of pre-revolutionary French life.[11]

A major consequence of the great debate, whose longer-term significance I attempted to take brief stock of in 1989, was a shift of historical attention away from the social to the intellectual and cultural significance of the Revolution.[12] Some prominent intellectuals of the age make their appearance here. Whilst I have analysed the career of Dupaty at much greater length elsewhere,[13] a brief conference paper views him as an exemplar of certain general conditions of intellectual life which have subsequently been explored in greater depth.[14] Mounier and Paine, meanwhile, were much more than exemplars. At certain moments both stood at the very centre of the tumultuous events of the Revolution; but, because sooner (in Mounier's case) or later (in Paine's) they were left behind by the movement they had once promoted with such enthusiasm, they have often been condemned as impractical moderates in extreme times. Here I argue that Mounier was less impractical,[15] and Paine less moderate than is usually thought.[16] What they both tried to be was consistent, but anybody attempting to remain true to a fixed set of ideals during the French Revolution was doomed to disappointment. So far from being unitary and pre-ordained in its course, two essays argue that it developed in ways quite unpredictable from the start, even if explicable enough with hindsight.[17] Another goes on to argue that the

[9] Chapter 5, pp. 105-40.
[10] *Venality: The Sale of Offices in Eighteenth-Century France* (forthcoming from Oxford University Press).
[11] Chapter 6, pp. 141-54.
[12] Chapter 9, pp. 173-8.
[13] 'Dupaty (1744-1788): A Career in the Late Enlightenment', *Studies on Voltaire and the Eighteenth Century*, 230 (1985), pp. 1-125. While technically an article, a study the length of a short book would unbalance the collection if included here.
[14] See especially S. Maza, *Private Lives and Public Affairs: The Causes Célèbres of Pre-Revolutionary France* (Berkeley and Los Angeles, 1993), esp. ch. 5.
[15] Chapter 10, pp. 179-96.
[16] Chapter 12, pp. 209-20.
[17] Chapters 8, pp. 163-72; and 11, pp. 197-208.

attempts of contemporaries to formulate explanations of why it occurred in the first place, if only to prevent recurrences, were perhaps not
as misguided as some later historians have tended to think.[18] It is in this
emphasis on the contingent and the accidental in the Revolution, rather
than in any sympathy with his views on what caused it, that I come closest
to Cobban; and stand detached from more recent interpreters, whose
reliance on culture as an explanatory key risks a determinism no more
flexible than that of older versions consigned to oblivion by the debates
to which most of these pieces have been contributions.

One justification for republishing some of these pieces is that they
appeared in relatively inaccessible places, or in French, or both. Two of
them now appear in English for the first time; and all passages originally
quoted in French have been translated. I have also taken the opportunity of resetting to correct grosser errors and expunge or amend the
occasional point or argument which no longer seems tenable. Inevitably
there will be some. But I should not think of reprinting these pieces at all
if I thought that many of their arguments had been disproved or
demolished.

Bath

February 1994

---

[18] Chapter 13, pp. 221-32.

Illustrations

Abbreviations

AD	Archives Departementales
AM	Archives Municipales
AN	Archives Nationales
BM	Bibliothèque Municipale
BN	Bibliothèque Nationale

1

The Parlements of France and the Breakdown of the Old Regime, 1771-88

Of all the commonplaces in the history of the French eighteenth century, few seem more self-evident than that the recall of the parlements in 1774 was a mistake. It seems clear that by reinstating the main organs of opposition to its will the government condemned itself to the financial crisis which precipitated the Revolution.

Historians have shown a remarkable degree of unanimity on this question. French historians of the old regime and the Revolution, who usually interpret the centuries preceding the Revolution as a struggle between monarchy and aristocracy, see the conflict with the parlements in the eighteenth century as the last stage in this struggle and the restoration of 1774 as the monarchy's final and fatal mistake.[1] The most notable recent history of the Revolution in English also condemns the restoration,[2] and so does the latest historian of the parlement of Paris itself.[3] The corollary of this view is, of course, that the reform of the parlements effected by Chancellor Maupeou in 1771 was wise, timely and potentially beneficial.

[1] On the old regime, see for example, Marcel Marion, *Dictionnaire des institutions de la France aux XVIIe et XVIIIe siècles* (Paris, 1923), p. 424; idem, *Histoire financière de la France depuis 1715* (Paris, 1914-28), i, p. 281; Hubert Méthivier, *Le siècle de Louis XV* (Paris, 1966), p. 126; and even Jules Flammermont, *Le Chancelier Maupeou et les parlements* (Paris, 1883), p. 592. Flammermont is the only substantial and serious work at present existing on the Maupeou coup as a whole. Jean Egret's *Louis XV et l'opposition parlementaire, 1715-1774* (Paris, 1970) appeared too late to be consulted in the writing of this essay. Among revolutionary historians, see Albert Mathiez, *La Révolution française* (Paris, 1922), pp. 1, 7; Georges Lefebvre, *The Coming of the French Revolution* (New York, 1957), p. 17.

[2] M.J. Sydenham, *The French Revolution* (London, 1965), p. 18.

[3] J.H. Shennan, *The Parlement of Paris* (London, 1968), p. 319.

The clearest expression in English of the whole interpretation, however, probably came from the late Alfred Cobban, whose views on this matter, at least, were completely orthodox.[4] For Cobban the parlements were 'the chief obstacles in the path of reform',[5] and 'the bitterest enemies of the monarchy'.[6] To expect them to concur in reform was hopeless.[7] So their recall in 1774 had been a mistake,[8] and accordingly[8] Maupeou had been right to suppress them in 1771. Maupeou, for Cobban, was the 'last of the great ministers of the Bourbon dynasty'.[9] If the old regime had a last chance, it was provided by Maupeou in 1771, only to be thrown away, with fatal results, in 1774. 'There was only one way out of the impasse, and that was the way of Maupeou.'[10]

This is the standard view, and it has seldom been critically examined. Yet close scrutiny of the role of the parlements between 1771 and 1787 shows that it is not the only possible interpretation. Such an inquiry must consider four problems. First, was Maupeou the clear-sighted and single-minded reformer that most historians portray? Secondly, what was the significance of his reforms? Thirdly, could he or his system have survived? Fourthly, how far did the restoration of 1774 lead to renewed obstruction of the government's policies? In the light of the conclusions on these matters, it should be possible, finally, to reassess the significance of the role of the parlements in the events leading to the collapse of the old regime.

There is very little evidence that Maupeou had any long-laid plans to reform the parlements when he left the parlement of Paris to become chancellor in 1768. Historians favourable to Maupeou infer the existence of such projects almost entirely from the memoirs of Charles-François Lebrun, Maupeou's secretary and later consul of the Republic.[11] Lebrun speaks of plans for sweeping judicial reforms that he drew

[4] See A. Cobban, *A History of Modern France* (London, 1957), i, passim; idem, 'The *Parlements* of France in the Eighteenth Century', *History*, 35 (1950), reprinted in *Aspects of the French Revolution* (London, 1968). All references are to the latter edition.

[5] Cobban, *History of Modern France*, i, p. 101.

[6] Ibid., p. 115.

[7] Ibid., p. 126.

[8] Ibid., p. 101.

[9] Ibid., p. 97.

[10] Ibid., p. 128.

[11] E.g., Pierre Gaxotte, *Le siècle de Louis XV* (Paris, 1933); Méthivier, *Siècle de Louis XV*; François Piétri, *La réforme de l'état au XVIIIe siècle* (Paris, 1935); and Jules de Maupeou, *Le Chancelier Maupeou* (Paris, 1942).

up and laid before Maupeou when he became chancellor. But, on Lebrun's own testimony, the chancellor dismissed them as both unwise and impracticable.[12] In the vindication of himself that Maupeou sent to Louis XVI in 1788, long after his disgrace, he went so far as to deny that he had any other ambition at this stage than to live at peace with the magistracy.[13] Certainly the months after this appointment saw him clearly striving, not without success, to conciliate and appease the parlements. He flattered the parlement of Paris and, as a result, was able in 1770 to push through a number of drastic financial measures with minimal opposition. He yielded to the parlement of Toulouse in a dispute over recruitment.[14] Above all, he attempted to end the most bitter and persistent *parlementaire* conflict of the decade, the quarrel between the parlement of Rennes and the duc d'Aiguillon, by dissolving the interim court at Rennes, the so-called *bailliage d'Aiguillon*, and recalling the old parlement from a two-year exile.[15] It was not Maupeou's fault that the king, on personal grounds, refused to reinstate the leaders of the previous disobedience; yet it was this issue which provoked a renewal of the d'Aiguillon quarrel, and that renewal which led to the confrontation of 1770.[16] When a confrontation came, therefore, it seems to have been in spite of Maupeou's initial efforts and not because of them. There was nothing new, or original, or radical, in his approach to the chancellorship. He simply changed one or two details of policy and certainly gave no sign of wishing to change the whole judicial system.

If, however, in the years 1768-70 Maupeou showed no sign of interest in reforms, much less a central preoccupation with them, he showed every sign of the most boundless personal ambition. All contemporaries agreed on this. Maupeou wanted to be not merely the chancellor, but the principal minister. To attain this he had to overthrow the duc de Choiseul; and all he did, from the moment of his accession to power, seems to have been directed toward this end.

---

[12] Flammermont, *Maupeou*, p. 38. A translation of the relevant passages of Lebrun's rare memoirs is printed in John Rothney (ed.), *The Brittany Affair and the Crisis of the Ancien Régime* (New York, 1969), pp. 240-58.

[13] See Maupeou's *Mémoire au roi*, printed at the end of Flammermont, *Maupeou*, pp. 599-635, esp. pp. 600-1 and 620.

[14] Flammermont *Maupeou*, pp. 35, 50.

[15] Ibid., ch. 2, passim; Marcel Marion, *La Bretagne et le duc d'Aiguillon, 1753-70* (Paris, 1898), ch. 16; and Barthélemy Pocquet, *Le duc d'Aiguillon et La Chalotais* (Paris, 1900-1), iii, chs 10 and 11.

[16] Flammermont, *Maupeou*, p. 65; Pocquet, *Duc d'Aiguillon*, iii, p. 65.

Ministers attacked their colleagues by attacking their policies, and the appointment of the abbé Terray as comptroller-general of finances in 1769 resulted from a direct confrontation between Maupeou and Choiseul over the state of the finances. The chancellor attacked the administration of Maynon d'Invau, Choiseul's nominee, with such force that the king was prevailed upon to dismiss him. Choiseul adroitly told the king that he could think of no replacement equal to Maupeou himself, since he knew so much about financial matters. This move, however, only left the way open for Maupeou to propose his own candidate – Terray, a clerical counsellor at the parlement of Paris – whom the king duly appointed.[17] From then on Maupeou had an ally on the king's council. He exploited this situation so skilfully that by the end of 1770 he had driven Choiseul and his cousin and ally, the duc de Praslin, from the council and captured it for himself.

Three issues dominated public life in 1770: Terray's partial bankruptcy; the d'Aiguillon case; and the Falklands Islands crisis. It was the latter which most preoccupied Choiseul in his dual capacity as secretary of state for foreign affairs and war. He bent most of his energies throughout the summer toward encouraging the Spaniards to resist the British, which would give France a pretext for renewing the colonial conflict, ended so ignominiously in 1763. By the autumn of 1770 the crisis was ripening nicely. However, in order to renew the war, Choiseul needed money and the prospect of more, and from this point of view the crisis could hardly have been more ill-timed. Terray had spent much of the year, for his part, in operating what amounted to a partial bankruptcy by slashing the interest rates on government debts.[18] The ordinary revenues were not adequate to cover the costs of the preparations involved even in the threat of war, and there were clashes between Choiseul and Terray on the council over the provision of extraordinary funds.[19] These clashes grew more frequent and more acrimonious, and by December were visibly annoying the king. Louis' own inclinations were against war, and Choiseul therefore took care to portray his preparations as defensive. But when Terray on 6 December declared the treasury empty, the announcement could not fail to strengthen the king's inclinations toward peace.

[17] Flammermont, *Maupeou*, pp. 38-42.
[18] Marion, *Histoire financière*, i, pp. 251-7.
[19] Flammermont, *Maupeou*, pp. 164-5, passim.

What settled matters, however, was the question of the parlements. Maupeou's policy of conciliating the parlement of Rennes was not a success. This parlement, angered at the royal refusal (for which the king himself was personally responsible) to reinstate certain leading members along with their colleagues in 1768, thought it saw the hand of d'Aiguillon still at work in the government's policies and consequently began proceedings against him. D'Aiguillon reacted by demanding that, to settle the affair once and for all, his case be examined by the parlement of Paris sitting as the court of peers; and the government eventually agreed. The trial, which the king attended personally at Versailles, created a great stir but, as the investigations probed more and more deeply into the workings of the government the latter became alarmed. At length it decided to bring the proceedings to a halt. In a *lit de justice* on 27 June 1770, the king quashed the case and declared d'Aiguillon blameless.

This flouting of judicial procedures predictably aroused a storm of protestations and remonstrances from the parlement, which suspended d'Aiguillon's peerage rights pending resumption of the case. When the king quashed this move, protests spread to the provincial parlements, which as usual were more unbridled in their language than the parlement of Paris. Reprisals followed against several provincial magistrates and, in another *lit de justice* on 2 September, the king confiscated all pieces relating to the d'Aiguillon affair and imposed a rule of silence regarding it. The beginning of the judicial vacation a few days later allowed time only for a formal protest, after which matters remained suspended until the end of November.

'Though it does not appear publicly', wrote the British ambassador on August 22, 'one may look upon the present situation of things as a secret struggle between the new party and the duc de Choiseul'.[20] Maupeou, in fact, by the way in which he was able as chancellor to conduct the d'Aiguillon case, was trying to effect what Linguet called the *coup de deux*.[21] Anything to the discredit of the government that came out in the case must harm Choiseul, the leading minister during d'Aiguillon's time in Brittany. Above all, a confrontation with the parlements would ruin Choiseul's hopes of an easy passage for war taxation. On the other hand,

[20] Quoted ibid., p. 154 n.1.

[21] [Simon Nicolas Henri Linguet], *Aiguilloniana ou anecdotes utiles pour l'histoire de France au dix-huitième siècle depuis l'année 1770* (London, 1777), pp. 11-14; see too J. Cruppi, *Un avocat-journaliste au XVIIIe siècle: Linguet* (Paris, 1895), pp. 228-30. Linguet was one of d'Aiguillon's lawyers.

the discredit of being vindicated by authority and not by a judicial acquittal would also spoil the ministerial ambitions of d'Aiguillon, favourite of Madame Du Barry. The well-known enmity between the two dukes prevented them from combining against Maupeou, and Choiseul took care not to involve himself in the affair while letting it take its course. The result was that by September it was beyond his capacity to influence matters anyway, and he sat helplessly by while Maupeou provoked the hostility of the only body which could ruin his foreign policy.

Throughout the autumn rumours abounded that Maupeou was about to attack the parlement before it attacked him; and this is what happened. The famous edict of November 1770 attacked the parlement in terms which it could never accept.[22] It was offensive not so much in its three articles as in the tone of its preamble, which sweepingly condemned a whole range of manoeuvres used by various parlements at various times to obstruct the government.

'L'édit en question', wrote Miromesnil, first president of the parlement of Rouen, 'paroit avoir été fait, moins pour établir une règle de discipline exacte et raisonnée, que pour faire passer les imputations flétrissantes contenuës dans la préambule'.[23] ['The edict in question . . . seems to have been intended less to establish an exact and reasoned rule of discipline, than to establish the insulting imputations contained in the preamble'.]

Strikes and suspensions of service, mass resignations and all links and co-operation between courts – the famous *théorie des classes* – were condemned in blunt terms; so were any *parlementaire* pretensions to be, in any sense, the representatives of the nation or the interpreters of the royal will. The first article of the edict forbade all co-operation between parlements, even down to the use of terms which implied the legality of such co-operation. The second forbade all judicial strikes and mass resignations, although it was the parlement of Rennes, not of Paris, which had been guilty of these offences most recently. The third article, which, while reaffirming the right of remonstrance attempted to define the point where legitimate resistance ended, also contained nothing with which the parlement could take real issue. But taken as a whole, the edict constituted a sweeping and, in the parlement's view, unjust attack on its

---

[22] The text is in Flammermont, *Maupeou*, pp. 116-20.

[23] Miromesnil to Bertin, 4 Feb. 1771, in Pierre Le Verdier, *Correspondance politique et administrative de Miromesnil (1767-1771)* (Rouen, Paris, 1903), v, p. 276.

public role over several decades. The insult was only aggravated when it was forcibly registered, after brutal language from Maupeou, at a *lit de justice* only four days after it had been laid before the court, when it normally took weeks to reach such extremes. The magistrates were provoked, as they were meant to be. They called a judicial strike; and this had the effect of setting the king in a fury against them.

In the first week of December 1770, everything came at once to a head. Terray had declared the treasury unable to finance Choiseul's military preparations only the day before the king confronted the recalcitrant parlement in his *lit de justice*. He did not need to add that the parlement in its current mood was unlikely to give a quiet reception to the new loans and tax increases that any war would necessitate. Louis wanted peace and no trouble from the parlements; the answer was clear. Maupeou underlined the lesson by suggesting to the king that Choiseul was encouraging the parlement of Paris in its resistance, and the suggestion did not need to be true to appear probable.[24] When the parlement refused to abandon its strike after being formally enjoined to do so, he put the issue with perfect clarity by offering his resignation rather than continue to serve with Choiseul.[25] It was this which decided Louis, and on 24 December Choiseul and Praslin were dismissed.

It has, of course, always been clear that the fall of the Choiseuls and Maupeou's attack on the parlement in December 1770 were connected; but it has usually been assumed that the removal of Choiseul was a necessary preliminary for attacking the parlement in earnest.[26] However, the evidence does not necessarily point this way, as some contemporaries noticed. Baron de Besenval observed that: 'Attaquer le parlement, c'étoit . . . attaquer M. de Choiseul qui ne pouvoit manquer d'embrasser sa défense, et par là donner matière à le noircir aux yeux du roi, fatigué de l'éternelle résistance de cette compagnie . . .'.[27] ['To attack the parlement was to . . . attack M. de Choiseul, who could not fail to take up its defence, and thereby give grounds to be blackened in the eyes of a king tired of the eternal resistance of this company . . .']

[24] Flammermont, *Maupeou*, pp. 189-90 and 196, discusses and dismisses the truth of this charge.

[25] Ibid., p. 192.

[26] See, e.g., John Lough, *An Introduction to Eighteenth-Century France* (London, 1960), p. 187.

[27] *Mémoires de M. le Baron de Besenval* (Paris, 1805), ii, p. 178. Rothney, in *The Brittany Affair*, pp. 229-30, impugns the authenticity and reliability of Besenval as a source. Undoubtedly he has a point. Nevertheless the author of these memoirs, whoever he was, shared the view here expressed with many contemporaries; and Lebrun's testimony, held up by Rothney in contrast, in no way contradicts it on this point. My argument is intended to show that this interpretation was a tenable one.

On 16 December the British ambassador noted: 'The struggle between the king and his parlement at this particular conjuncture may be considered as a contest for the ascendancy in the cabinet without which things might not have been carried such lengths.'[28] It seems that far from attacking Choiseul in order to attack the parlement, Maupeou attacked the parlement in order to attack Choiseul.

It may be, of course, that by this stage he had become a convert to reform. Having captured the council, at last he would be free to throw off the veil. The fact is, however, that after the fall of Choiseul the crisis seemed to lose much of its urgency. The government no longer reacted promptly to the moves of the parlement. Only four days had passed between the presentation of the November edict and its forcible registration. Up to the time of the *lettres de jussion* of 20 December, which formally ordered them back to work, the king was prompt as well as firm in rejecting the defiant *arrêtés* of the striking magistrates. Yet, despite an immediate refusal to obey, Maupeou now waited two weeks before renewing the royal orders.[29] Moreover, when they came, they were in a tone quite different from the blunt strictures of the November edict. It is well attested, finally, that the prince de Condé was acting as unofficial mediator between the government and the parlement.[30] By all these means the magistrates were induced to believe that a gesture of goodwill would lead to a suitable modification of the November edict, and on 7 January they actually called off their strike and resumed their service. All this seems to indicate that, having eliminated Choiseul, Maupeou was now seeking to withdraw from the extreme position he had adopted and settle the quarrel with some compromise involving perhaps a modification of the edict. The parlement clearly thought so. This would indicate that on the chancellor's part no deep commitment to reform had yet developed.[31]

---

[28] Quoted in Flammermont, *Maupeou*, p. 151. Flammermont shared this important opinion, although he did not give it the emphasis it deserves. Robert Villers, '*L'organisation du parlement de Paris et des conseils supérieurs d'après la réforme de Maupeou* (Paris, 1937), pp. 31 and 46-49, takes the same view. See too Jacob Nicolas Moreau, *Mes souvenirs* (Paris, 1898-1901), i, p. 237, for a contemporary of the same opinion.

[29] Admittedly it was the Christmas holiday, but clearly Maupeou was using the coincidence to allow tempers to cool.

[30] Besenval, *Mémoires*, ii, pp. 185-6; Moreau, *Souvenirs*, i, pp. 244-5; Flammermont, *Maupeou*, pp. 196-7.

[31] It is only fair to note that Flammermont does not believe that Maupeou was sincere in this (*Maupeou*, p. 197). The negotiations were sponsored by his colleagues, notably Terray. This still indicates, however, that the government as a whole was not committed to reform.

In the event, the parlement's gesture led nowhere. The government declared bluntly that it would not alter the November edict; in reaction the magistrates resumed their strike. Again, it was not out of principle but out of conciliar tactics that Maupeou had acted. He seems to have felt that if a quarrel that he had fanned were to be resolved by Condé, the prince would soon become another Choiseul.[32] He had to stay firm and browbeat the magistrates into some concession. Ministerial success with the parlements meant procuring for Louis XV a quiet life; whether by authority or conciliation did not matter greatly. Condé had pre-empted conciliation. To outmanoeuvre him Maupeou had to stick to authority, and for the moment he was able to win the exasperated king to this course. Thus the sides took up their positions. The parlement ignored repeated orders to resume work; Maupeou had therefore to carry out his threats or admit failure. And so he was driven to the famous expedient of sending soldiers to wake each magistrate in the small hours of 20 January and demand by a simple answer of yes or no whether they would resume their service. Thirty-five refused to reply directly; fifty agreed, though conditionally, to resume; seventy refused.[33] But when the refusers were exiled the next night, the attitude of the rest hardened. Maupeou had hoped to retain a rump to carry on business; but within a week there was near unanimity among them not to resume. Again, Maupeou had no real alternative; he invoked the penalties of the November edict; he deprived all the magistrates of their offices; and dispatched them to remote exiles all over France.

This was how the Maupeou reform began. Increasingly committed despite himself to firm policies, repeatedly he miscalculated the resistance he would meet, and repeatedly was forced to ever greater extremes to overcome it. After the incident of the exiles there was no turning back. Since he could induce no magistrates to remain, and since everyday judicial business had to go on, he had to draft in new magistrates. Since most members of other sovereign courts refused to help, justice had to be administered until April 1771 by an *ad hoc* court made up of councillors of state. This left nobody to staff the council of state itself, and so its own, mainly judicial, business came to a standstill. After January 1771, therefore, the rebuilding of the judicial structure was unavoidable.

---

[32] Flammermont, *Maupeou*, p. 199.
[33] Ibid., p. 209.

Yet the new order was not instituted until April. This delay provides the best evidence that Maupeou had not planned any reform in advance. If he had, presumably he would have imposed it at once or as soon as he had gathered personnel for the reformed order. Either course indicates a lack of preparation. His contemporaries saw this too. The *procureur* Régnaut, who kept a journal of the events, believed that Maupeou was proceeding 'from day to day', with no preconceived plan, and that he was forced to extreme measures by the strength of the resistance.[34] Jacob-Nicolas Moreau, who was close to the centre of power throughout this period, declared that Maupeou 'n'avait pas compté que les choses iraient aussi loin, son plan n'était point fait; il espéra d'abord diviser la compagnie; il se crut assuré, pendant le mois de janvier et celui de février, de conserver une partie des anciens membres du Parlement. Lorsqu'il dut renoncer à cette espérance il avoit tiré l'épée.'[35] ['had not calculated that things would go so far, he had no plan; he hoped at first to divide the company; he felt sure, during the month of January and that of February, of retaining part of the old membership of the Parlement. When forced to give up this hope, he drew the sword.'] Besenval, looking back at the renewal of its strike by the parlement, declared that: 'Par cette démarche les choses en étoient venuës à un point, qu'il falloit un part décisif. L'incertitude et la lenteur de la cour à prendre ce parti, démontrèrent, de reste, qu'elle s'étoit engagé légère-ment, et qu'en commençant cette grande affaire, on n'avoit pas prévu où elle pouvoit aller, ni les déterminations les plus convenables dans les différens cas . . .'[36] ['By this step matters reached a point where decisive action was necessary. The court's uncertainty and slowness in making a move showed, in any case, that it had committed itself thoughtlessly, and that in starting this great affair it had not foreseen where it would lead, or what should best be done in different cases . . .'] Above all, Maupeou himself admitted in his vindication that: 'La marche lente et indécise en apparence des premières opérations dut démontrer au public et aux magistrats, qu'il n'y avait point eu de plan irrévocablement arrêté . . .'[37] ['The slow and apparently irresolute pace of the first operations

---

[34] Cited in Félix Rocquain, *L'esprit révolutionnaire avant la Révolution, 1715-1789* (Paris, 1878), p. 297 n. 1; also Villers, *Parlement de Paris*, p. 49. Lebrun also emphasised the escalation of the affair: Rothney, *Brittany Affair*, pp. 272-4.

[35] J. N. Moreau, *Souvenirs*, i, p. 245. Moreau, later Historiographer Royal, was a member of the Dauphin's household and played a major part in the Maupeou reforms in Provence.

[36] Besenval, *Mémoires*, ii, p. 186.

[37] Flammermont, *Maupeou*, pp. 626-7.

should have shown to the public and to the magistrates, that there had been no plan irrevocably decided on . . . ']

This implies, of course, that there *was* a plan but that he was hoping not to have to implement it. We may wonder. That the reforms which did take place followed the ideas of Lebrun only shows that Maupeou now found them useful, not that he had been convinced by Lebrun's suggestions before 1771. When Maupeou also admitted that later, 'il fallait agir pour ne pas donner plus longtemps le spectacle d'une administration . . . qui n'avait su ni prévenir le mal ni préparer le remède',[38] ['it was necessary to act so as no longer to provide the spectacle of an administration . . . which had not known how to prevent the malady or to prepare the remedy,'] it seems likely that it was not so much an impression that he wished to keep from the public as the truth.

Only the discovery of new sources, and sources of a more reliable sort than those already known, may prove conclusively whether Maupeou was a single-minded reformer with cunningly laid plans, or whether he became a reformer despite himself and was forced into strong action through miscalculating the vigour of the parlement's reactions. What is certain is that we cannot discover what was intended to happen merely by arguing from what did happen. To be sure, the answers resulting from this process, though logically invalid, may be coincidentally true. However, there is enough evidence both in the pattern of events and the opinions of contemporaries to suggest that the conventional picture of Maupeou on the eve of his reforms is, to say the least, distorted. This evidence also suggests that the reforms of Maupeou came about, not through clear vision and fixity of purpose on the chancellor's part, but because he lost control of a situation that he himself had pushed to crisis in the first place, largely to gratify his own ambition and to overthrow Choiseul. As he himself admitted to Louis XVI, 'La révolution de 1771 ne fut que l'ouvrage de la nécessité, mais d'une nécessité imprévu . . .'[39] ['The revolution of 1771 was no more than the work of necessity, but unforeseen necessity . . .']

It was inevitable that Maupeou's reforms should extend to the whole of France. Cardinal de Bernis, who had for some time handled the affairs of the parlements for the government in the 1750s, confided prophetically to his memoirs that: 'On ne peut exiler ni suppléer le parlement de

---

[38] Ibid., p. 627.
[39] Ibid., p. 632.

Paris sans que les autres parlements du royaume prennent fait et cause pour lui; il faudrait donc se résoudre à les supprimer tous à la fois . . .'[40] ['You cannot exile or replace the parlement of Paris without the other parlements of the kingdom supporting them to the hilt, so you would have to resolve to abolish them all at the same time . . . '] Maupeou, looking back, declared that: 'Après la révolution qu'avait subie le parlement de Paris, il était impossible que les parlements de province ne fussent pas soumis à la même opération.'[41] ['After the revolution which the parlement of Paris had undergone, it was impossible that the provincial parlements should not undergo the same operation.']

Just as they had done in August and September 1770, the provincial and other sovereign courts protested in vehement language at the measures taken against the Paris parlement. The *cour des aides* of Paris and the parlement of Rouen saw no answer to governmental power but the estates-general, and they called for it in widely circulated remonstrances.[42] Nearly all the provincial parlements sent remonstrances condemning what had happened, and they continued to renew their protests as Maupeou's measures moved steadily forward throughout the spring. They felt certain that he would have to act against them eventually; and indeed between August and November, one by one all the provincial parlements were dissolved and remodelled. They suffered not because they had quarrelled directly with the government, but because they took the side of Paris in its quarrel. As President de Brosses of Dijon put it: 'Quelles sont les causes de la persécution que nous éprouvons? Des faits auxquels nous n'avons aucune espèce de part: une intrigue de Cour pour chasser un ministre, la vengeance qu'on vouloit prendre contre le Parlement de Paris. Pour donner à ceci d'autres apparences et quelque espèce de suite, on nous enveloppe dans cette étrange révolution . . . '.[43] ['What are the causes of the persecution we are suffering? Matters in which we have no part: a court intrigue to drive out a minister, and a desire to be revenged on the Parlement of Paris. To give all this a different aspect and some consequence, we are engulfed in this strange revolution . . . ']

---

[40] Frédéric Masson (ed.), *Mémoires et lettres de François Joachim de Pierre, cardinal de Bernis (1715-1758)* (Paris, 1878), i, p. 322. These memoirs were dictated late in the 1760s.

[41] Flammermont, *Maupeou*, p. 630.

[42] Ibid., pp. 255, 268-71.

[43] Quoted in Théophile Foisset, *Le président de Brosses: histoire des lettres et des parlements au XVIIIe siècle* (Paris, 1842), pp. 319-20. De Brosses to Marquise de Damas d'Antigny, autumn 1771.

The parlements were not abolished; most were simply remodelled.[44] Only Rouen, Douai and Metz suffered the extreme fate; the first on account of its previous militancy, the others on account of their small importance as parlements. In addition, several *tribunaux d'exception* such as the *cour des aides* of Paris, the *châtelet*, the *grand conseil* and the *cour des comptes* of Aix were abolished and not replaced. But when Maupeou suggested in April 1771 that all the parlements be abolished and replaced with *conseils supérieurs*, the king rejected the idea because of the despotic impression it would create.[45] For similar reasons, the powers of the remodelled parlements were not substantially diminished either; they remained sovereign courts of justice and they retained the right, guaranteed in the edict of November 1770, to remonstrate with the king before registering the measures that he sent to them. It was on this right that the parlements had built their whole political importance in the eighteenth century.

Maupeou could afford to maintain the trappings of the old institutions because he effectively emasculated them in other ways. The parlement of Paris, for instance, had its judicial competence diminished from below by the establishment of six *conseils supérieurs* in its area of jurisdiction.[46] These bodies were not set up all over the kingdom, nor did they replace parlements except at Rouen and Douai. In the jurisdiction of Paris, however, new courts were established at Arras, Blois, Châlons, Clermont-Ferrand, Lyons and Poitiers.[47] Their powers were to judge in the last resort all civil and criminal cases emanating from their immediate areas, except for cases concerning the peerage and certain other matters; there would in the future be no appeal from them to the parlement of Paris. On the other hand, these new courts had no political role. They registered laws, as all courts in the judicial hierarchy did, but they could neither remonstrate nor delay registration. These powers remained the monopoly of the parlement of Paris within its jurisdiction.[48] The overall result of these dispositions was that the

---

[44] Some authoritative historians appear to believe that they were abolished, e.g. Robert R. Palmer, *The Age of the Democratic Revolution* (Princeton, 1959), i, pp. 97.

[45] Flammermont, *Maupeou*, p. 437.

[46] Villers, *Parlement de Paris*, passim.

[47] The powers of the parlement of Toulouse were diminished by the establishment of a *conseil supérieur* at Nîmes, and the old *ressort* of Rouen was divided between two such councils at Rouen and Bayeux.

[48] Edict of 23 Feb., 1771. François-André Isambert et al., *Recueil générale des anciennes lois françaises* (Paris, 1822-33), xxii, pp. 512-15. Similar provisions governed the new courts at Rouen, Douai, Bayeux and Nîmes.

judicial competence of the parlement was confined to the area immediately surrounding the capital, and this obviously had the effect of
diminishing the influence it could exert. Nevertheless, the remodelled
provincial parlements, except that of Toulouse, continued to enjoy all
the powers and attributions of their predecessors without diminution.

A more serious change was that of personnel; but even here the break
was far from complete. Maupeou knew that the position of his reforms
would be stronger if he could persuade some of the old magistrates to
support them by co-operation in them. It would divide his enemies. In
Paris, however, he had little success in this direction. The *parlement
Maupeou*, when it was set up in April 1771, contained no members of the
old court. It was made up of ex-members of the *grand conseil* and the *cour
des aides* – both of which Maupeou now suppressed – and an assortment
of government clients from the provincial and subordinate magistracy.
Protracted negotiations had failed to persuade the members of the *grand
conseil* to allow themselves to be transformed at one blow into the
parlement.[49] Yet such drastic steps seemed necessary in order to release
enough magistrates of sufficient competence to staff the new courts. At
Aix-en-Provence, for instance, the parlement was suppressed and its old
rival, the *cour des comptes*, merely took its place with the title of
parlement.[50] All the new parlements had about half the number of
magistrates of the old. At Besançon, where the parlement had been torn
for a decade between two factions, the dominant faction was simply
ejected and what remained constituted as the new court.[51] At Rouen,
only two ex-magistrates joined the new *conseil supérieur*, and it had to be
recruited from lower jurisdictions.[52] However, at Grenoble, Dijon and
Toulouse significant numbers of the old magistracy were persuaded to
remain;[53] and at Douai and Bordeaux the new courts were made up
almost entirely of the old.[54] At Pau, Nancy, Perpignan and Colmar there

[49] Flammermont, *Maupeou*, p. 347.
[50] Moreau, *Souvenirs*, i, chs 14, 15, gives a detailed and first-hand account of the negotiations
leading to this result.
[51] Flammermont, *Maupeou*, pp. 439-42.
[52] P.A. Floquet, *Histoire du parlement de Normandie* (Rouen, 1840-43), vi, p. 672.
[53] Jean Egret, *Le parlement de Dauphiné et les affaires publiques dans la deuxième moitié du XVIIIe
siècle* (Paris, Grenoble, 1942), i, pp. 289-92, for Grenoble; Foisset, *Président de Brosses*, p. 340,
and Flammermont, *Maupeou*, p. 473, for Dijon; Geneviève Crébassol, 'Le parlement Maupeou
à Toulouse, 1771-1775' (unpublished *mémoire*, Toulouse 1949), for Toulouse. I am grateful to
Professor Jacques Godechot of the University of Toulouse for lending me a copy of this last
work.
[54] G.M.L. Pillot, *Histoire du parlement de Flandres* (Paris, 1849), i, pp. 327-9, for Douai; C.B.F.
Boscheron des Portes, *Histoire du parlement de Bordeaux* (Bordeaux, 1878), ii, pp. 315-21, for
Bordeaux.

was no need even to suppress and recreate the old courts; their terms of service were merely amended.[55] Nevertheless, for all the old magistracy consenting, more or less willingly, to serve under the new order, enough newcomers were brought in to make the magistracy a very different body from what it was before its reformation. The newcomers owed their position to the new order, and for that reason were unlikely to act to its prejudice. The old magistrates who remained – the *restants* or *remanants* as they were known – had equally burnt their boats. Any breakdown in the new order would surely bring their rancorous colleagues back from exile in no kind mood. All Maupeou's magistrates, therefore, whatever their background, had every interest in making his system work and very little in disrupting it.

Besides, the government now had a final sanction that it had not had before. Magistrates were no longer irremovable. This was the corollary of the most radical part of the Maupeou reforms – the abolition of venality.[56] This step was first announced in the edict of February 1771, which created the *conseils supérieurs*, and it formed part of all subsequent reforms. 'La vénalité', declared Maupeou on 23 February, 'introduite par la nécessité des circonstances, semble avilir le ministère le plus auguste en faisant acheter le droit de l'exercer'.[57] ['Venality, introduced by the necessity of circumstances, seems to debase the most august functions in making the right to exercise them purchasable.']

This made, as it was meant to, a good impression on those who believed genuinely in reforms. However, the real point was, as Maupeou wrote in his defence in 1774, that venality 'est devenue une chaîne qui lie le souverain et un retranchement contre sa puissance'.[58] ['has become a chain binding the sovereign and a constraint on his power'.] Under the new order the upper magistracy remained to an extent self-recruiting, but it was not possible to buy offices. Courts chose a shortlist of three worthy candidates for vacancies, from which the king made the final choice. And since office in the parlements had thereby ceased to be property, heredity disappeared, too. There are grounds for thinking that the government did not expect this to make much difference in practice, since office in the new courts still conveyed nobility, and this

---

[55] Flammermont, *Maupeou*, pp. 477-8. There were *conseils souverains*, half-parlements, at Perpignan and Colmar.

[56] Even then, of course, the reform only applied to the upper magistracy. Lower offices remained venal.

[57] Quoted in Flammermont, *Maupeou*, p. 275.

[58] *Mémoire destiné à être lu au conseil*, printed in ibid., pp. 635-46.

nobility was to be transmissible after three successive generations in a court. Nevertheless, the government was now free to dismiss magistrates to whom it objected, without laying itself open to the charge of depriving them of their property. It took care to avoid giving this impression even in the case of the initial suppressions which inaugurated the reforms. All magistrates who sent in claims were awarded the right to compensation,[59] although this was to be paid over a long period, and many exiled magistrates refused to put in a claim so as not implicitly to recognise the legality of the suppression.

The efficacy of these combined reforms was undoubted. The edict of November 1770 can be regarded, in retrospect, as the manifesto of the reform, with its condemnation of strikes, mass resignations, and concerted action between parlements. None of these occurred between 1771 and 1774. However, remonstrances and delayed registrations were not entirely eliminated. Nor could the government really complain, since both were specifically allowed under the edict, which had not been formally submitted to the provincial parlements anyway.

Terray's tax increases of 1771, practically the first public measures to be laid before the remodelled parlements, provoked a shower of remonstrances throughout the winter from Paris, Toulouse, Grenoble, Bordeaux, Aix, Dijon and Rennes.[60] A forced registration of various of these measures was necessary at Rennes,[61] and the new parlement of Bordeaux, made up almost entirely of former magistrates, carried resistance and remonstrance to such extremes in the spring of 1772 that it was seriously debated at Versailles whether it should be suppressed and remodelled yet again.[62] None of the others, however, pushed matters this far, and most refrained from exciting public opinion by having their remonstrances and *arrêtés* printed and publicly distributed. Most of those who did raise protests did so mainly for form's sake, simply feeling bound, however impotently, to make some show of independence in order not to appear complete time-servers. In any case, the predicament of the new courts was considerably eased by the fact that after Terray's financial measures no more nationally important measures were laid before them. After the grain shortage of 1773 the

[59] The belief that this was not the case is common. See, for example, Cobban, *History*, i, p. 93; and Norman Hampson, *The Enlightenment* (London, 1968), p. 177.

[60] Flammermont, *Maupeou*, p. 517.

[61] Arthur Le Moy, *Le parlement de Bretagne et le pouvoir royal au XVIIIe siècle* (Angers, 1909), pp. 426-30.

[62] Flammermont, *Maupeou*, p. 517.

parlements of Bordeaux and Toulouse protested at Terray's restrictive grain policy, but their interest was strictly regional.[63] So it was with such other remonstrances as were sent in by Maupeou's parlements. The parlement of Paris was silent after the end of 1771. The extremes condemned by the edict of 1770 were avoided; and the parlements from 1772 to 1774 were quieter than they had been for years.

Maupeou did, therefore, succeed in bridling the parlements. Whether the government took any real advantage of the situation he had created to push through more fundamental reforms is another question.

The most pressing problem facing the state was undoubtedly that of the finances. Terray's programme for restoring financial order contained two basic elements: to cut the level of debts; and to increase the yield of taxes. The first was brought about by a partial bankruptcy in which the interest rates on a whole range of government *rentes* were reduced and perpetual annuities were changed into life annuities.[64] Yet most of these operations took place early in 1770, long before the reform of the parlements, and even before the crisis which precipitated it. Terray did not need to dispense with the parlements before he could operate a bankruptcy.[65] In fact, the parlements created comparatively little stir over his measures. The parlement of Paris remonstrated,[66] and the fortunes of some of its members were undoubtedly damaged by Terray's operations; nevertheless, it avoided pushing matters to extremes. No force was needed to persuade the parlement, after protesting, to register the new edicts, for they chiefly penalised one of the regular objects of the magistrates' attack – the financiers, the speculators and the money-lenders; and while the parlement felt bound to protest at the violation of public faith, having protested it did not obstruct the process further. The bankruptcy, after all, was mainly directed at the '*capitalistes*' whom the magistrates considered, in part at least, to be responsible for the disorders in the finances.[67]

---

[63] Crébassol, 'Parlement Maupeou à Toulouse', pp. 75-82, for Toulouse; *Journal historique de la Révolution opérée dans la constitution de la monarchie française par M. de Maupeou* (London, 1775), v, pp. 83-4, for Bordeaux. See too Georges Weulersse, *La Physiocratie à la fin du règne de Louis XV, 1770-1774* (Paris, 1959), pp. 174-83.

[64] Marion, *Histoire financière*, i, pp. 252-3.

[65] There was, however, a further reduction in *rentes* in June 1771; Flammermont, *Maupeou*, p. 425.

[66] J. Flammermont, *Les remontrances du parlement de Paris au XVIIIe siècle* (Paris, 1888-1908), iii, pp. 78-103; 11 Feb. 1770, 14 March 1770.

[67] Marion, *Histoire financière*, i, p. 259. See too pp. 231-2 for *parlementaire* opinion on the flaws in the financial system.

If the old parlements were no obstacle to a partial bankruptcy, the history of the 1760s made it seem unlikely that they would take an increase in taxes so quietly. Terray used this argument to some effect against Choiseul in 1770. Indeed Terray only brought forward his major tax increases when the remodelling of the parlements was almost complete.[68] The impact of the edict of November 1771 concerning the *vingtièmes* was, as we have seen, so great as to provoke protests even from the Maupeou parlements.[69] By this edict the first *vingtième* became in effect perpetual, and the second, due to expire in 1772, was prolonged until 1781. Various surcharges were also imposed, and above all, a complete reassessment of liability was planned, so that the full weight of the *vingtièmes* should fall more equitably. Thanks to the reforms of Maupeou this edict and several others of less importance passed the parlements, not without some resistance certainly, but without modification. For the first time in years the government did not have to bargain over its financial policy.

How far Terray's policy was the one to solve the state's problems, is a different question. His bankruptcy, if it reduced the debt, shook credit and made further loans more expensive and harder to raise. Yet he could not avoid recourse to such loans to keep the government going. It is unlikely that a heavy *vingtième* alone, even one more equitably assessed, would by itself have solved the state's financial problems. Yet more radical solutions never seem to have been considered. Terray's policy was simply to decrease what he owed and to increase what he was owed. Maupeou may have suppressed venality in the higher judiciary (and incidentally loaded the treasury with a heavy burden of compensation), but far from attempting to suppress venality generally, Terray's policy was merely to make a greater profit from it. Indeed he actually extended the system by making municipal offices, elective since the reform of Laverdy, venal once again.[70] Even his policy on the grain trade was conservative, at a time when some of the parlements

---

[68] Did then Terray, if not Maupeou, have long-term plans for which the reform of the parlements was an essential prerequisite? It seems not. Late in 1770 he still thought he could do without the tax increases. These followed from, rather than necessitated, the reform of the parlements. See Douglas Dakin, *Turgot and the Ancien Régime in France* (London, 1938), pp. 154-5.

[69] The preamble is in Isambert et al., *Anciennes lois*, xxii, pp. 540-44.

[70] Marion, *Histoire financière*, i, pp. 273-4; Maurice Bordes, *La réforme municipale du contrôleur-général Laverdy et son application (1764-1771)* (Toulouse, 1967), ch. 7.

themselves were in favour of greater freedom for the trade.[71] In short, Terray was a conservative, not a reformer. His crisis measures were supremely orthodox. Although it is undeniable that he reduced the gap between income and expenditure, reduced the debt and reduced anticipations, he made no economies, incurred new debts and badly shook the king's credit.[72] Turgot's programme of 'no bankruptcy, no loans, no tax increases' was the antithesis of all that Terray stood for, and was Turgot's reaction to the chaos that he found in 1774.

If there was, then, no serious reform of the finances in this period, at least things seemed different in the administration of justice. Maupeou accompanied his attack on the parlements in 1771 with loud proclamations that reforms would not be confined to the structure of the judicial system but would extend to the stuff of justice itself. Advocates of legal reform, like Voltaire and Condorcet, were excited and completely won over to Maupeou when he let it be known that he was contemplating a whole new code of law.[73] Yet, although Maupeou claimed afterward, as well as at the time, that he wished to reform the law,[74] he made no serious attempt to do so during his tenure of power beyond the provisions which were already contained in the edict of February 1771. In order to give the impression of purifying justice, however, this edict did not confine itself to abolishing venality. Setting the pattern for all subsequent reforms, it claimed also to make the courts more accessible to litigants and to end payments by them to their judges (*épices*), so making justice free. The first claim was fair enough; in the *ressort* of Paris the *conseils supérieurs*, because they were final courts of appeal for their areas, were more convenient to litigants than the distant parlement. The same must have been true in eastern Languedoc, although dwellers in other *ressorts* were less well provided for.

Free justice, however, was not as simple as it appeared. Magistrates in the old parlements were in general very poorly paid, and were clearly not expected to live on their incomes from office alone. This income came from two sources, the *gages* and the *épices*. *Gages* were paid by the government and strictly speaking, represented interest on the capital value of judicial offices. *Epices*, levied on a time basis, were payments

---

[71] See Weulersse, *Physiocratie*, ch. 7, passim. The remonstrances of Bordeaux and Toulouse in 1773 were directed *against* restrictions in the corn trade such as Terray had imposed.

[72] See Dakin, *Turgot*, pp. 154-5.

[73] See Rocquain, *Esprit révolutionnaire*, p. 296 n.3; Flammermont, *Maupeou*, p. 254; Peter Gay, *Voltaire's Politics* (Princeton, 1959), pp. 327, 352.

[74] Flammermont, *Maupeou*, pp. 277, 618, 645. See too Moreau, *Souvenirs*, ii, p. 64.

made by litigants to the court, which were then redistributed to magistrates. Together these payments usually fell far below a realistic living wage for a magistrate, and did not even constitute a conspicuous return on the capital invested in office.[75] Maupeou abolished them both, declared justice to be free, and introduced more realistic fixed salary scales both for the new parlements and the *conseils supérieurs*. However, these new salaries had to be paid from somewhere, and the money was usually found by adding a surcharge to the tax assessment of each locality. Justice was therefore free only in the sense that everybody, not merely litigants, now paid for it.[76] The lavish pensions accorded to the leading magistrates of the new courts, to ensure their loyal co-operation, augmented the cost further. It was not even as if the litigants' burden was eased. *Epices* in lower jurisdictions were not abolished, and an edict of June 1771[77] raised all the fees payable on the dispatch of legal documents by as much as two-and-a-half times.[78] As one Maupeou parlement even admitted publicly in 1773:

> Dans le moment que cette gratuité a été annoncée, et que les Magistrats ont cessé de percevoir les émoluments accoûtumés, les droits de Greffe, de contrôle, et autres qui se perçoivent sur les actes judiciaires, ont été si prodigieusement augmentés . . . que les fraix de Justice excèdent de beaucoup ce qu'il en coûtoit auparavant, et avant la suppression des épices . . . [79]

> [At the moment when this gratuity was proclaimed, and Magistrates ceased to charge the accustomed fees, registration dues, duties and others payable on legal documents were so prodigiously increased . . . that the costs of justice far exceed what it cost previously, and before the abolition of *épices* . . .]

In the end, under Maupeou, justice was not only not free but probably even dearer than before his reform. As Malesherbes put it later: 'Cette prétendue justice gratuite n'a été annoncée que pour éblouir le feu roi et

[75] See François Bluche, *Les magistrats du parlement de Paris au XVIIIe siècle, 1715-1771* (Paris, 1960), pp. 168-72; Egret, *Parlement de Dauphiné*, i, pp. 28-9; P. de Peguilhan de Larboust, 'Les magistrats du parlement de Toulouse à la fin de l'ancien régime, 1775-1790' (unpublished *mémoire*, Toulouse, 1965), pp. 72-6; Jean Meyer, *La noblesse Bretonne au XVIIIe siècle* (Paris, 1966), ii, pp. 946-53; William Doyle, 'The Parlementaires of Bordeaux at the End of the Eighteenth Century, 1775-90' (unpublished D.Phil. thesis, University of Oxford, 1967), p. 134.

[76] Villers, *Parlement de Paris*, pp. 72-4; see too [anon.], *Essai sur la dernière révolution de l'ordre civil en France* (London, 1782), i, pp. 150ff.

[77] Flammermont, *Maupeou*, pp. 482-4.

[78] Villers, *Parlement de Paris*, p. 73.

[79] AM, Bordeaux, Fonds Ancien, FF 5b. *Arrêt d'enregistrement*, 2 Aug. 1773.

se jouer de ses sujets.'[80] ['This pretended free justice was only proclaimed to dazzle the late king and mislead his subjects.']

In restraining the political role of the parlements, therefore, Maupeou did create an opportunity for a bold government to initiate, with the minimum of opposition, contentious reforms. However, the government of which he was a member clearly did not regard his work as a means to this end but rather as an end in itself. There was no radical reform; indeed, there was very little reform of any sort after 1771. The government was not interested. Terray's financial operations were short-term and short-sighted. The reforms in the administration of justice were superficial and largely illusory. 'On finit par la réforme de tous les parlemens', Voltaire later wrote, 'et on espéra de voir réformer le jurisprudence. On fut trompé; rien ne fut réformé . . .'['In the end all the parlements were reformed . . . and there was hope of a reform in jurisprudence. The hope was false; nothing was reformed.'] But he was not being ironical about the restoration of 1774.[81] He was reporting what happened, or rather what failed to happen, under Maupeou.

It is easy to forget how absolutely a minister depended for his position upon the favour of the king. Maupeou had undermined Choiseul's position by shaking the king's confidence in Choiseul's policies and his capability. Having usurped Choiseul's pre-eminence in the royal counsels, he then had to see that nobody undermined his own position by the same means. Louis gave Maupeou his confidence because the chancellor's policies procured him a quiet life. Maupeou could not therefore afford to let them fail. Malesherbes, first president of the *cour des aides*, had suffered from the reforms of 1771 and knew very well what was at stake. 'Dans le fait', he wrote, 'le roy n'a pas une inclination particulière pour cet homme, mais il a un grand attachement pour le despotisme, et une grande aversion pour les parlemens et pour les affaires que ces corps luy suscitoient.'[82] ['In fact . . . the king has no particular liking for this man, but he has a great attachment to despotism, and a great aversion for the parlements and for the problems which these bodies caused him.']

[80] Quoted in Pierre Grosclaude, *Malesherbes, témoin et interprète de son temps* (Paris, 1961), p. 302.

[81] Cobban, in 'The *Parlements*', p. 79, cites this passage (from the 1879 edition of the *Dictionnaire philosophique*) clearly believing that it refers to the 1774 restoration.

[82] P. Grosclaude, *Malesherbes: nouveaux documents inédits* (Paris, 1964), p. 71; Malesherbes to Mme—, 24 June, 1772.

To keep the king's confidence, Maupeou had to show that he had settled the problem of the parlements once and for all. In April 1771, when he established the new parlement of Paris, Louis XV declared that he would never change, and he never did.[83] But this was only thanks to the constant efforts deployed by Maupeou in defending and consolidating his reforms. It was true that in principle the king's support was the only support that he needed, but this support was always uncertain, and liable to be conditioned by circumstances in part, at least, outside Maupeou's control.

For instance, with the exception of the clergy and isolated individuals like Voltaire, there was almost universal public hostility to the reforms. The dissolution of the parlements, wrote Diderot, would turn France into little more than a Turkish despotism.[84] Terray's tax increases, immediately following the remodelling of the parlement only confirmed the worst fears. Madame d'Epinay, whose fortune had been ruined by Terray's operations, took the same view.

> Il est certain [she wrote in her most brilliant and perceptive comment on Maupeou's work], que, depuis l'établissement de la monarchie française, cette discussion d'autorité, ou plutôt de pouvoir, existe entre le roi et le parlement. Cette indécision même fait partie de la constitution monarchique; car si on décide la question en faveur du roi toutes les conséquences qui en résultent le rendent absolument despote. Si on la décide en faveur du parlement, le roi, à peu de chose près, n'a pas plus d'autorité que le roi d'Angleterre; ainsi, de manière ou d'autre en décidant la question, on change la constitution de l'Etat au lieu qu'en laissant subsister les choses telles qu'elles ont été de tout temps, quel est . . . le cas où, malgré la résistance des parlements, la volonté du souverain n'a pas prévalu . . . ?[85]

> [It is certain that . . . from the foundation of the French monarchy this debate over authority or rather power, has gone on between the king and the parlement. This very uncertainty is part of the monarchical constitution; for if the question is settled in favour of the king, all the resulting consequences render him absolutely a despot. If it is settled in favour of the parlement, the king, virtually, has no more authority than the king of England; and so, settling the question one way or another changes the state's constitution; whereas if

---

[83] At the *lit de justice* of 13 April, 1771. Flammermont, *Maupeou*, p. 361.

[84] A much-quoted passage; e.g. Lough, *Eighteenth-Century France*, p. 192.

[85] Eugène Asse (ed.), *Lettres de l'abbé Galiani à Mme d'Epinay* (Paris, 1882), i, p. 22. Mme d'Epinay to Galiani, 11 April 1772. Partially quoted in Elie Carcassone, *Montesquieu et le problème de la constitution française au XVIIIe siècle* (Paris, 1927), pp. 456-67, in a section which fully chronicles the extent of the opposition to Maupeou.

things are left to go on as they always have, has there ever been . . . a case where, despite the parlements' resistance, the sovereign's will has not prevailed . . . ?]

For Turgot, the reform seemed a step towards 'legal despotism'.[86] For the bulk of the political nation, however, despotism had nothing to do with legality. If the king could destroy with impunity the only apparent checks on his power, there was nothing that he could not do. This was why the *cour des aides* of Paris and the parlement of Rouen called, in the spring of 1771, for the Estates-General – the ultimate answer to the ultimate problem. Moreover, the court nobility, led by the Princes of the Blood themselves, made certain that the king was aware of the sense of outrage felt by the political nation. In April 1771 the princes issued a formal protest, which was later printed,[87] against the whole judicial revolution. They were banished from the presence of the king as a result. Not until December 1772 did they make their submission; even so, most of the princes and peers boycotted the new parlement of Paris throughout its existence. In short, the volume and the persistence of the protest could not fail to reach the king. Louis XV, although he disliked the parlements, did not like to think of himself as a despot, and it must have disturbed him to know how widespread and persistent was the opinion that he was one.

His confidence was further shaken by the fact that the new system did not establish itself smoothly. Trouble began with the refusal of the whole parlement of Paris in January 1771 to submit to authority, and it continued when the bar refused to plead before the interim parlement and various noblemen withdrew their suits.[88] At Toulouse and Rennes after the reform, long intrigues were necessary to make up the new courts, and at Rennes and Dijon there were strikes of the bar.[89] Moreover, no sooner were these troubles over than Terray's tax increases brought the wave of remonstrances and resistance of the winter of 1771-72. For a time it seemed that Maupeou's elaborate *coup d'état* had solved nothing, and that the new parlements, in one way or another, were proving just as troublesome as the old. Nor could the old

[86] Gustave Schelle, *Oeuvres de Turgot* (Paris, 1913-23), iii, p. 475. Turgot to Du Pont de Nemours, 8 Feb. 1771.

[87] Printed in Flammermont, *Maupeou*, pp. 380-3.

[88] Ibid., pp. 249-51.

[89] *Essai sur la dernière révolution*, ii, pp. 46ff, and Crébassol, 'Parlement Maupeou à Toulouse', pp. 40-41, for Toulouse, along with Flammermont, *Maupeou*, p. 451; ibid., pp. 470-2 for Rennes; and p. 475 for Dijon.

system be laid silently to rest. Maupeou's concern for the appearance of legitimacy had made him promise compensation for suppressed offices, yet this compensation could only be paid if magistrates sent in documents proving the value of their offices. Those who had joined the new courts did this willingly enough but, as noted earlier, a number of intransigents among the exiles of the Paris courts refused to co-operate. To 'liquidate' would be implicitly to recognise the legality of the suppression. These refusals made Maupeou postpone several times the closing date for sending in claims, and it was not until the submission of the princes at the end of 1772 that the ranks of the recalcitrants began to waver; and even then submission was not unanimous.[90] 'Voilà deux années qui n'ont rien ajouté à la solidarité du nouvel édifice', wrote an exiled magistrate of Bordeaux, 'et tant que les ruines subsisteront on leur redemandera toujours l'ancien. Il faudra détruire jusqu'aux ruines même . . . '.[91] ['Two whole years now have added nothing to the solidity of the new edifice . . . and so long as the ruins remain there will always be calls to bring the old one back. The very ruins themselves will have to be destroyed . . . ']

Maupeou, in fact, never succeeded in making the parlements a closed question.[92] Both the new and the old orders gave enough trouble to keep them in the forefront of the king's attention, and this gave hope to Maupeou's enemies. The best sign of hope, however, was that after the summer of 1771 the council was once more divided. The essential prerequisite of Maupeou's coup had been his capture of the council. But in June 1771, despite all Maupeou's previous efforts, after six months of intrigue the duc d'Aiguillon became secretary for foreign affairs. He set to work at once to undermine the position of the dominant minister – in this case Maupeou himself. Maupeou, Terray and d'Aiguillon have been linked together by historians as the 'triumvirate', but they were as little united in reality as their original namesakes. When the new parlements, especially that of Bordeaux, created so much trouble over Terray's tax increases in the spring of 1772, d'Aiguillon led an attack on Maupeou in the council, declaring that this resistance showed that the reform had achieved nothing. Terray and his ministerial colleague, Bertin, knowing the king's views, also came out against Maupeou by

[90] Flammermont, *Maupeou*, pp. 519-32.

[91] Bibliothèque de la Rochelle, MS 1903, fos 244v-245. Dupaty to de Sèze (Dec. 1772 or Jan. 1773).

[92] A point made by Jean Louis Soulavie, *Mémoires historiques et politiques du règne de Louis XVI* (Paris, 1801), i, p. 197.

opposing vigorous action to crush the Bordeaux parlement.[93] In 1773, when the famous lawsuit between the playwright Beaumarchais and the counsellor Goezman had brought down general public ridicule on the new parlement of Paris, d'Aiguillon and Bertin entered into negotiations with various exiled magistrates with a view to replacing the new parlement with members of the old.[94] That any such change would involve the fall of Maupeou was taken for granted. Moreover, in the spring of 1774, d'Aiguillon seemed to be gaining ground, as he added the portfolio of war to that of foreign affairs. Moreau believed that, when Louis XV fell into his final illness in May 1774, he was on the point of a new revolution in the judiciary and had resolved to dismiss the chancellor.[95]

In other words, Maupeou and his revolution were inseparable. They stood or fell together. Since Maupeou's position never seemed completely unshakeable, neither did the work for which he was responsible. While Louis XV lived the failure of policies was the only ground on which Maupeou could be attacked effectively; if he succumbed to these attacks, naturally the policies would succumb, too. His system never achieved a convincing air of permanency because neither did his own position.

Even if Maupeou's position under Louis XV did not seem immune from danger, outside court circles his dismissal remained a subject for propaganda and secret speculation rather than real hope. The system, after initial troubles, was working. Louis XV might remain impervious to d'Aiguillon's machinations. If the question of the parlements had not been closed, it could only seem a matter of time. Unfortunately, time was what Maupeou did not have. The death of the king in 1774 and the accession of a new monarch could only renew the hopes of his enemies. Nobody knew for certain where the new king stood, and this uncertainty meant that the question of the parlements not only remained an open one but became, as it had been in 1771, the central one in politics. It had to be settled one way or another before the new reign could proceed peacefully.

Why then were the parlements restored? In general terms it was because Louis XVI and nearly all his subjects wanted a break with the bad old ways. The scale of this break was not foreseen or planned; it

[93] Flammermont, *Maupeou*, pp. 517-18.
[94] Ibid., p. 549; Moreau, *Souvenirs*, ii, p. 89.
[95] Ibid., pp. 89-90.

confined itself in the first instance to the recall to favour of Maurepas, exiled since 1749 and a martyr to the spite of Louis XV's mistress. However, 'sans parlement, point de monarchie' was Maurepas' opinion.[96] Not that the king shared it initially; it was he who had written, in 1770, that Maupeou's disciplinary edict was 'le vrai droit public'.[97] Moreover, in dismissing d'Aiguillon at the insistence of the queen within three weeks of his accession, he seemed to be removing Maupeou's greatest enemy. He gave other signs too that he intended to maintain the reformed order, and resisted all suggestions, emanating notably from the Princes of the Blood, of a restoration of the old parlements.[98]

It was now that the power of public opinion came into play. In old regime politics, public opinion merely meant what the governors thought the governed were thinking – 'le qu'en dira-t-on'. The information did not need to be true; it merely needed to be believed. Further, it was only important when members of the government and especially the king thought it was. In the months following the accession of Louis XVI, however, they undoubtedly did think it important.

The king was hailed with great popular enthusiasm in the early days of his reign but as the suspicion grew that he intended no action on the question of the parlements, enthusiasm began to wane quite noticeably. The king, as anxious as anybody for a new start, soon came to believe that public opinion would accept no other token of his good intentions. Any change at all could only appear an overture to this, and that was indeed how the recall of Maurepas and the replacement of d'Aiguillon and Bourgeois de Boynes had been interpreted.[99] Although two of the new ministers, the comte de Vergennes and the comte du Muy, were enemies of the parlements and opposed their recall until the last moment, the other newcomer and the most sensational new appointment, Turgot, was in favour of a qualified recall.[100] By early August, therefore, Maurepas had been able to bring the king to realise that 'rien ne pouvait être entrepris sur les affaires parlementaires avec M. de Maupeou, soit pour, soit contre le Parlement ancien ou nouveau'.[101]

---

[96] Jacques M. Augeard, *Mémoires secrets* (Paris, 1866), p. 77.

[97] Flammermont, *Maupeou*, p. 115.

[98] In fact, he exiled the duc d'Orléans and the duc de Chartres for refusing to recognise the Maupeou parlement in public.

[99] Secretary of the navy since the fall of Choiseul-Praslin. A creature of Maupeou's.

[100] See Henri Carré, 'Turgot et le rappel des parlements', *La Révolution Française*, 43 (1902), passim; also Dakin, *Turgot*, pp. 136-48; Edgar Faure, *12 mai 1776: la disgrâce de Turgot* (Paris, 1961), pp. 117-48; and Villers, *Parlement de Paris*, pp. 315-17.

[101] Jehan de Witte (ed.), *Journal de l'abbé de Véri* (Paris, 1929-30), i, p. 159.

['nothing could be undertaken on parlementary affairs with M de Maupeou, either for or against the old or new Parlement'.] It was under these circumstances that, on 24 August, Maupeou and Terray were simultaneously dismissed.

The news was greeted with vast popular enthusiasm and seems to have restored the king's personal popularity overnight. The fallen ministers were burned in effigy and, more significantly, there were demonstrations in Paris against Maupeou's parlement.[102] Maupeou's fall was taken as a sign that his system was condemned; and this sudden loss of what respect the system had hitherto commanded only made it the more certain that it would be condemned. The appointment of Miromesnil, a leading *parlementaire* martyr to Maupeou's policy, as his successor seemed added confirmation. It would have been the height of folly, and would have irrevocably ruined the new king's prestige, popularity, and perhaps his credit, if the government had not gone on at this stage. Maurepas, Miromesnil and Turgot knew this, and Vergennes and du Muy were overridden. By October the king was convinced that the recall of the parlements was not only the right policy but his own policy;[103] and so they were recalled. In less than a year Maupeou's whole system was abandoned and the judiciary was restored, in personnel and in structure, to the position it had occupied before 1771.

If men and their policies were so closely linked it is obvious that Maupeou could not have stayed in office after the repudiation of his policies; hence his dismissal preceded it. But there was no real chance, either, of these policies surviving after his fall. 'Public opinion' would have been outraged. As Malesherbes had shrewdly predicted: 'Dès l'instant que cette disgrâce sera sçue, toute l'espèce d'armée levée par cet homme sera dissipée . . . le roy sera donc dans la nécessité absolue et connue de tout le monde de rappeller les parlemens.'[104] ['The moment this dismissal becomes known, the whole of the army, so to speak, raised by this man will disband . . . the king will then be known by all to be absolutely compelled to recall the parlements.']

The chancellor is reputed to have declared, at the moment of his dismissal, that he had won for the king a case which had dragged on for centuries.[105] But the whole point was that, in 1774, he had *not* won the

---

[102] Flammermont, *Maupeou*, pp. 568-9; Faure, *12 mai 1776*, pp. 134-5.

[103] Véri, *Journal*, i, p. 202.

[104] Grosclaude, *Nouveaux documents*, p. 71.

[105] Joseph Droz, *Histoire du règne de Louis XVI* (Paris, 1839), i, p. 138.

case; it was still (to prolong the metaphor) subject to appeal. With the advent of a new order all his work was called at once into question. If it was inevitable that the new reign would bring changes – and it was – it was inevitable too that there would be a demand for the most important change of all – the recall of the parlements. This and the fall of Maupeou were ideas as inseparable under Louis XVI as under Louis XV.

In 1774, therefore, there was no real hope either for the chancellor or for his new judicial order. Many wondered whether there was any more hope of a settled state of affairs in the future. So long as the king gave his confidence to factions, either of personalities or of policies – and the one usually implied the other – then any policy was likely to be changed at the next turn of the political wheel. If there was to be any hope there had to be a new *style* of government. As Bertin told Moreau in 1774, with the experience of the years since 1771 behind him: 'Toute besogne qu'il sera possible d'attribuer à un tel ou à un tel ne réussira point: il faut qu'elle soit celle du Roi seul . . . '.[106] ['Whatever work can be attributed to one person or another cannot succeed: it must be the king's alone . . . '.]

Louis XVI's government did not restore the parlements because it was bankrupt of ideas, nor was it blindly yielding to ephemeral public pressure. The ministers had a plan. The situation of before 1771 was not restored in every detail. The parlements returned only under certain conditions.

Informed public opinion supported this course. Only the clergy seem to have been rootedly opposed to any restoration.[107] Even Condorcet, perhaps the bitterest enemy of the parlements among the *philosophes*, condemned the recall of the parlements only if it were unconditional.[108] Malesherbes, son of a chancellor and the most famous victim of the Maupeou reforms, also favoured restrictions. 'Il n'est pas douteux qu'il n'y ait des mesures à prendre contre l'abus du pouvoir parlementaire', he wrote in August 1774. 'Je le pense moy personellement parce que je crois que les parlemens ont quelquefois usé de ce pouvoir contre le bien public et trop rarement pour le bien public et qu'après un retour sans conditions et sans précautions les abus seraient encore plus communs et plus considérables.'[109] ['There is no doubt that

---

[106] *Souvenirs*, ii, p. 100.

[107] Flammermont, *Maupeou*, pp. 571-2; Dakin, *Turgot*, pp. 144-5.

[108] Charles Henri, *Correspondance inédite de Condorcet et de Turgot* (Paris, 1882), pp. 201-2; Oct. or Nov. 1774.

[109] Quoted in Grosclaude, *Malesherbes*, p. 293.

there are measures to be taken against the abuse of parlementary power ... I think so myself because I believe that the parlements have sometimes made use of this power against the public good and too rarely for the public good, and that after an unconditional return without precautions abuses would be more common still and more considerable.']

Above all, this was the view of Miromesnil, the new head of the judiciary. When the parlement of Paris was restored, therefore, it was under a series of conditions, some of which were drawn from Maupeou's famous edict of 1770 and some of which Miromesnil had complained at the time were absent from that edict.[110]

First of all, Maupeou's new courts were abolished and most of those which he himself had abolished were restored. On the other hand, a separate edict raised the level of competence of the *présidiaux*, the old inferior courts, so that the full extent of the old parlement's judicial power was not restored and the spirit of the *conseils supérieurs* remained.[111] The new edict of discipline, like that of 1770, forbade all strikes, mass resignations and prolonged obstructions of the legislative process. Miromesnil now also introduced a series of clauses designed to reduce general assemblies of chambers to a minimum, to bolster the power of the stolid *grand'chambre* at the expense of its turbulent juniors, and to increase the power of the first president. All contraventions of these provisions were to be judged by a new plenary court, composed of princes, peers, ministers, various councillors of state and masters of requests; and if the *parlementaires* were found guilty they were to be replaced by members of the *grand conseil*, exactly as Maupeou had attempted to arrange things in 1771. Similar edicts of discipline were imposed on the provincial courts as they were restored. The government believed that these restrictions would be enough to prevent the parlements in the future from getting out of hand. Admittedly not everybody felt so sure. Moreau believed that three-quarters of the court were dissatisfied with the arrangements.[112]

The British ambassador wrote that: 'The young king thinks that his authority is sufficiently secured by the regulations he has made. He may

---

[110] Compare articles 5, 8, 10, and 21 of the edict (Isambert et al., *Anciennes lois*, xxiii, pp. 50-7) with the remarks of Miromesnil to Bertin, 4 Feb. 1771, in Le Verdier, *Correspondance de Miromesnil*, v, pp. 275-6.

[111] Isambert et al., *Anciennes lois*, xxiii, pp. 43-56.

[112] *Souvenirs*, ii, p. 111; Soulavie, *Mémoires historiques*, ii, pp. 174-5ff, gives a list and analysis of the opposed parties at court and in public life.

probably find himself deceived by the end of his reign . . . '.[113] From England, however, Horace Walpole commented more optimistically that the restored parlement would not be troublesome except 'when the power of the crown is lessened by reasons that have nothing to do with the Parliament . . . '.[114]

Both these foreign judgments shared the same premise – that the key to the power of the parlements lay not in themselves but at Court. Bertin's remarks to Moreau assumed the same thing.[115] And herein lay a further reason for ministerial confidence. Henceforth France was to be governed by a ministry united under the king. Louis XV had ruled by dividing his ministers; Louis XVI was to rule by uniting them, initially at least, under the co-ordinating hand of Maurepas. This would ensure firm and consistent government, and in the face of that, the *parlementaire* problem would be unlikely to reassert itself.

'Rien n'est si préjudiciable', Miromesnil had written in 1771, 'qu'un gouvernement vacillant, qui change sans cesse de principes et de conduitte, et dont les actions se contredisent presque en tout occasion.'[116] ['Nothing is more prejudicial . . . than a government which vacillates, which constantly changes its principles and its conduct, and whose actions contradict each other on almost every occasion.'] And as he later wrote to the king: 'Rien ne déconcerte les Intriguants Comme l'union des ministres Entre Eux, et avec le premier Président . . . '.[117] ['Nothing disconcerts Intriguers like unity among Ministers, and with the first president . . . '] He always believed that with a firm and united government the parlements were not to be feared; this was clearly the spirit in which in 1774, Louis XVI's ministers were resolved to act, and so they looked forward with confidence.

In the case of the parlement of Paris events justified their confidence. Apart from its opposition to Turgot the parlement of Paris was unprecedently quiet concerning public affairs between 1774 and the middle of the 1780s. As the first president d'Aligre wrote to Vergennes in 1782: 'Depuis que Le Roy est sur le Trône il n'a Eprouvé aucune difficulté de la part du Parlement de Paris. Tout y a toujours été

---

[113] Quoted in Dakin, *Turgot*, p. 146.
[114] Mrs Paget Toynbee (ed.), *The Letters of Horace Walpole* (Oxford, 1903-25), ix, 104. Walpole to H.S. Conway, 27 Nov. 1774.
[115] See above, n. 106.
[116] Le Verdier, *Correspondance de Miromesnil*, v, p. 267.
[117] AN, K 163. Miromesnil to Louis XVI, 11 Dec. 1785.

enregistré tout de suite . . . '.[118] ['Since the king has been on the throne he has met with no difficulties from the parlement of Paris. Everything has been registered there at once . . . ']

Broadly speaking, it was true. In the eight years to which d'Aligre was referring there had only been a need for three *lits de justice*, including one by which the parlement was re-established. Up to the time of his letter there had been seventeen sets of remonstrances, about two a year, and seven of those sets were on fairly minor matters. Only twice had the court been moved to repeat its remonstrances on a particular issue. The conditions of re-establishment evoked two sets of remonstrances, and Turgot's various measures three. Taxation and the government's finances, apart from Turgot's measures, led to six sets, and another a few days later after d'Aligre wrote.[119] But all this still did not amount to much, and not even in the case of Turgot's measures did the parlement prevent the government from getting its way. It is probable that the only reason why matters went as far as *lit de justice* in this case was that the parlement was encouraged by just such a split in the ministry as Miromesnil had sought to avoid. Ironically enough, Miromesnil himself was responsible for this, through his implacable and overt opposition to Turgot's six edicts.[120] Condorcet opined to Voltaire that Miromesnil had agents directly serving him in the parlement. The Abbé de Véri, who knew many government secrets, was of the same opinion.[121] Nevertheless, it was not the parlement which brought about the fall of Turgot, nor did it defeat his measures, although it certainly did contribute to the atmosphere in which he was dismissed. This dismissal, like Maupeou's, naturally entailed the abandonment of his measures. 'Sans doute', complained the provincial magistrate Felix Faulcon in 1783 of the parlement of Paris, 'il fut un temps où les magistrats de ce tribunal auguste, animés par l'amour du bien public . . . s'opposaient avec force aux tentatives ruineuses des ministres . . . Aujourd'hui, énervés par les plaisirs d'une vie voluptueuse, guidés par l'ambition, ils souscrivent avec une déférence aveugle aux volontés du monarque . . . '.[122] ['Doubtless

---

[118] Archives des Affaires Etrangères, Quai d'Orsay, Mémoires et Documents, *France* 1392, fo. 170, 6 July, 1782.

[119] Calculated from Flammermont, *Remontrances*, iii.

[120] Dakin, *Turgot*, pp. 226-42; Faure, *12 mai 1776*, p. 447.

[121] Theodore Besterman (ed.), *Voltaire's Correspondence* (Geneva, 1953-65), xciv, p. 174, letter 19054. Condorcet to Voltaire, June-July 1776; also Véri, *Journal*, ii, pp. 54-5.

[122] Gabriel Debien, *Correspondance de Félix Faulcon*, i, p. 180, Société des árchives historiques du Poitou, 51, (1939); Faulcon to Texier, 5 Dec. 1783. I am grateful to Colin Lucas for drawing my attention to these remarks, as well as for his many other valuable suggestions.

. . . there was once a time when the magistrates of this august tribunal, moved by the love of public good . . . would strongly oppose the ruinous schemes of ministers . . . Today, worn out by the pleasures of a voluptuous life, led by ambition, they subscribe with wilful blindness to the monarch's will']

In fact historians as well as contemporaries have not failed to notice the relative tranquillity of the parlement in the late 1770s, but they have explained it away by the fact that during the ministry of Jacques Necker no contentious measures, above all financial ones, were laid before it. Necker's loans enabled him to finance the war without new taxation and therefore without obstruction from the parlement.[123] There is certainly some truth in this. However, the parlement of Paris (unlike its provincial equivalents) also had to register all major loans, and it did so consistently under Necker with little demur. The parlement's relative complaisance continued even when new taxes were at last introduced, when the second *vingtième* was prolonged in 1780 and the third one introduced in 1782.

> Les sots et la multitude . . . [wrote the farmer-general Augeard in his memoirs] n'ont cessé de dire et de répéter que M. de Maurepas avoit perdu le royaume en faisant revenir le Parlement; qu'il étoit la cause de tous les malheurs de la France, et que le Roi auroit dû brider davantage l'autorité du Parlement; comme si depuis 1774 jusqu'au mois de décembre 1786, le Parlement n'avoit pas été le plus obséquieux possible à toutes les volontés de MM. les ministres; comme s'il n'avoit pas enregistré en 1781, dans l'espace de 6 mois, les deux sous pour livre et les . . . vingtièmes sans aucune remontrance.[124]

> [Fools and the multitude . . . have ceaselessly said and repeated that M de Maurepas lost the kingdom when he brought back the Parlement; that it caused all France's ills, and that the King should have further bridled the Parlements' authority; as if between 1774 and the month of December 1786, the Parlement had not been as obsequious as could be to all the wishes of ministers; as if it had not registered in 1781, in the space of six months, the five per cent surtax and . . . the twentieths without any remonstrance . . .]

Clearly it was not the presence or absence of contentious issues which determined whether the parlement was troublesome or not.

If the relations between the government and the parlement of Paris deteriorated at all before 1787, it was not until the accession to power of Calonne (November 1783). Although there were still no *lits de justice*

---

[123] See, for example, Cobban, 'The *Parlements*', p. 80; E. D. Glasson, *Le parlement de Paris* (Paris, 1901), pp. 411-12; and Shennan, *Parlement of Paris*, p. 320.

[124] Augeard, *Mémoires secrets*, p. 80.

there were seventeen sets of remonstrances – more than five a year – between that moment and the convocation of the Assembly of Notables. Four of these sets repeated previous remonstrances, and three concerned loans, which had provoked no protest under Necker. Necker's had been war loans and these were not, but there was more behind the increasing restlessness of the parlement than this. The death of Maurepas at the end of 1781, for instance, had robbed the ministry of the co-ordinating power of a principal minister. Certainly this did not have the immediate effect of harming relations between the government and the parlement, since Necker had been succeeded by Joly de Fleury and d'Ormesson, two comptrollers-general who had close family and professional links in the parlement. Calonne, on the other hand, soon quarrelled with the first president d'Aligre. He had affronted his family, and also seems to have thought that president Lamoignon (later keeper of the seals) would be a better choice. Certainly d'Aligre did not extend himself as he normally did to secure an easy passage for the new loans.[125] Above all, the ministry was once more divided, for Calonne was hostile to the baron de Breteuil, who had become secretary of the household almost at the same time as he himself had come to power.[126] The results of their clashes were as might be expected. Talleyrand, who even then was near the centre of affairs, recalled that:

La majorité que le président d'Aligre conservait pour la cour allait chaque jour s'affaiblissant et se perdit au moment où M. de Calonne et M. de Breteuil se brouillèrent. Quoique M. d'Aligre portât aux membres du parlement qui votaient avec lui la faveur de M. de Miromesnil, garde des sceaux; de M. de Breteuil . . . de la reine . . . il vit sa majorité se fondre au moment où il fut en guerre ouverte avec le contrôleur-général.

[The majority which president d'Aligre had put together for the Court grew daily enfeebled and was lost the moment M de Calonne and M de Breteuil fell out. Although M d'Aligre lent the members of the parlement who voted with him the favour of M de Miromesnil, keeper of the seals; of M de Breteuil . . . , of the queen . . . he saw his majority dissolve the moment he and the comptroller-general declared open war . . . ']

As to the parlement: 'L'intrigue y pénétrait de toute part. M. Necker, M. de Calonne, M. de Breteuil y avaient chacun leurs créatures qui

---

[125] Augeard, *Mémoires secrets*, pp. 152-4; also AN, K 163, Miromesnil to Louis XVI, 5 Aug. 1786.
[126] Augeard, *Mémoires secrets*, pp. 152-4; O. Browning (ed.), *Despatches from Paris, 1784-7* (London, 1909), Camden third series, 16, p. 102, 23 Feb. 1786, and pp. 109-10, 27 April 1786.

défendaient ou attaquaient les mesures du ministre qu'on voulait soutenir ou renverser.'[127] ['Intrigue suffused it. M Necker, M de Calonne, M de Breteuil each had their clients there who defended or attacked the measures of whatever minister they wished to support or bring down.']

The deterioration in the relations between the parlement and the government was exemplified when, in December 1785, a deputation was summoned to Versailles to hear the king emphasise his support for Calonne and to be instructed expressly to register his third loan.

The assembling of the notables, therefore, took place after twelve years of relatively tractability on the part of the parlement of Paris. The restoration of 1774 inaugurated a period of docility unparalleled since early in the century. In the last four years the docility did indeed show signs of breaking down; but this was, as Horace Walpole had foreseen, for reasons that had nothing to do with the parlement.

Matters had not, however, gone so well in the provinces, even though not all national public measures which had been laid before the parlement of Paris were submitted to the provincial ones as well. Not all Turgot's measures, for instance, reached the provincial parlements before he fell and they were reversed. Of the major measures considered by the parlement of Paris between 1774 and 1787 only the edicts of restoration, certain of Turgot's measures, and the second and third *vingtièmes* came before provincial parlements.

Concerning the restoration, some provincial courts followed the Parisian line, protesting in remonstrances or by reservations in registration either about the new disciplinary regulations or about the augmentation of the competence of the *présidiaux*.[128] Others did not. Of Turgot's measures, only the freeing of the corn and wine trades and the abolition of the *corvée* reached the provinces, and here again there was no unity of action. If Paris registered the corn edict without demur, Rouen put up a lively opposition.[129] The wine edict, registered at once by Toulouse and Grenoble, whose areas stood to gain by the abrogation of privileges in the wine trade, was opposed in remonstrances by the parlement of Bordeaux, a city which held a privileged position.[130] As to the *corvées*, the

---

[127] Duc de Broglie (ed.), *Mémoires du Prince de Talleyrand* (Paris, 1891), pp. 90, 94.

[128] Of those which did, e.g. Bordeaux, Boscheron des Portes, *Parlement de Bordeaux*, ii, pp. 336-7; Rennes, Le Moy, *Parlement de Bretagne*, pp. 457, 461. Of those which did not, e.g. Grenoble, Egret, *Parlement de Dauphiné*, ii, p. 4.

[129] Dakin, *Turgot*, p. 179.

[130] Ibid., pp. 252-3.

matter hardly had the chance to be considered before the edict was abrogated; it was not in fact submitted to all the parlements.[131] Of those parlements which did consider it, not all took the Parisian line of hostility. The parlement of Rouen expressed itself in favour of the suppression with minor reservations. So did that of Grenoble.[132] Diversity and disunity characterised the reactions of the parlements as a whole to these reforming measures. There was certainly no united and sustained opposition to the government's policies.

The problem of the assessment and collection of the *vingtièmes* preoccupied certain provincial parlements, as it did that of Paris,[133] some time before these taxes were extended and then increased by a third in the early 1780s. The protests against the arbitrary revision of assessments for the tax made by the parlement of Rouen were quashed in a military session (the provincial equivalent of a *lit de justice*). However, the magistrates took no notice of this; the struggle continued and culminated in 1778 in the mass resignation of the parlement, contrary to the edict of discipline of 1774. The government chose to ignore this and the crisis passed. When the second *vingtième* was extended, in 1780, Rouen followed the example of Paris and registered the measure almost without demur.[134] So did most of the others, although in their formulae of registration they tended to express fears as to the weight of taxation and hopes that it would soon be diminished. At Bordeaux, at least, a military session was necessary.[135] The imposition of the third *vingtième*, had a more mixed reception. Douai, a traditionally docile parlement, registered the edict at once; and several, with a far more turbulent tradition, such as Bordeaux and Rouen, raised only formal difficulties.[136] But there were vehement remonstrances from Grenoble, Besançon, Rennes and even from Nancy, traditionally almost as docile as Douai. A military session was necessary at Grenoble, and a deputation from Besançon was called to Versailles and severely reprimanded.[137]

---

[131] The edict was laid before the parlement of Paris on 7 Feb. and rescinded on 11 Aug.

[132] Floquet, *Parlement de Normandie*, vii, pp. 52-3, for Rouen; Egret, *Parlement de Dauphiné*, ii, p. 127, for Grenoble.

[133] Flammermont, *Remontrances*, iii, pp. 394-439; remonstrances of 23-26 Jan. 1778.

[134] Floquet, *Parlement de Normandie*, vii, pp. 57-83.

[135] AD, Gironde, 1B 56, fo. 115 (registers of the parlement), 21 Sept. 1780.

[136] Pillot, *Parlement de Flandres*, i, p. 409; Floquet, *Parlement de Normandie*, vii, p. 85; AD, Gironde, 1B 56, fo. 162v.

[137] Egret, *Parlement de Dauphiné*, ii, pp. 145-9, for Grenoble; Droz, *Louis XVI*, i, pp. 386-8, and Lough, *Eighteenth-Century France*, p. 214, for Besançon; Le Moy, *Parlement de Bretagne*, pp. 504-5, for Rennes; Hubert de Mahuet, *La cour souveraine de Lorraine et Barrois (1641-1790)* (Nancy, 1959), p. 102, for Nancy.

Sometimes the government only got its way, or avoided trouble after it did, by making local concessions.

The important point is surely that it did get its way. If the provincial parlements were an obstacle they were certainly not an effective one. There was clearly a complete lack of unity, both among themselves and with the parlement of Paris. The *théorie des classes* was dead insofar as it had ever been a reality outside the sonorous phrasing of remonstrances.

On the other hand, for all their ineffectiveness as obstacles to the central government's policies, the provincial parlements constantly disrupted the smooth running of local affairs under Louis XVI. This disruption began with the judicial system itself. In those parlements with members who had consented to serve under Maupeou the restoration began a period of bitter internal feuding and vendetta. The *rentrés* came back determined to persecute the *restants*, and the prosecution of such feuds occupied a good deal of public time in the mid 1770s at Rouen, Rennes, Toulouse, Grenoble, Dijon and even Douai.[138] At Bordeaux, where half the parlement had served under Maupeou, there were strikes and counterstrikes, endless petitions to the government by both sides, with the last dispute arising out of these recriminations settled only in 1786.[139] These disputes embarrassed the government, held up the normal course of both public and private business in the provinces, brought the judicial system into disrepute, and above all distracted the magistrates' attention from public issues.

Local government was also disrupted, as it had been throughout the century, by disputes between the parlements and other local authorities. The parlement of Aix was in open war against the *cour des comptes*, after the latter court had supplanted it under Maupeou.[140] The parlement of Rennes squabbled in the 1780s with the estates of Brittany over which side had the right finally to approve the levying of the third *vingtième* in the province. More important still was its conflict with the intendant, in his capacity as head of the local fiscal system, over the operation of the tobacco monopoly.[141] Dijon, too, conducted a lengthy struggle with the

---

[138] Floquet, *Parlement de Normandie*, vii, pp. 33-7, for Rouen; Le Moy, *Parlement de Bretagne*, pp. 448-51, for Rennes; Egret, *Parlement de Dauphiné*, ii, pp. 6-27, for Grenoble; Pillot, *Parlement de Flandres*, i, pp. 338-40, for Douai.

[139] Boscheron des Portes, *Parlement de Bordeaux*, ii, pp. 393-7, chronicles the opposition to the *procureur-général* Dudon *fils*. The quarrels are also briefly touched upon in A. Grellet-Dumazeau, *La société bordelaise sous Louis XV* (Paris and Bordeaux, 1881), pp. 389, 408.

[140] Flammermont, *Maupeou*, p. 592.

[141] Le Moy, *Parlement de Bretagne*, pp. 505-24; Henri Fréville, *L'intendance de Bretagne* (Rennes, 1953), iii, pp. 129-205.

intendant.[142] Above all, the parlement of Bordeaux joined forces with the local *cour des aides* to obstruct the attempts of the intendant Dupré de Saint-Maur to operate a scheme for the commutation of the *corvée* in Guienne. A commission of inquiry was sent from the council, and as a result of its findings Dupré was replaced.[143] The parlement of Bordeaux also conducted a five-year struggle with the royal domain over the status of certain alluvial deposits along the Gironde, which culminated in the court being summoned in a body to Versailles in 1786. Once there it was given a hero's welcome by the courtiers, and the government, despite this show of authority, surrendered, or at least clarified, its pretensions.[144]

Provincial parlements, therefore, were by no means as docile as that of Paris before 1787. On a local level they certainly were a major obstacle to reform. Tenacious resistance on their part could often bring about changes of policy and personnel. That their conduct weakened the overall pattern of authority seems certain. Yet the fact remains that on major national questions of universal and not just local importance any resistance they did put up was ineffective. This was partly the result of a complete lack of unity among themselves, although this was nothing new. More important, it was the result of the very docility of Paris. Although the provincial parlements, far away from the subtle and complex political world of the capital, habitually took a firmer and more extreme line on public affairs than that of Paris, they were shouting in the wilderness unless Paris made common cause with them. A provincial protest on a national issue was easily overridden; it took the adherence of the court of peers to make a protest truly national and therefore forceful. Otherwise provincial courts only met with success on provincial issues.

The intense preoccupation with purely local matters which is visible among the provincial courts in these years seems partly at least to have stemmed from this isolation. The provincial particularism which characterised the noble agitation of 1788 seems to have originated in part with the call of the local parlements in earlier years for the erection or revival in the *pays d'élection* of provincial estates (as opposed to the client

---

[142] Jean Egret, *La Pré-Révolution française* (Paris, 1962), p. 211.

[143] C. Dartigue-Peyrou, *Dupré de Saint-Maur et le problème des corvées* (Mont-de-Marsan, 1936), passim. Dupré's face was saved by a nomination to the council of state.

[144] Alain Plantey, 'Un exemple de continuité des principes du droit public français: l'affaire des alluvions (Bordeaux, 1781-6)', *Revue de droit public et de science politique*, 71 (1955), passim.

assemblées of Necker and Calonne). This cry had in fact been raised as early as 1759 by the parlement of Rouen,[145] but after 1774 it became widespread as the *cour des aides* of Paris (1775) and the parlements of Grenoble (1776), Bordeaux (1779) and Besançon (1782) all took up the demand.[146] Estates were seen above all as an antidote to the arbitrary power of the intendants and as institutions which, as in the *pays d'états* like Languedoc and Brittany, really could bargain over taxation. They were on a local scale like the estates-general, the ultimate answer to the ultimate problem of controlling arbitrary power; and in fact certain parlements called for both.[147] In the meantime, appeal to local liberties and privileges seemed the best way to limit the power of an arbitrary central authority and its agents, and this was perhaps the most constant theme of provincial remonstrances between 1774 and 1788.

If the parlements, both in Paris and the provinces, really were as weak as an analysis shows them to have been, it is remarkable that Calonne should have gone to the trouble of convoking the notables to avoid their opposition. But it seems questionable whether in fact this was his intention. After the event he declared that it had been, when he could see where events had led.[148] But the facts that, after the notables should have approved his plan, he still envisaged its registration by the parlements and that the largest single contingent in the assembly was drawn from the parlements suggest that he was not seeking a way around the sovereign courts. Certainly, he must have hoped that the approval of the notables would discourage further discussion of his plans in the parlements afterward, and that they would be implemented 'sans qu'il puisse y avoir lieu à aucune réclamation'.[149] ['with no complaint possible'] He wanted a semblance of universal approval, and in this the parlements must play their part; but to avoid them would only defeat the real object by making the government look as if it were afraid of them.

---

[145] Cobban, *History*, i, p. 127.

[146] Egret, *Parlement de Dauphiné*, ii, p. 129, for Grenoble; Grosclaude, *Malesherbes*, p. 315, for the *cour des aides*; AD, Gironde, C 1989, for the Bordeaux remonstrances of 26 Aug. 1779; Claude Fohlen (ed.), *Histoire de Besançon* (Paris, 1965), i, pp. 216-17, for Besançon.

[147] At Bordeaux, for example, the remonstrances of 1779 called for provincial estates, and remonstrances of 1785 (on the colonial trade) called for the estates-general.

[148] Of the two foremost modern authorities on the Notables, Albert Goodwin, 'Calonne, the Assembly of French Notables of 1787 and the Origins of the "Révolte nobiliaire" ', *English Historical Review*, 61 (1946), nowhere states that this was Calonne's intention; Egret, *Pré-Révolution française*, p. 9, only cites Calonne's retrospective justification of 1789 to prove that it was.

[149] Quoted in Goodwin, 'Calonne', p. 21.

For the real problem of the finances since 1783 was not that reforms were obstructed but that loans would not fill: 'toutes les caisses étaient vides, tous les effets publics baissés, toute circulation interrompue; l'alarme était générale et la confiance détruite'.[150] ['all accounts were empty, all public stocks fallen, all circulation interrupted; alarm was general and confidence destroyed'.] The recourse to the notables, wrote the British envoy, 'under whatever pretext it may be disguised, has certainly been adopted with a view to reanimate, if possible, the calamitous credit of Government, and to pave the way to fresh loans'.[151]

The reason for this lack of confidence did not lie in the parlements' obstruction since 1774. It is more likely that confidence had disappeared, at least in part, because the parlements had been unable or unwilling to modify, in any substantial way, the government's rapacious and irresponsible policies.

Weakness, then, not strength, characterised the position of the parlements on the eve of the revolution. Foreigners, and especially those with experience of the British constitution, perhaps saw this weakness more clearly than the French themselves; for the similarity in the names of parlement and parliament, far from confusing them, only underlined the contrast between the two institutions. Chesterfield told Montesquieu earlier in the century that the parlements might raise barricades but never barriers.[152] 'Those bodies', observed de Lolme, the celebrated Swiss commentator on the English constitution, 'being at bottom in a state of great weakness, have no other means of acquiring the respect of the people than their integrity, and their constancy in observing certain rules and forms'.[153] Even in France itself, perceptive observers saw this. Malesherbes declared that: 'Je regarde la magistrature comme un corps nécessaire à conserver dans notre constitution, parce que ce corps est le gardien des loix qui règlent les intérêts des citoyens, et qui font leur unique sauve-garde contre les entreprises du despotisme. Je conviens que ce frein est très faible dans les affaires publiques . . . .'.[154] ['I regard the magistracy as a body necessary to preserve in our constitution,

---

[150] Quoted ibid., p. 248.

[151] Browning, *Despatches*, xvi, p. 164. Hailes to Carmarthen, 30 Dec. 1786.

[152] Quoted in Droz, *Louis XVI*, i, pp. 144.

[153] Jean-Louis de Lolme, *The Constitution of England*, trans. of 4th edn (London, 1784), p. 163.

[154] Grosclaude, *Nouveaux documents*, p. 138; Malesherbes to Breteuil, 27 July 1776. See also Grosclaude, *Malesherbes*, p. 280.

because this body is the guardian of the laws which regulate the interests of citizens, and which are their sole safeguard against the wiles of despotism. I own that this brake is very weak in public affairs . . . ']
Miromesnil, whose concern they were, told Louis XVI in 1787 that:
'Ceux qui craignent les Parlements ne connaissent ou ne veullent pas paroître connaître, combien ils sont peu à craindre . . . '.[155] ['Those who fear the Parlements do not know or do not wish to appear to know how little they are to be feared . . . ']

It is possible that this fundamental weakness was not so clear before 1771. De Lolme, who wrote in the 1760s, thought that despite their weakness the parlements commanded enough public respect to prevent the king from making them 'the tools of his caprices'.[156] Cardinal de Bernis thought (before it happened) that a *coup d'état* like that of Maupeou would be so dangerous as to be impossible; and that therefore no final sanction could ever by effectively employed against the parlements.[157] In the 1760s the parlements themselves certainly intervened with great confidence and frequency in public affairs, sometimes even at the request of the government. It seems unlikely that they, any more than Maupeou, foresaw the measures the king would subsequently find it possible to employ against them.

The events of 1771 clarified matters in the most brutal way. Chancellor Lamoignon had declared that the king of France was a sovereign to whom everything was not permitted but everything was possible.[158] Chancellor Maupeou proved it – there was nothing the king could not do, permitted or not, if he were determined. The parlements could no more prevent their own reformation than Terray's tax increases or anything else. In the view of most magistrates and many others besides, Louis XV had crossed the narrow divide between monarchy and despotism, and it was clear, if it had not been before, that there were no effective regular checks on government in France.

Such arbitrary measures harmed the government's reputation, except with that minority who believed that the state's salvation lay in strong measures. Even the latter were quickly disillusioned as it became clear that Maupeou did not intend to use the opportunity he had created to carry through more radical reforms. Maupeou's coup was not so much

[155] AN, K 163, Miromesnil to Louis XVI, 4 Jan. 1787.
[156] De Lolme, *Constitution of England*, p. 163.
[157] Masson, *Mémoires de Bernis*, i, pp. 322-3.
[158] Grosclaude, *Malesherbes*, p. 279.

an attempt at reform as the debris of a misfired political manoeuvre, irrelevant to the deeper problems of the state; besides, a really determined but more skilful government, as Malesherbes at least was well aware,[159] could have had its way with the parlements without going to such extremes. Nevertheless, such a spectacular operation could not fail to have repercussions, and the most important was to show clearly the essential weakness of the parlements' position. This is what those aristocratic ladies, mesdames de Mesmes and d'Egmont, meant when they told Gustavus III that Maupeou had given a lesson in French history to those who might otherwise never have known it.[160]

It seems clear that this lesson was not lost on the restored parlements after 1774. A sense of their own weakness disposed the parlements to act cautiously in affairs of national importance and never to push matters to the extremes of 1771. The mere rumour of Maupeou-like reforms in the mid 1780s was enough to put eminent Parisian magistrates in a panic.[161] Maupeou's work, although it was destroyed, had a permanent chastening effect on the parlements.

All this leaves a capital problem unexplained. If the parlements really were so vulnerable, why did their position appear superficially so strong? For one thing, ministers probably did not realise themselves how much lay in their power until circumstances forced them to put matters to the test. Maupeou's rejection of Lebrun's proposals seems evidence of this. Even more important were two sets of circumstances on which the parlements could normally rely.

The first of these was an atmosphere of confidence in the political system. 'Le Parlement', wrote Cardinal de Bernis, 'n'a de force que par celle de la voix public; les fermentations des compagnies ne sont rien si elles ne sont appuyées par la fermentation générale . . . Dès que Paris dit que le Roi a raison et qu'il faut que le Parlement obéisse, sa résistance est non-seulement inutile, mas elle devient aussi importune au public qu'elle l'a été à la cour . . . Il faut que les parlements cèdent dès qu'ils sont abandonnés par le public.'[162] ['The Parlement only has strength through the public's voice; ferment in companies is nothing if not supported by general ferment . . . The moment Paris says the King is

---

[159] Ibid., p. 280.

[160] Flammermont, *Maupeou*, p. 425. Cited also in Lough, *Eighteenth-Century France*, pp. 190-1.

[161] Archives des Affaires Etrangères, mémoires et documents, France, 1395, fos 38-9. Anonymous report to Vergennes, 12 Nov. 1783.

[162] Masson, *Mémoires de Bernis*, i, p. 338.

right and that the Parlement must obey, its resistance is not only useless, but it becomes as unwelcome to the public as it had been to the Court . . . The parlements must yield once they are abandoned by the public.']

Parlementaire resistance, therefore, followed what it took to be public opinion as much as it led it. Militancy was sometimes an obligation and not always a willingly accepted one, but if the parlements did not voice some opposition to the government on controversial matters then they would show themselves to be no obstacle and therefore no protectors to the public. Ministries, which always contained a number of ex-magistrates, knew this as well as anybody and were therefore well aware that *parlementaire* opposition was often not as serious as it sounded. Besides, they also knew that if the public believed in the power of *parlementaire* resistance it must also believe that the power of the government was not unlimited and that the French monarchy was not a despotism. Not only was this good for credit; it also kept the king happy. In a curious way, therefore, the government needed the opposition of the parlements. As Augeard claimed to have told Maurepas:

> Il faut que le Roi soit maître absolu dans son royaume, mais ce qui est encore plus nécessaire non-seulement au bonheur de ses peuples, mais au maintien des opérations du crédit, c'est qu'il faut que personne ne se doute que son pouvoir est au-dessus de la loi, car si les peuples le croyoient despote, il lui seroit impossible d'ouvrir des emprunts; ou s'il prenoit cette voie, elle lui seroit . . . coûteuse . . . Il faut que le Roi soit maître du Parlement, mais que personne ne le croie.[163]

> [The King must be absolute master in his kingdom, but what is yet more necessary not only for the well-being of his peoples, but for the operation of credit, is that none should believe that his power is above the law, for if people thought him a despot, it would be impossible for him to raise loans; or if he did so, it would be . . . costly . . . The king must be master of the Parlement, but none must believe him so.]

Resistance, in fact, was a matter of not obstructing the government while appearing to; government was a matter of ignoring resistance while appearing not to.

This, of course, kept the question of where final power lay conveniently in the background. What happened in 1771 was that this elaborate game of confidence broke down. For once both sides meant more of what they said than usual, and both sides miscalculated their responses. Each new manoeuvre aggravated the situation, until the

---

[163] Augeard, *Mémoires secrets*, p. 81.

question of where sovereignty lay could no longer be avoided and the crown had to assert that it had the last word. Yet even as he was making this brutally clear, Maupeou took care to leave his new courts the powers whose exercise bred confidence – registration and remonstrance. His failure was that, despite this, he never really succeeded in rebuilding on a new basis the atmosphere of confidence which he had shattered in 1771.

The second source of strength possessed by the parlements was division in the ministry. Maupeou could not have attacked the parlements so effectively if he had not first captured the royal council and united it, however briefly, behind him; and if Louis XV had not departed from his usual style of government. Since the death of Fleury Louis XV had governed by dividing his ministers. Louis is usually spoken of as a weak monarch, and the impact he made on the working of government doubtless was a weakening one. But in the face of his immediate subordinates the king was remarkably strong. He remained the effective head of the government and never let himself become dominated, at least until the time of Choiseul, by an indispensable first minister. The rivalry between Machault and d'Argenson in the middle of the reign is perhaps the best example of this style of government in action,[164] but the hostility between Choiseul and Maupeou after 1768 is equally typical. The king knew that division gave him the last word and kept him out of the pocket of any of his subjects. In policy he favoured now one side of the divided council, now the other, so that nobody was ever able to take him for granted. This conduct naturally resulted in vacillating policies; Louis remained strong by keeping his government weak.

Rival ministers sought the confidence of the king for their respective policies because the king alone could authorise their execution. The struggle did not end, however, when the king decided on one of the policy alternatives before him. The unfavoured minister or group then bent all its energies towards discrediting their rivals with the king by showing that the policies adopted did not work in practice – by sabotaging them if necessary. This was the role of the parlements. Only there could policies and measures be delayed, obstructed and criticised in such a way as to shake the king's confidence in them. The parlements were, therefore, always useful to some minister in his struggle with his rivals. It seems fairly clear that it was standard practice for ministers to

---

[164] See M. Marion, *Machault d'Arnouville* (Paris, 1891), pp. 303-10.

maintain groups of friends in the parlement of Paris, at least, who could be relied upon to act as they directed. Equally it was standard practice for ministers to accuse each other of fomenting trouble in the parlements, whether they were or not, as Maupeou accused Choiseul in December 1770.[165] Maupeou's whole campaign against Choiseul was an object lesson in how conciliar politics and the parlements interacted under Louis XV's style of government. Whereas the rivalry between Machault and d'Argenson had ended with the king dismissing them both simultaneously, that between Maupeou and Choiseul ended in complete victory for Maupeou. He thus captured the council on an *antiparlementaire* policy; for the first time in years the parlement of Paris found itself without protectors on the king's council, and it was in those circumstances that he was able to strike his blow.

Under Louis XVI the strength of the parlements was diminished by the new king's style of government. Louis XVI, until 1781 at least, put himself largely in the hands of a first minister. It was Maurepas who made and unmade ministers during these years. Therefore it was his confidence, not the king's, that it was essential to retain. Maurepas filled the council with picked men, so the parlements had little opportunity or encouragement to exploit ministerial disunity. It was no coincidence that the only major confrontation between the government and the parlement of Paris while he lived came in 1776, when the ministry was divided. Similarly, even after the death of Maurepas, the parlement of Paris only became restive again when the split between Calonne and Breteuil came to dominate the council. The strength or weakness of the parlements in politics, was directly related to the degree of unity or disunity in the ministry; that in turn depended upon the style of government adopted by the monarch.

As long as general confidence in the system was maintained and the ministry was divided, the parlements not only survived but were able to exercise some influence on policy. In 1771 a united ministry destroyed confidence and the parlements fell. Under Louis XVI confidence was restored for a time, but relative unity in the ministry meant that the parlements remained weak, and the confidence of 1774 slowly ebbed away as more and more people came to see this weakness. The 'Pre-

---

[165] In addition to the examples to be found elsewhere in this article, see also Marion, *Machault*, pp. 336-42, and J.M.J. Rogister, 'New Light on the Fall of Chauvelin', *English Historical Review*, 72 (1967), passim.

Revolution', therefore, began in a very real sense as a crisis of confidence in French public life.

It is clear that the Assembly of Notables was intended to change everything by introducing a completely new element into the political equation. It failed; but it did so because too little had changed. Rival ministers tried to manipulate the notables, and the notables exploited this ministerial division to their own advantage, just like a parlement. This only resulted in the accession to power of a united and determined ministry under Cardinal Loménie de Brienne, which proceeded to override and ignore the notables when they proved recalcitrant – again, just like a parlement.

This situation was inauspicious for the parlements as the government began to send its measures to them for registration. Whenever it was provoked, the Brienne-Lamoignon ministry acted ruthlessly against the parlements, with the exiles of Paris and Bordeaux, the arrest of individual magistrates of Paris and Toulouse, and the overriding of a stream of protests which flowed in over various aspects of its policies throughout the winter of 1787-8. These firm measures, when it became clear that they alone could not silence the sovereign courts and force them to comply in the ministry's programme, culminated in the famous edicts of May 1788. The programme these edicts represented was far more radical than Maupeou's. The parlements' judicial competence was savagely diminished from below, while the vesting of the sole right of registration and remonstrance in the plenary court destroyed the vehicle of their political power from above. The fact that they were put at once into vacation seemed to suggest that the future of the parlements in any form was uncertain. Once again the government had demonstrated that, with determination, it could brush the parlements aside.

Of course, the whole experiment collapsed within months; but this had nothing to do with the parlements. It was simply that the treasury was empty and loans exhausted.[166] And this was because public confidence had been utterly destroyed. It was only restored by the abandonment of the despotically imposed Lamoignon reforms, the recall of Necker the wonder-worker, and the firm promise of the estates-general. This final crisis clearly demonstrated the need for public confidence. This was why the ministry waited so long before striking its blow. The notables had not created the hoped for credit to float new loans; it was essential that the parlement of Paris should. So its exile of

---

[166] Egret, *Pré-Révolution*, p. 192.

August 1787 was rescinded and the land tax abandoned in return for the registration of a prolongation of existing taxes and, above all, a new loan. The apparent reconciliation between government and parlement had the desired effect – the loan of November 1787 was a rapid success. Any attack on the parlements after the disastrous royal session of 19 November might shatter this reviving confidence, as the events of the summer of 1788 were to prove. So the ministry stayed its hand and tolerated months of non co-operation by the sovereign courts; not because it did not have the power to override them but because it did not wish to look as if it had. In short, the government did not wish to appear despotic.

For despotism was the cry that the parlements raised, in 1787 as in 1771, and this cry was taken up by the whole political nation.[167] The history of France between 1771 and 1774 had shown, if it had not been clear before, that the power of the government was irresistible and that there existed no effective permanent checks on it. It was clear by 1787 that the restoration of 1774 did not alter matters substantially; the finances seemed to have been ruined by an authority responsible only to itself. Yet it was this same authority which was now proposing to impose sweeping reforms and new taxes to rectify the situation. What was worse, it did not seem clear how this imposition could be prevented. This was despotism indeed: absolute, irresistible power, not responsible to those subject to it, observing no rules, capricious, incorrigible. However the government wished to appear in 1787-88, there is no doubt that this is how it did appear. All its actions in overriding the parlements to impose its programme seemed to show that the errors of despotism were only to be rectified by more despotism.

Historians, as well as certain contemporaries, have been surprised that, in 1787-88, the parlements should call so unanimously for the estates-general, a body which was bound to end their power. But the years since 1771 had shown them and the public too how little power they had. Only the estates-general, it now seemed, could provide the checks on the government that the parlements so manifestly could not. The argument at local level, for provincial estates, was similar. The success of such demands was uncertain, and in any case not dependent upon any pressure that the parlements or their public supporters could apply. When the government conceded the demand it was (as with the

---

[167] On the importance of this concept in the origins of the Revolution, see the penetrating remarks of Frédéric Braesch, *1789 – l'année cruciale* (Paris, 1941), pp. 38-45.

convocation of the notables) primarily another financial expedient to win confidence and credit. Without this circumstance it is difficult to see how the government's hand could have been forced, since the impotence of the governed in the face of the government lay behind the demand in the first place. The parlements encouraged the people because all else failed. The people supported the parlements because there was nothing else. Neither invoked the estates-general from a position of strength. It was their last hope.

2

Was There an Aristocratic Reaction in Pre-Revolutionary France?

Amid the turmoil of debate which has characterised the study of the French Revolution and its origins in recent years, it might seem that no aspect could escape renewed and critical scrutiny. Yet this impression is deceptive. The history of the revolution continues to be charted with reference to many landmarks seemingly so well-established that historians take them for granted. One such landmark is the 'aristocratic reaction' of the last years of the old regime. Emphases differ, and some historians use the idea in a far broader sense than others, but it finds its place in most of the standard works,[1] and writers of monographs feel equally obliged to take account of it. Most descriptions of the aristocratic reaction comprise one or more of four elements:

1 *Political Reaction.* This was the campaign of the nobility, beginning in 1715 and culminating in the 'noble revolt' of 1787-88, to recover the political power it had lost under Louis XIV. The main vehicles of the movement were the parlements, which became the spearhead of all noble pretentions over the century.[2]

---

[1] E.g. R.R. Palmer, *The Age of the Democratic Revolution*, 2 vols (Princeton, 1959), i, pp. 458-60; A. Goodwin, *The French Revolution* (London, 1959), pp. 24-5; N. Hampson, *A Social History of the French Revolution* (London, 1963), pp. 2-13; M.J. Sydenham, *The French Revolution* (London, 1969), pp. 25-6; F. Furet and D. Richet, *The French Revolution* (London, 1970), p. 23; G. Lefebvre, *The Coming of the French Revolution* (New York, 1947), pp. 14-19; A. Mathiez, *La Révolution Française*, 3 vols (Paris, 1922-4, i, pp. 8-9, 17; A. Soboul, *La France à la veille de la Révolution: économie et société* (Paris, 1966), pp. 79-86.

[2] The classic statements of this case are J. Egret, 'L'opposition aristocratique en France au XVIIIe siècle', *L'information historique*, (1949), pp. 181-5; and F.L. Ford, *Robe and Sword; The Regrouping of the French Aristocracy after Louis XIV* (Cambridge, MA, 1953), passim.

2 *Ideological Reaction.*[3] This was exemplified by the works of such writers as Saint-Simon, Fénelon, Boulainvilliers and Montesquieu; and the remonstrances of the parlements, all of which were manifestos for noble control of the state.

3 *Social Reaction*, 'caste spirit' or 'noble exclusivism'.[4] This refers to the aristocracy of Louis XVI's ministers, the noble monopoly of high ecclesiastical positions and the exclusion of commoners from the parlements. It is most classically exemplified by the famous Ségur ordinance of 1781, excluding non-nobles from the officer corps of the army.

4 *Feudal or Seigneurial Reaction.* This means the reconstruction by aristocratic landlords of their terriers, and the revival of obsolete or moribund rights and dues, which took place in the last two decades of the old order and so incensed the peasantry in 1789.

Some historians only stress some of these aspects, others attempt to synthesise them all into one great movement. But however it is used, the idea of a reaction helps to dramatise the revolution's break with aristocracy and all it stood for; it emphasises the difference between the incorrigible old order and the radical new.

Some doubts have indeed been raised. Vivian Gruder has used the conclusions of her work on eighteenth-century intendants as a departure point for a critique of the idea of a social reaction, while in France François Furet has raised a whole series of terminological doubts.[5] But clichés die hard. Others who have come within intellectual striking distance of questioning the concept of a reaction have preferred to use their conclusions to add nuances to the old picture instead.[6] Yet if such doubts are well founded, we shall sooner or later be compelled to revise our whole view of the origins of the revolution. Important theses on broader topics, which attach some weight to the reaction, might also

---

[3] Well summarised in Ford, *Robe and Sword*, chs 9, 10, 12; and more briefly in Soboul, *La France à la veille*, pp. 79-82.

[4] The terms are Soboul's, *La France à la veille*, p. 83.

[5] V.R. Gruder, *The Royal Provincial Intendants; A Governing Elite in Eighteenth-Century France* (Ithaca, NY, 1968), ch. 8, passim, and pp. 219-24; F. Furet, 'Le catéchisme révolutionnaire', *Annales, ESC*, 26 (1971), pp. 255-89

[6] A. Goodwin, 'The Social Origins and Privileged Status of the French Eighteenth-Century Nobility', *Bulletin of the John Rylands Library*, 47 (1964-5), pp. 393-4, comes close to questioning it but does not follow his conclusions through, although in 'The Recent Historiography of the French Revolution', *Historical Studies*, 6, ed. T.W. Moody (London, 1968), pp. 132-3, he goes somewhat further. A. Cobban, *The Social Interpretation of the French Revolution* (Cambridge, 1964), p. 52, prefers to question the nature of the 'feudal' reaction rather than the thing itself. F. Furet, 'Le catéchisme revolutionnaire', pp. 263-9, takes this line too.

be undermined.[7] So the question is perhaps worth pursuing. Was the aristocratic reaction an illusion? Even if we cannot reply definitively, we can at least review some of the evidence which suggests that it was; and in so doing we can perhaps indicate where further research might prove more conclusive.

Much of the argument about a political reaction turns not upon what we know of the eighteenth century, but upon what we know of the seventeenth. The eighteenth-century evidence which gave rise to the idea is not open to question; what is in doubt is the singularity of that evidence. If the policies of Louis XIV were not anti-aristocratic, and if under him the nobility were not stripped of all power, then what has looked like a new set of developments in the eighteenth century may turn out to have been far less important. Had the nobility lost so much that it took a century to recapture it? A clear view of the reign of Louis XVI, from this point of view, depends on an accurate knowledge of that of Louis XIV.

There can be little doubt that Louis XIV was not hostile to aristocracy as such. His whole way of life, surrounding himself at Versailles with the cream of the nobility, and upholding their privileges and social standing, shows how profoundly he accepted it and its values.[8] The search after false nobles, of which some historians still make so much,[9] far from being anti-aristocratic, was directed against those who adulterated nobility and usurped its privileges. Many legitimate nobles welcomed it.[10] The expansion of the nobility's ranks throughout the sale of venal ennobling offices was a fiscal expedient, not a hostile policy.[11] Arguably it strengthened rather than weakened the position of the nobility in society by making noble status a constantly attainable aspiration.[12] The

[7] E.g. C. Brinton, *The Anatomy of Revolution* (New York, 1965), pp. 36-7; Barrington Moore, Jr, *Social Origins of Dictatorship and Democracy* (London, 1969), pp. 63-6; Palmer, *The Age of the Democratic Revolution*, i, ch. 3.

[8] P. Goubert, *L'ancien régime*, 2 vols (Paris, 1969-72), i, p. 155; R. Mandrou, *La France aux XVIIe et XVIIIe siècles* (Paris, 1967), pp. 149-50; G. Pagès, *La monarchie d'ancien régime en France* (Paris, 1928), pp. 178, 191; J.B. Wolf, *Louis XIV* (New York, 1968), p. 271; and Ford, *Robe and Sword*, pp. 9-18.

[9] E.g., P. Goubert, *Louis XIV et vingt millions de Français* (Paris, 1966), pp. 66-7.

[10] See Mandrou, *La France aux XVIIe et XVIIIe siècles*, p. 93; P. Deyon, 'A propos des rapports entre la noblesse française et la monarchie absolue pendant la première moitié du XVIIe siècle', *Revue historique*, 231 (1964), pp. 354-6.

[11] Cf. Goubert, *Louis XIV*, p. 67.

[12] See G. Pagès, 'La vénalité des charges dans l'ancienne France', *Revue historique*, 169 (1932), pp. 492-3.

campaign to strengthen the law of derogation (*dérogeance*), shocking as it may have been to the commercial noblemen of Brittany, can only with perversity be described as anti-noble.[13] Despite Saint-Simon's jibes, all Louis's ministers enjoyed nobility.[14] His anti-aristocratic reputation in fact seems to rest mainly on his diminution of the political power wielded by a few *great* noblemen, a tiny handful of over-mighty subjects.

Most of the aristocracy, for example, were left quite untouched by Louis's decision in 1661 not to call any prince, duke, peer or ecclesiastic to his policy-making councils. Such distant metropolitan manoeuvres were governmental changes, but hardly a new social policy. It was the same when Louis imposed restrictions on the powers and tenure of provincial governors, and indeed when he concentrated the magnates of the realm around his person at Versailles away from their provincial power bases. Those affected were a relatively small group of notables. Moreover, when we examine the precise nature and the subsequent history of these innovations, we find either that they were not entirely novel, and were only partly reversed in the eighteenth century; or that, once made, they survived until the old order ended.

There was obviously a clear reaction in 1715 against the exclusion of princes, peers and clerics from policy-making. A system of *polysynodie* was introduced, an attempt to govern the kingdom through a series of executive councils staffed at least by great nobles;[15] but the most notorious fact about *polysynodie* is its short life, its failure to work. Within three years the experiment was abandoned. It is true that even after the collapse the categories excluded from policy-making by Louis XIV continued to play a part in the process. Princes like Orléans and Conti, peers like Choiseul, d'Aiguillon and Castries, clerics like Fleury, Bernis, Terray and Brienne are examples. To this extent there was something of a reaction, although it was century-long and certainly did not intensify as time went on. Yet it is arguable that a better description than reaction would be diversification of recruitment. Most of the personnel of the royal councils continued to be recruited from the upper echelons of the venal hierarchy, from the masters of requests and, ultimately, the

---

[13] See J. Meyer, *La noblesse bretonne au XVIIIe siècle*, 2 vols (Paris, 1966), i, pp. 46-7, ch. 6, passim, and ii, pp. 1245-6 for the conclusion that such measures strengthened noble exclusivism rather than broke it down; see too R.B. Grassby, 'Social Status and Commercial Enterprise under Louis XIV', *Economic History Review*, 2nd series, 13 (1960-1), pp. 19, 25-6, 35.

[14] See below, p. 59.

[15] See M. Antoine, *Le conseil du roi sous le règne de Louis XV* (Paris and Geneva, 1970), pp. 80-100.

sovereign courts. Louis XIV's innovation had been to confine recruitment to these groups, all noble,[16] but certainly not composed of men of 'high consideration'[17] who might delude themselves that their power was independent of the king's. Most of the personnel of the royal councils, in fact, was already drawn from their ranks before 1661,[18] and all Louis did was to exclude others and so in a sense professionalise his administration. This made it more exclusive too.[19] The eighteenth-century trend was to broaden recruitment once again, not restrict it.[20]

In other respects, the eighteenth century was remarkable for changing nothing. The concentration of the great at Versailles, for example, went from strength to strength, and the complex restrictions on access to the 'honours of the court' which were elaborated in the eighteenth century were mainly a logistic device to stem the demand.[21] Similarly, provincial governorships, which Louis XIV kept as the preserve of the great nobility, remained in their hands until 1789. Admittedly Louis had restricted tenure of these offices to periods of three years, and this restriction apparently did not survive into the eighteenth century. But even under Louis himself appointments were normally renewed, the term being merely the guarantee of good conduct. He did deprive the governors of control of royal patronage, through which in the early seventeenth century they had been able to build up an extensive and semi-independent network of clientage, but this too was a permanent development. Indeed the eighteenth century saw a further decline in the governors' provincial power in the sense that from 1750 they were forbidden to reside in their provinces without royal permission.[22] The intendants too survived, concentrating in their own hands powers of justice, taxation and public works which the governors had often been able to usurp during years of internal disorder.[23] The powers of governors were above all military, and it is no coincidence that Louis

---

[16] See below, pp. 59-60.

[17] *Mémoires de Louis XIV* (Paris, 1806), i. p. 7.

[18] R. Mousnier (ed.) *Le conseil du roi de Louis XII à la Révolution* (Paris, 1970), pp. 23-31.

[19] See below, pp. 63-4, for other links between exclusivism and professionalisation.

[20] See below, p. 60.

[21] F. Bluche and P. Durye, *Les honneurs de la cour* (Paris, 1959); P. Du Puy de Clinchamps, *La noblesse* (Paris, 1959), p. 62.

[22] On the governors, who deserve more attention, see P. Viollet, *Le roi et ses ministres pendant les trois dernières siècles de la monarchie* (Paris, 1912), pp. 324-34; M. Marion, *Dictionnaire des institutions de la France aux XVIIe et XVIIIe siècles* (Paris, 1923), pp. 259-61.

[23] G. Zeller, *Aspects de la politique française sous l'ancien régime* (Paris, 1964), ch. 12, passim; also J.H. Shennan, *Government and Society in France, 1461-1661* (London, 1969), pp. 60-2.

XIV singled out those of frontier provinces as the most dangerous.[24] The policy of Louvois was to diminish these powers too by appointing subordinate commandants or lieutenants-general to exercise the military authority theoretically at least still vested in the governors. These officers also continued into the eighteenth century, but since they were normally peers or great magnates of similar social standing to the governors themselves, the significance of their institution was limited.[25] On the other hand, we should beware of thinking that Louis reduced the governors to complete ciphers, and that ciphers they remained. In provinces with estates especially, where local notables had to be managed and conciliated, the king relied heavily on their help.[26] From the mid-eighteenth century, when quarrels with provincial parlements became more bitter, the government resorted more and more to the help of the governors or commandants in order to coerce parlements undaunted by the authority of mere intendants; this led to such famous disputes as those between the parlement of Toulouse and the duc de Fitz-James, or that of Rennes and the duc d'Aiguillon.[27] It was the governors and commandants who remodelled the provincial parlements on behalf of Maupeou in 1771, and they who received back the old ones in 1774-75.[28] But such a growth in the political role of these officers was hardly a sign of reaction; it was an institutional response to opposition among provincial parlements.

The parlements and the provincial estates were also aristocratic institutions. In these spheres at least Louis XIV's policies affected more than the great nobility, although how far the latter would have regarded their position as linked in any way to those institutions is dubious. Louis kept a tight rein on the estates, and the meetings of some were allowed to lapse. Yet most survived in all their aristocratic glory, and kept their

---

[24] *Mémoires de Louis XIV*, i, pp. 15-16.

[25] Viollet, *Le roi et ses ministres*, pp. 361-5.

[26] Ibid., p. 362, alludes to this neglected fact, but does not elaborate. For further substantiation, however, see A. Rebillon, *Les états de Bretagne de 1661 à 1789: leur organisation, l'évolution de leurs pouvoirs, leur administration financière* (Paris and Rennes, 1932), pp. 161, 183-5, 190; M. Bordes, 'Les intendants de Louis XV', *Revue historique*, 203 (1960), pp. 46-51; and R.C. Mettam, 'The Role of the Higher Aristocracy in France under Louis XIV, with Special Reference to the "Faction of the Duke of Burgundy" and the Provincial Governors' (University of Cambridge Ph.D. thesis, 1966), pp. 200-384. Dr Mettam shows that the active role of the governor in Brittany, often cited as an exception, had its counterparts in the Lyonnais, Boulonnais and Languedoc.

[27] For convenient summaries, See J. Egret, *Louis XV et l'opposition parlementaire, 1715-1774* (Paris, 1970), pp. 149-56, 158-70.

[28] Ibid., p. 194.

powers, without increasing them, until the old order fell. In the case of the parlements, 1715 admittedly quite clearly saw a reaction against Louis's policies. In 1673 he had crowned a policy hostile to the pretentions of the sovereign courts ever since 1661 with the rule that henceforth remonstrances should follow the registration of laws and not precede it. In 1715 the government of the regency reversed this rule and allowed remonstrances once more to precede registration.[29] The parlements built their whole constitutional position throughout the eighteenth century upon this reversal. By 1715 the aristocracy of their members was not in doubt.[30] Were they not, then, the vehicles of a broader aristocratic reaction? To prove rather than assume this we should have to demonstrate, first that they conducted a fairly conscious and successful campaign to increase their power in the state, and secondly that the policies they advocated were concerned with the promotion of aristocratic power. Neither of these propositions is self-evident.

The pattern of *parlementaire* resistance to royal authority over the eighteenth century is not one of crescendo. Up to about 1750 the provincial parlements remained relatively quiescent, and that of Paris was only sporadically active. They made no constitutional advances on what they had already achieved in 1715.[31] Nor were religion and finance, the two main issues which agitated the parlement of Paris in the troubled decades that followed, new ones. The religious question had been contentious even before Louis XIV died, and had been at the centre of the crises of the regency and the early 1730s.[32] It had nothing whatever to do with the nobility and its aspirations. The finances had also been a constant subject of disagreement since 1715.[33] Naturally, in their protests against increasing taxation the magistrates sometimes alluded to the privileges of the nobility; but far more often they reiterated that the nation as a whole was overtaxed and would be ruined

[29] Ibid., p. 9.

[30] Ford, *Robe and Sword*, p. 59.

[31] Egret, *Louis XV et l'opposition.*, pp. 45-9.

[32] J.D. Hardy, Jr, *Judicial Politics in the Old Regime: The Parlement of Paris during the Regency* (Baton Rouge, LA, 1967), chs 2, 3, 7; J.H. Shennan, 'The Political Role of the Parlement of Paris, 1715-23', *Historical Journal*, 8 (1965), pp. 183-5, 194-5; idem, 'The Political Role of the Parlement of Paris under Cardinal Fleury', *English Historical Review*, 81 (1966), pp. 526-40; Egret, *Louis XV et l'opposition*, pp. 17-33.

[33] Egret, *Louis XV et l'opposition*, pp. 34-43; Hardy, *Judicial Politics*, chs 4, 6, 8; Shennan, 'The Political Role of the Parlement', *Historical Journal*, pp. 186-94; idem, 'The Political Role of the Parlement of Paris under Cardinal Fleury', pp. 522-6.

by further impositions.[34] Indeed the theme of *national* rights and *national* sovereignty is a far more striking feature of their remonstrances in the later eighteenth century than their occasional espousal of specifically noble interests.[35]

These remarks also apply to the provincial parlements, who began to make the pace in opposition after about 1750. Their main preoccupations were with taxes again, and with the powers of the government's local agents – intendants, governors, commandants. What was at stake was local autonomy; and it was not the localities and their parlements which sought change. If they were 'reacting', it was not against a *status quo* going back to Louis XIV, but rather in defence of a *status quo* threatened by the ever-increasing encroachments of a revenue-hungry government. Allegations that the cry of public interest was a mask for noble ambitions will only take us so far; the parlements could not have achieved support as they did without a genuine and persistent defence of the interests of all, not just the nobility.[36] Support for the convocation of the estates-general only spread when it became clear, from 1771, that the parlements were no longer defending the interests of all. This was not because they ceased to be willing to do so. It was because the work of Maupeou showed that in the last analysis they had not the power to do so. The last twenty years of the old regime, when we should expect to find the aristocratic reaction at its height, were in fact years of great weakness for the parlements, when their influence on the government fell back almost to pre-1750 levels.[37] The tax increases and extensions of the early 1780s passed with unprecedented ease. Even if we could call the zenith of their power, that is to say the 1750s and 1760s, part of a reaction (which is dubious), we should still have to admit that by the time of Louis XVI it had manifestly failed. The 'noble revolt' of the summer of 1788 was not the confident knock-out blow aimed at a government tottering from previous aristocratic onslaughts. It was a desperate movement of non-cooperation with a government which had shown itself contemptuous of institutional checks on its power.

---

[34] Egret, *Louis XV et l'opposition.*, pp. 107-9, 131-2. See too the remarks of Shennan, *English Historical Review*, p. 526.

[35] R. Bickart, *Les parlements et la notion de souveraineté nationale au XVIIIe siècle* (Paris, 1933), passim; see too Mathiez, *La révolution*, i, p. 8.

[36] Egret, *Louis XV et l'opposition.*, pp. 230-1; see too Meyer, *Noblesse bretonne*, ii, p. 1250, for the conclusion that the Breton nobility was on the defensive, and p. 1252 for noble defence of the general interest.

[37] W. Doyle, 'The Parlements of France and the Breakdown of the Old Regime, 1771-1788', above, pp. 1-47.

That the rule of Louis XIV provoked an 'ideological' reaction in certain noble circles is well established. Around the prospect of the duc de Bourgogne coming to power congregated a group of great noblemen and supporters who saw France's salvation in an end to Colbertian mercantilism, the encouragement of agriculture and the suppression of the intendants. The assumption behind these ideas was that in implementing them great noblemen would resume the place in the state of which Louis was felt to have deprived them.[38] Fénelon, Boulainvilliers and Saint-Simon, the most notable leaders of the group, are often cited as the ideological prophets of the aristocratic reaction, which reached its most articulate expression in Montesquieu.[39]

It is undoubtedly true that all these writers were in favour of aristocratic power in the state; but it must be asked whether this general common feature was more important that the very considerable differences between them. Saint-Simon, for instance, was interested mainly in the claims of the peerage, a much more restricted group than the aristocracy as a whole.[40] Belesbat, Fénelon and Boulainvilliers, in favour of power for the aristocracy as a whole, nevertheless conceived of this body as essentially hereditary and were hostile to ennoblement. This implied condemnation of the political and social pretentions of the magistracy, the whole category of nobles of the robe. Yet it was from this group that Montesquieu came, and it was the institutional power of the parlements that he saw as the best guarantee that the French monarchy would remain true to its nature and subject to the check of aristocratic intermediary bodies. Evidently there was no agreement among the ideologues of aristocracy as to what the aristocracy was, what powers it should have or how they should be exercised. This suggests uncertainty and loss of direction rather than a new and self-conscious assurance.

It has, on the other hand, been argued that the events of the regency proved the incompetence of the higher aristocracy, and that consequently they were led to abandon their own theorists and turn to support the parlements, with their well-established constitutional position.[41] Accordingly the full elaboration of Montesquieu's views in the *Esprit des lois* of 1748 was a synthesis of all the various noble positions

---

[38] L. Rothkrug, *Opposition to Louis XIV: The Political and Social Origins of the French Enlightenment* (Princeton, NJ, 1965), pp. 175-7, 242-86, 328-71; also Mettam, 'The Role of the Higher Aristocracy', pp. 68-106.

[39] E.g. Soboul, *La France à la veille*, pp. 79-82.

[40] Ford, *Robe and Sword*, pp. 182-7; Mettam, 'The Role of the Higher Aristocracy', pp. 120-2.

[41] Ford, *Robe and Sword*, ch. 10.

reflecting this 'regrouping' over the previous half-century.[42] Yet it is also admitted that Boulainvilliers' theories 'remained the symbol of the *thèse nobiliaire* prior to 1748',[43] and that the similar feudal fantasies of La Curne de Sainte-Palaye could appear ten years after the *Esprit des lois*.[44] Above all it is assumed, but not proved, that the parlements united in the second half of the century, armed with Montesquieu, to press the claims of the whole nobility against the king. Undoubtedly they often did cite Montesquieu in their remonstrances, and at no time more frequently than during the crisis of 1788.[45] But he was never their consistent point of reference. They pillaged him, as they did many other writers when they found it convenient, in a wide range of causes. So did their opponents.[46] In any case all references to the authority of theorists were strictly secondary to arguments from the law. Indeed it has been argued that the remonstrances of the parlements between 1660 and 1789 show a marked decline of interest in political theory, and an ever-growing emphasis on legal technicalities.[47] There is no *prima facie* reason why legal arguments should always have the object of defending or refurbishing 'privilege', however convenient it may be to assume this. Nor need an increasing concern for legalistic constitutionalism always have been directed, consciously at least, towards concentrating power in aristocratic hands.

If, indeed, the aristocratic reaction is thought to have gathered pace over the eighteenth century, the conventional view of its ideological aspect has a further weakness. Why are its spokesmen all writers of the seventeenth or the first half of the eighteenth century? One would expect to find more, even if not greater, writers articulating aristocratic principles as time went on, if the reaction accelerated. But even lesser works, like those of Mirabeau or the chevalier d'Arc, all appeared before 1760. As Albert Soboul, who defines the 'ideological reaction' most succinctly, is constrained to admit, after Montesquieu the aristocratic current 'remained stationary' until the eve of the Revolution.[48] The fact

---

[42] Ibid, ch. 12, especially pp. 244-5.

[43] Ibid, p. 227.

[44] Ibid, p. 245.

[45] E. Carcassonne, *Montesquieu et le problème de la constitution française au XVIIIe siècle* (Paris, 1927), ch. 11, passim.

[46] Ibid, ch. 6, passim and pp. 562-3.

[47] W.F. Church, 'The Decline of French Jurists as Political Theorists, 1660-1789', *French Historical Studies*, 3 (1967), pp. 1-40, passim.

[48] Soboul, *La France à la veille*, p. 79.

that it was still Montesquieu whose name was most invoked by discontented nobles in 1788 shows that the early masters had no heirs.

It might be said, of course, that the theory was for the struggle, and that the years of triumph after mid century required none. But it has already been suggested that in political terms the eighteenth century saw and required no struggle, and therefore no triumph. This is even clearer if we turn to social developments.

The idea of a social reaction is one of the clearest and most persistent in the historiography of the old regime. Evidence by which it may be undermined accumulates daily, yet its significance is still largely ignored. So we may read, in a recent authoritative work by a group of very distinguished French historians, that:

> Kings no longer followed the prudent policy of Louis XIV. Under Louis XVI, all ministers, all councillors of state, all intendants (save one), all bishops and all abbots were nobles of old or very old 'extraction'; new rules ... effectually reserved for them the high ranks of the army; in the navy, they alone had access to the 'grand corps'. Against common or freshly ennobled talent, the doors were closing one by one.[49]

Here again, clearly, much of the argument depends on what we know of Louis XIV and those in office under him. As we have seen, Louis chose his advisers from the ranks of those already experienced in royal service but dependent for their continued worldly success on royal favour.[50] This alone ensured that they were noble, since most of the higher offices in the royal bureaucracy conveyed nobility on their holders; but, in any case, the families of Louis's secretaries of state had all enjoyed nobility for at least one generation, and that of most of them went back a good deal further. Such lineages were undistinguished compared to those of the dukes and peers whom Louis excluded from policy-making, but they still were noble ones; and what distinction they lacked in age, these families soon made up in alliances with the most ancient stock. The conclusion is clear:

> The personal reign of Louis XIV witnessed, in the high posts of the government, no commoners and no new men in the juridical sense of the word. This should be noted. We therefore conclude with a proposition exactly the

---

[49] F. Braudel and E. Labrousse (eds), *Histoire économique et sociale de la France: des derniers temps de l'âge seigneurial aux préludes de l'âge industriel (1660-1789)* (Paris, 1970), p. 595.

[50] See above, pp. 52-3.

contrary of that which is still held: Louis XIV governed without recourse to the collaboration of a single *bourgeois*.[51]

This then was Louis's 'prudent policy'. How far did matters change in the eighteenth century?

It is true that in the eighteenth century the king's ministers and secretaries of state included a number of princes, dukes and peers and clerics – men like Choiseul, d'Aiguillon or Brienne. But it is equally true that men of very humble extraction, such as Dubois or Sartine, could also attain these heights.[52] Most ministers and secretaries of state continued to be drawn under Louis XVI, as under Louis XIV, from the personnel of the privy council of state. The difference was that under Louis XVI more were recruited from outside its ranks. This meant that some great nobles attained office, but it also meant that other outsiders did so too. It is certainly difficult to believe that Louis XIV would ever have appointed a non-noble Swiss banker, like Necker, to manage his finances. Far then from closing, the doors to ministerial office seem to have been open to a wider and more diverse social range in the late eighteenth century than in the late seventeenth.

Of course, if most ministers and secretaries of state still came within reach of high office through being masters of requests, intendants or councillors of state, the true accessibility of the highest offices would reflect that of those subordinate ranks. But here the impression is confirmed. It was easier for newcomers to become councillors of state under Louis XV than under his predecessor, and there is no reason to believe that this state of affairs changed in the last years of the old order.[53] A study of the intendants yields similar conclusions.[54] Louis XIV's intendants were noble, like those of Louis XVI; having risen through the hierarchy of venal offices, they progressed in their careers through similar stages. It is the continuity of the pattern, rather than any change, which is striking. But in so far as it did change, there seems to have been a slight relative easing of access to intendancies for men of obscure origin under Louis XVI. In the last years of the old order the

[51] F. Bluche, 'L'origine sociale des secrétaires d'état de Louis XIV (1660-1715)', *XVIIe siècle*, 42-3 (1959), pp. 15-16; see also Furet, 'Le catéchisme', p. 274.
[52] F. Bluche, 'L'origine sociale du personnel ministériel français au XVIIIe siècle', *Bulletin de la société d'histoire moderne*, 12th series (1957), pp. 9-13; and *Les magistrats du parlement de Paris au XVIIIe siècle, 1715-1771* (Paris 1961), p. 67; and Goodwin, 'Social Origins', p. 397.
[53] Antoine, *Le Conseil du roi*, pp. 255-60; see too his communication in Mousnier, *Le conseil du roi de Louis XII*, p. 44, and Furet, 'Le catéchisme', p. 274.
[54] Gruder, *Royal Provincial Intendants*, ch. 8, passim.

body of intendants, like that of the masters of requests from which it was recruited, comprised men of shorter lineage and more diverse background than ever before.

Admittedly this could not be said of the church hierarchy. There is no evidence of a diversification in its recruitment at the end of the old order: nobles practically monopolised the bench of bishops. But even under Louis XIV, between 1682 and 1700, at least 88 per cent of bishops were noblemen.[55] Any reaction there may have been was hardly significant statistically.

If the church stood still, other institutions were following the pattern of the royal councils and diversifying their recruitment. Provincial academics became broader in their interests and broader in their socio-professional recruitment as the century went on.[56] These were the very bodies singled out by Franklin Ford as noteworthy in the earlier part of the century for their aristocratic exclusivism, and their contribution to the evolution of an aristocratic ideology.[57] But, of course, Ford's book did not prove the existence of an aristocratic reaction; it took its existence for granted and set out to explain it.[58] This obviously affected both his researches and his findings. If the aristocratic reaction turns out to have been an illusion, we may find ourselves questioning more important points in his thesis – for instance, that 'robe' and 'sword' had united behind the parlements between 1715 and 1748 to form a solid aristocratic front down to 1789. Then we might remember that the spring of 1789 saw plenty of bickering between magistrates and other nobles,[59] and that magistrates ennobled by office were no more welcome

---

[55] N. Ravitch, *Sword and Mitre: Government and Episcopate in France and England in the Age of Aristocracy* (The Hague and Paris, 1966), pp. 69-71. It is true that Ravitch also concludes that there was a trend towards more exclusively 'sword' recruitment, but such a category is dubious in itself, and he provides no means of checking his categorisations. Gruder, *Intendants*, p. 222 n. 23, points out that the sources of Ravitch's data on types of nobility are not always reliable. On the other hand independent research cited by Furet, 'Le catéchisme', has yielded similar conclusions to his.

[56] D. Roche, 'Milieux académiques provinciaux et société des lumières. Trois académies provinciaux au XVIIIe siècle: Bordeaux, Dijon, Châlons sur Marne', in G. Bollême et al., *Livre et société dans la France du XVIIIe siècle* (Paris and The Hague, 1965), pp. 112-20.

[57] Ford, *Robe and Sword*, pp. 235-7.

[58] See his preface, pp. vii-ix.

[59] E.g. in Franche Comté – H. Carré, *La fin des parlements, 1788-90* (Paris, 1912), pp. 94-5; or Guyenne – M. Lhéritier, *La révolution à Bordeaux dans l'histoire de la Révolution Française: la fin de l'ancien régime et la préparation des états-généraux (1787-1789)* (Paris, 1942), pp. 205-9, 222-5, 242-55.

at court under Louis XVI than under Louis XIV.[60] We might conclude that, despite the social fusion between 'robe' and 'sword' which seems conclusively proved, political and professional rivalry between different sections of the nobility fatally persisted until the old order fell.[61] Indeed, as more and more evidence emerges of social fusion even in the seventeenth century,[62] we might begin to wonder if these famous categories were ever more than professional ones, whose social signific-ance was extremely limited. Clearly this would rob the Ford thesis of much of its point.

We should not, however, deceive ourselves that the notion of a social reaction is based on no evidence at all. At the centre of it lies the all-too-solid evidence of the decisions of various parlements designed to exclude non-nobles and newcomers, and a series of military ordinances which restricted access to the officer corps. We cannot deny the existence of these; but we can investigate why they were passed, and whether they were enforced.

In the case of the parlements, the circumstances in which the excluding decisions of Rennes, Aix, Grenoble, Nancy and Toulouse were passed deserve further study. It may be that some of them emerged in the same way as that of Bordeaux in 1780, that is to say as bargaining counters in an internal quarrel, directed at a specific individual.[63] This would diminish their importance as assertions of general principle. In the case of Rennes some form of restrictive regulation had already been in force during the seventeenth century, so this was no new develop-ment.[64] Similarly, if the personnel of eighteenth-century parlements was noble, and included magistrates of very old lineage too, the situation was often foreshadowed in the seventeenth century.[65] The proportion of magistrates of noble extraction in the parlement of Paris in 1771 was

[60] See Bluche and Durye, *Les honneurs de la cour*; and Goodwin, 'Social Origins', p. 396. R. Mousnier, *La société française de 1770 à 1789* (Paris, 1970), pp. 87, 107-110, is clearly sceptical of any claims that divisions within the nobility had disappeared.

[61] Furet, 'Le catéchisme', p. 275, suggests that what had been called an aristocratic reaction was the manifestation in reality of just such conflicts. See also below, p. 65.

[62] See the remarks of P. Goubert in P. Goubert and J. Meyer, 'Les problèmes de la noblesse au XVIIe siècle', paper read at the Thirteenth International Congress of Historical Sciences (Moscow, 1970), p. 4; also Goubert, *Ancien régime*, i, p. 165.

[63] W. Doyle, 'Aux origines de l'affaire Dupaty', *Revue historique de Bordeaux et du département de la Gironde*, new series, 17 (1968), pp. 5-16.

[64] Meyer, *Noblesse bretonne*, ii, pp. 930-7.

[65] J.C. Paulhet, 'Les parlementaires toulousains à la fin du XVIIe siècle', *Annales du Midi*, 76 (1964), pp. 6-8; also Goubert, 'Les problèmes de la noblesse', p. 4.

overwhelming, but this was equally the case in 1715.[66] Any changes were very minor and self-cancelling. The author of these conclusions believes that they demonstrate a noble reaction; but he provides no earlier evidence to substantiate the assertion. Even if he could, clearly it would not be a matter of the classic reaction of the last decades before the Revolution, but rather something of very long standing indeed. Similar conclusions emerge from an analysis of the recruitment of the parlements as a whole between 1774 and 1789, which shows that, although the vast majority of those admitted to office in the parlements were noblemen, many had not the four quarterings or three degrees stipulated by the restrictive decisions even in places where such decisions existed (and they did not exist everywhere).[67] The majority of new recruits were in any case newcomers, with no *parlementaire* tradition behind them. Among these were the sons of both *parvenus* and old nobility. Again the impression is one of great diversity in recruitment,[68] and certainly no clear exclusivist trend.

The military evidence seems at first sight less ambiguous. In the navy, the *grand corps* of officers afloat was exclusively noble, and after 1775 entrance to officer cadet schools was confined to noblemen. In the army, the famous Ségur ordinance of 1781, 'the classic example of the aristocratic reaction',[69] restricted entrance to the officer corps to those who enjoyed at least four degrees of nobility, following the restriction of military academies to noblemen in the 1770s. But these were not new principles of policy. The *grand corps* in the navy always had been noble by definition and Louis XIV had announced his desire to recruit naval cadets exclusively from the ranks of the nobility as long before as 1683.[70] The recruitment of army officers had been restricted as closely as in 1781, in 1718 and 1727.[71] Moreover there were important qualifications. The naval cadet schools, whose status and prestige fluctuated spectacularly over the century, never monopolised entrance to the officer class, and outside the *grand corps* the only requirements for recruits remained professional rather than social. The Ségur ordinance

[66] Bluche, *Les magistrats*, pp. 76-7, 82-5.

[67] J. Egret, 'L'aristocratie parlementaire française à la fin de l'ancien régime', *Revue historique*, 208 (1952), pp. 6-9, see too Furet, 'Le catéchisme', p. 274.

[68] Egret, 'L'aristocratic parlementaire', pp. 6, 11-12.

[69] M. Reinhard, 'Elite et noblesse dans la seconde moitié du XVIIIe siècle', *Revue d'histoire moderne et contemporaine*, 3 (1956), p. 11.

[70] Marion, *Dictionnaire des institutions*, p. 365.

[71] E.G. Léonard, *L'armée et ses problèmes au XVIIIe siècle* (Paris, 1958), pp. 101 and 165; Mousnier, *La société française*, p. 126.

did not apply either to those already serving in the army (still in 1789 one quarter of all officers), or to the technical branches like the artillery, or to sons of *chevaliers de Saint-Louis*.[72] It was also to an extent, like the Bordeaux *arrêt* of 1780, the result of particular political circumstances rather than general policy, being issued on the personal insistence of the comte d'Artois, brother of the king.[73] All these circumstances make both the aims and results of the measures restricting the recruitment of officers less self-evident than would appear.

What then was their intention? They were the culmination of two long-term trends. One was towards the professionalisation of the armed forces. Ever since the 1750s the ideal of army reformers had been to diminish the influence of money, eliminate purchase by creating a professionally trained officer corps of noblemen. This had been the object of the edict creating a 'military nobility' of 1750, and of the Saint-Germain reforms of the 1770s.[74] Such a policy could only favour the petty nobility, too poor to pay the inflated price of commissions but traditionally dependent on the army as a means of livelihood. Yet it did not necessarily exclude non-nobles either, if they chose to rise on their talents rather than their money. The military nobility of officers envisaged by the chevalier d'Arc and other mid-century writers was designed, like the higher judiciary, to ennoble recruits as well as to recruit nobles.[75] Between 1750 and 1781 this was official policy too, and the 1781 ordinance explicitly claimed to be continuing it. In fact, by excluding those without a formidable noble lineage, it abandoned half the policy. Professionalisation was sacrificed to another policy trend – making provision for the poor nobility.

Most of the apparent signs of reaction attributable to the government were part of this second trend. The restriction of access to the naval and military cadet schools was to keep out the rich and guarantee a career to the poor nobleman with no other resources. Similarly, if ecclesiastical benefices in the crown's gift were restricted to noblemen, the intention was explicitly to help the poor nobility.[76] The problem was not new.

[72] Gruder, *Intendants*, pp. 223-4; Léonard, *L'armée*, p. 286; Viollet, *Le roi et ses ministres*, p. 378.

[73] Léonard, *L'armée*, p. 286.

[74] Ibid., p. 163-90, 244-50; Viollet, *Le roi et ses ministres*, pp. 369-70; Reinhard, 'Elite et noblesse', pp. 7-12; and A. Corvisier, *L'armée française de la fin du XVIIe siècle au ministère de Choiseul: le soldat*, 2 vols (Paris, 1964), i, pp. 126-7.

[75] Léonard, *L'armée*, pp. 181-90.

[76] Mme Campan, *Mémoires sur la vie de Marie-Antoinette, reine de France et de Navarre* (Paris, n.d.), p. 163. Also quoted in Ravitch, *Sword and Mitre*, p. 52.

Even in the seventeenth century the question of the poor nobility had preoccupied political writers. Then, as in the later period, they were torn between the conflicting solutions of urging the poor nobles into trade by suspending the law of *dérogeance*, or reinforcing their social separation by reserving certain positions for them alone.[77] It is possible that over the eighteenth century the problem became more acute. Certainly awareness of it was widespread, a fact reflected in the writings of the chevalier d'Arc, the abbé Coyer, or the marquis de Mirabeau. In a society where wealth opened every door, and yet where poor noblemen were largely debarred by their status from accumulating it, the pressure for some special provision became enormous.[78] Yet it was not so much against the competition of commoners that the poor nobility sought and were granted protection, as the glittering, well-connected courtiers of Versailles, and the new rich who so easily bought themselves ennoblement. It was against the nepotism of the former that the ecclesiastical appointments policy was mainly directed,[79] and against the wealth of the latter that the 1781 ordinance was framed.[80] If these measures were signs of a reaction, it was not so much noble against commoner, as one type of noble against another. They illustrate the deep chasms between rich and poor nobles, old and new nobles, metropolitan and provincial nobles, which remained a far more significant feature of old regime society than any possible fusion between the dubious categories of 'robe' and 'sword'.

On the other hand, the very consciousness of these divisions fostered attitudes, which from outside could only look reactionary. Petty provincial nobles reacted to the economic gap between themselves and the great at Versailles by attempting to play down other differences, falling back on doctrines of the unity and indivisibility of the nobility.[81] Rather than be treated as a separate and potentially inferior category, much less

[77] Grassby, 'Social Status', passim, for the seventeenth century; Reinhard, 'Elite et noblesse', pp. 13-19, for the eighteenth. How far a feeling of poverty in the poor nobility reflected their true position is, of course, a different matter. See J. Meyer, 'Un problème mal posé: la noblesse pauvre. L'exemple breton, XVIIe siècle', *Revue d'histoire moderne et contemporaine*, 18 (1971), passim, but especially pp. 166, 188.

[78] See J. McManners, 'France', in A. Goodwin (ed.), *The European Nobility in the Eighteenth Century* (London, 1953), pp. 36-8; and H. Carré, *La noblesse de France et l'opinion publique au XVIIIe siècle* (Paris, 1920), pp. 157 and 163.

[79] Campan, *Mémoires*, p. 163.

[80] Furet, 'Le catéchisme', p. 275.

[81] McManners, 'France', pp. 36-8; E. Champion, *La France d'après les cahiers de 1789* (Paris, 1867), pp. 89-90; Carré, *La noblesse*, pp. 348-9.

allow the court nobility a superior status, they resigned themselves to sharing the benefits of the Ségur ordinance with them, and ostentatiously applauded the decisions of those parlements which announced that they would no longer admit those whose only credentials were money. So that exclusivist or 'reactionary' moves were finding a more receptive audience among some members of the nobility as the old regime ended, and from outside the Ségur ordinance and the restrictive rulings of the parlements must have looked like vehicles of aristocratic reaction. In practice there was little movement towards greater exclusivism. This was of little consolation to the aspiring bourgeois to whom even an unchanging degree of it might appear for various reasons increasingly intolerable. But that is another question.

The idea that the last years of the old regime saw a 'feudal' or 'seigneurial' reaction in the countryside seems to go back to the last years of the nineteenth century.[82] As then outlined, it had two main features. On the one hand, lords or their agents fraudulently or unilaterally increased the burden of seigneurial rights and dues by new assessments.[83] On the other, old rights of undoubted legality which had fallen into disuse were revived and exercised, as terriers were remade by a zealous breed of agents (*feudistes*).[84] These developments contributed to the aggravation of the burden borne by peasants in 1789 and thus played a crucial role in the peasant risings of that summer.

As early as 1902 the suggestion that dues were arbitrarily increased came under attack,[85] and the greatest agrarian historian of the next generation remained unconvinced.[86] By 1946, even the father of the idea felt constrained to admit that 'It is difficult to prove a direct and written increase',[87] and most modern authorities carefully avoid committing themselves on this aspect,[88] confining themselves to the better-

---

[82] A. Chérest, *La chute de l'ancien régime*, 3 vols (Paris, 1884), i. pp. 48-56; Champion, *La France d'après les cahiers*, pp. 150-1; P. Sagnac, *Quomodo jura dominii aucta fuerint regnante Ludovico sexto decimo* (Le Puy, 1898).

[83] Champion, *La France d'après les cahiers*, pp. 149-50. I cannot claim to have read, or even to be able to read, Sagnac's thesis, but it is fairly fully summarised in Mousnier, *La société*, pp. 166-75.

[84] Champion, *La France d'après les cahiers*, pp. 152-3.

[85] M. Marion, *Etat des classes rurales au XVIIIe siècle dans le généralité de Bordeaux* (Paris, 1902), pp. 74-6.

[86] G. Lefebvre, *Les paysans du Nord pendant la Révolution Française* (new edn, Bari, 1959), pp. 158-60.

[87] P. Sagnac, *La formation de la société française moderne*, 2 vols (Paris, 1946), ii, p. 221.

[88] E.g., Soboul, *La France à la veille*, p. 85, and, at greater length, idem, 'De la pratique des terriers à la veille de la Révolution', *Annales, ESC*, 19 (1964), p. 1049; but A. Davies, 'The

established fact that many terriers were remade and old rights revived under Louis XVI, and quite legitimately too. This at least seems irrefutable, and has passed into most textbooks. Revival of obsolete or half-forgotten dues when terriers were remade still meant that there was a reaction in which the peasants' burden increased.

Yet even this did not find universal acceptance when it was first suggested. In 1914 Alphonse Aulard, while admitting that he did not have the volume of evidence to demolish it completely, suggested that the *cahiers*, the most persuasive source for the idea, were not always reliable as precise evidence, being often vague and general in their allegations.[89] He also pointed out the dangerous complexities in the use of other evidence, such as the comparison of terriers,[90] and the selection of untypical cases of profiteering and abuse among *feudistes*.[91] His conclusion was that 'there is no certainty about the degree of worsening of feudalism under Louis XVI, if indeed this feudalism did worsen'.[92] The only certainty was that people complained more about the burden, and that for reasons like foreign examples of alleviation, and the spread of enlightenment, they found it less tolerable.[93]

Curiously enough nobody followed this lead. General works ignored the doubts,[94] while particular studies seemed to confirm that revision of terriers, revival of old dues, and therefore a seigneurial reaction, did occur.[95] Most leading historians therefore continue to take them for granted. Even Alfred Cobban, who forced us to look afresh at so much in this period, accepted the fact of a reaction, although he did suggest that the increase in the peasants' burden came from a 'growing commercialisation' in the management of rights, rather than a return to archaic demands and harsher ways of management.[96] After all, evidence has continued to accumulate that pre-revolutionary landlords *were*

Origins of the French Peasant Revolution of 1789', *History*, new series, 49 (1964), p. 36, is reluctant to abandon the idea entirely.

[89] A. Aulard, *La Révolution Française et le régime féodal* (Paris, 1919), pp. 58-9, 66-9. The book was in fact written in 1914. For a translation of Aulard's earlier views on the subject, see R.W. Greenlaw (ed.), *Economic Origins of the French Revolution: Poverty or Prosperity?* (Boston, MA, 1958). Only recently have new doubts arisen as to the exact value and meaning of the *cahiers* as evidence: see Furet, 'Le catéchisme', pp. 266-8.

[90] Aulard, *La Révolution Française*, pp. 57-8.

[91] Ibid., pp. 60-1.

[92] Ibid., p. 69.

[93] Ibid., pp. 69, 75.

[94] Mathiez, *La Révolution*, i, pp. 16-17.

[95] Lefebvre, *Paysans du Nord*, pp. 157-71.

[96] Cobban, *Social Interpretation*, p. 52.

remaking terriers and reviving dues,[97] which seems to confirm the repeated complaints of the rural *cahiers*.

Unfortunately much of this evidence remains inconclusive on logical grounds alone. The remaking of terriers and complaints about it only prove that a reaction was taking place if they were not being remade, or were being remade much less extensively, in previous years. The discovery of new terriers in the 1780s means far less if they can also be found in the 1750s, for example, or even earlier. It is the same methodological problem which lies at the heart of other aspects of the so-called reaction. Long histories of individual fiefs are needed, and in large numbers, if we are ever to resolve this aspect of the problem satisfactorily.[98] Meanwhile, our materials are as statistically inadequate as Aulard's were, and certainly not enough to justify our dismissing him out of hand. Quite the reverse, in fact: there is evidence to suggest that a thorough inquiry might do much to vindicate his doubts.

First of all historians have uncovered 'feudal' or 'seigneurial' reactions in other, earlier, periods. From the Hundred Years' War onwards seigneurial administration became better organised and more regularly documented throughout France;[99] the reconstruction of domains in the Bordelais after that war demonstrates many of the classic elements of 'reaction' – renewal of half-forgotten obligations, foreclosures on accumulated debts, prior purchase by lords (*retrait féodal*), and reconstruction of terriers.[100] More significantly, a similar process of reconstruction occurred on lands around Dijon after the Thirty Years War in the seventeenth century; in this area ravaged by war and plagued by lost records, the reaction seems to have been far more severe than anything the eighteenth century might have witnessed.[101] But terriers were being reconstructed in the seventeenth century even where war did not rage, as the case of the Beauvaisis shows.[102] It has been suggested that this was

---

[97] See R. Forster, *The Nobility of Toulouse in the Eighteenth Century: A Social and Economic Study* (Baltimore, MD, 1960), pp. 49-53, for a much-cited example; and Davies, 'The Origins', pp. 35-7, for a general statement of the case.

[98] See the appeal in Mousnier, *La société*, pp. 191-2.

[99] M. Bloch, *Les caractères originaux de l'histoire rurale française*, 2 vols (Paris, 1964), i, p. 135.

[100] R. Boutruche, *La crise d'une société: seigneurs et paysans du Bordelais pendant la Guerre de Cent Ans* (Paris, 1963), pp. 333-9. On p. 338 he actually calls it 'an attempt at seigneurial reaction'.

[101] G. Roupnel, *La ville et la campagne au XVIIe siècle: étude sur les populations du pays dijonnais* (Paris, 1955), pp. 250-67.

[102] P. Goubert, *Beauvais et le Beauvaisis de 1600 à 1730: contribution à l'histoire sociale de la France du XVIIe siècle* (Paris, 1960), pp. 530-2. On p. 543 he speaks of a 'sort of first "feudal" reaction'.

going on, and that *feudistes* were at work, all over France in that period.[103] There was, then, nothing unique about what happened under Louis XVI. It had happened before.

This suggests a further reflection; perhaps it was always happening, all the time. In any system where lordship and ownership are not congruent, any records of debts owed and properties on which they are owed are bound to become outdated very quickly as land changes hands; and as soon as they do, exact dues may cease to be levied. On the other hand, if dues went unexacted for thirty years, then rights lapsed. This meant that terriers had to be revised every twenty-nine years at the least, which explains why arrears which peasants complained had built up, were seldom more than twenty-nine years behind.[104] Every generation of lords had to remake its terriers, or lose its rights for ever. This would mean that the main characteristics of what has been called a reaction were in fact permanent features of that structure of property which for convenience we call 'feudal' or 'seigneurial'. It would mean that the reaction which supposedly began around 1770,[105] was in fact only the last phase of a perpetual process, complained about by those peasants who happened at the time to be undergoing it.[106] It would certainly mean that we could no longer accept massive accumulations of evidence for a reaction under Louis XVI, such as those for the Nord,[107] unless it could also be demonstrated that such evidence could not be found in the same area for the earlier decades of the century. It the present state of knowledge, this cannot be taken for granted, as a brief survey reveals.

The seigneurial burden was probably generally lighter in southern than in northern France,[108] but even there terriers were remade and old rights exacted. But when? Foreclosures and prior purchases cited as examples of seigneurial reaction in the Bordelais are drawn from the

[103] In Braudel and Labrousse, *Histoire économique et sociale*, pp. 591-2. See too Goubert, *Ancien Régime*, i, p. 170.

[104] Soboul 'De la pratique des terriers', pp. 1062-3; Meyer, *Noblesse bretonne*, ii, pp. 788-9. In some areas the limit of legal memory was twenty years. It is noteworthy that the two seigneurial offensives of the Saulx-Tavanes family, in 1765 and 1785, coincided with the estates changing hands: R. Forster, *The House of Saulx-Tavanes: Versailles and Burgundy, 1700-1830* (Baltimore and London, 1971), p. 92. It is only fair to add that the sharpening of seigneurial demands in this Burgundian duchy after 1750 seems irrefutable evidence of a reaction there. It remains astonishing, however, that there had been no general revision of terriers since 1610 (p. 95).

[105] Sagnac, *La formation*, ii, pp. 129-30.

[106] Mousnier, *La société*, pp. 191-2, employs a similar argument, suggesting that terrier renovation occurred whenever a fief was sold.

[107] Lefebvre, *Paysans du Nord*, pp. 158-9.

[108] Goubert, *Ancien régime*, i, pp. 83-123; Furet, 'Le catéchisme', pp. 264-5.

whole century.[109] The two examples of collections of accumulated
arrears in a study of the nobility of Toulouse come from 1750 and
1724.[110] In Auvergne the burden, though light, increased over the
century, but only as a proportion of net produce.[111] In lower Provence
there was no reaction at all either in the long or short term, either by the
extension of seigneurial domains or in the increase of burdens on the
peasants.[112] It was the same in the Albigeois.[113] Even further north there
were areas where the burden was slight. In what was to become the
department of the Sarthe, seigneurial rights were very unremunerative,
disturbed the peasants little and did not obviously increase in weight
with the remaking of the terriers. Their historian concludes that terriers
were only remade at all as part of the waste-clearing mania of the 1760s,
and because they were bound to get out-of-date as owners changed.[114]

Even in parts of northern France, like the Nord, terriers were being
remade at least as early as 1759.[115] Admittedly in certain areas of a
traditionally heavy seigneurial burden, like Burgundy, some aggravation may have taken place in the old regime's last years.[116] In the duchy
of Saulx-Tavanes, the courtier landlord was determined to squeeze the
last penny from his rights, and used the occasion of his elevation to a
dukedom in 1786 to double his demands for the year under a custom
not invoked since the thirteenth century.[117] A general study of the whole
of northern Burgundy also emphasises a more intensive approach to
exercising seigneurial rights later in the century.[118] Yet the same study

---

[109] R. Forster, 'The Noble Wine Producers of the Bordelais in the Eighteenth Century',
Economic History Review, 2nd series, 14 (1961-2), pp. 29-30.

[110] Forster, *Nobility of Toulouse*, p. 51.

[111] A. Poitrineau, *La vie rurale en Basse Auvergne au XVIIIe siècle, 1726-1789*, 2 vols (Paris,
1965), i, pp. 342ff.

[112] R. Baehrel, *Une croissance: la Basse-Provence rurale (fin XVe siècle à 1789)* (Paris, 1961), pp.
451-2.

[113] P. Rascol, *Les paysans de l'Albigeois à la fin de l'ancien régime* (Aurillac, 1961), pp. 102-13.

[114] P. Bois, *Paysans de l'Ouest: des structures économiques et sociales aux options politiques depuis
l'époque révolutionnaire dans la Sarthe* (Le Mans, 1960), pp. 391-4.

[115] Lefebvre, *Paysans du Nord*, p. 149.

[116] R. Robin, *La société française en 1789: Semur en Auxois* (Paris, 1970), p. 153, calls this a
certainty, on the grounds that lords were employing the right to a segment of divided commons
(*triage*) more frequently. The examples she gives for her own community, however (pp. 154-7),
do not relate to this practice, nor does she prove there was anything about them peculiar to the
pre-revolutionary decades.

[117] Forster, *House of Saulx-Tavanes*, pp. 100-1; for the general intensification of pressure on
this estate see pp. 92-108.

[118] P. de Saint-Jacob, *Les paysans de la Bourgogne du Nord au dernier siècle de l'ancien régime*
(Paris, 1960), p. 425.

also reveals renovation of terriers and scrupulous attention to seigneurial rights throughout the first half of the century.[119] Its author concludes
that the reaction was century long, and that what happened later in the
century was merely a 'new chapter' in proceedings by no means new in
themselves.[120] In Brittany noble concern for exactitude in the levy of
dues went back to the late seventeenth century or even before. It
resulted, moreover, not so much from the greed of landlords as the
policies of a royal administration determined to deprive them of all
rights they could not document;[121] and from constant attempts by a
resourceful peasantry to whittle away their lords' rights whenever their
vigilance relaxed. Such tendencies forced lords to make their claims
precise, either in periodic new terriers or at each change of ownership.
As the historian of the Breton nobility puts it:

> The expression 'seigneurial reaction' is inadequate because it has been applied
> to too short a period (the end of the eighteenth century), when its judicial
> symptoms were appearing from the end of the sixteenth. It is also incomplete in
> that is leaves aside not only the permanence of seigneurial pressure, but also
> that of erosion by the peasants (*grignotage paysan*).[122]

The overall impression left by recent studies, therefore, is that the
maintenance of seigneurial rights was a constant process, of which the
remaking of terriers under Louis XVI, where it occurred, was merely
the last manifestation. Only very occasionally were new dues levied or
old ones increased. It was mostly a question of not allowing existing ones
to lapse.

This is not to say that the seigneurial order saw no new developments
as the eighteenth century progressed. The rise in prices must have
diminished the weight of dues in cash, a positive alleviation of the
burden.[123] On the other hand, it must have increased the weight of dues
in kind. Improved surveying techniques must have made terriers more
precise as time went on.[124] A new table of duties payable on terrier work,
of 1786, certainly increased the cost of revising these documents, costs

---

[119] Ibid., pp. 223-5, 243-4. Roupnel, *La ville et la campagne*, pp. 250-67, shows it going on
earlier still.

[120] Saint-Jacob, *Les paysans*, pp. 249, 425, 434.

[121] Meyer, *Noblesse bretonne*, ii, pp. 784-5.

[122] Ibid., p. 788.

[123] E.g. in Provence, a point made by Baehrel, *Une croissance*, pp. 450-1.

[124] Davies, 'The Origins' (cited n. 88), pp. 36-7; Soboul, 'De la pratique', pp. 1058-63; Meyer,
Noblesse bretonne, ii, pp. 790-1.

which the tenant rather than the lord usually bore.[125] It seems too that more lords were farming out their assets to professional agents or farmers, who were perhaps harsher managers than the lords themselves.[126] In these ways the burden of the seigneurial structure may have been increasing. For these reasons, the peasants complained when the *cahiers* presented them with the opportunity. But little of this resulted from any 'reaction' among lords. The rise in prices and the improvement of surveying techniques were beyond their control. So was royal fiscal policy. The employment of farmers suggests disinterest in the means of assuring returns, rather than renewed attention.[127] The remaking of the terriers, collection of arrears, and all the other multifarious exactions of the system, were processes as old as the system itself, which had no occasion to be revived, since they had never died out.

Those historians who have tried to synthesise all the elements analysed here into one immense reaction have often been shown to be vulnerable. Critics have seized upon their convenient confusion of terms, like 'noble' or 'aristocratic' or 'feudal' or 'seigneurial', none of which are entirely synonymous and some of which are very different indeed.[128] The foregoing survey should add to these doubts. The 'feudal' or 'seigneurial' reaction was an idea developed quite independently of the others, and whatever tenuous connection it could be said to have with political or social reactions, in that it was conducted by aristocrats,[129] now seems weaker than ever. Similarly, if there was an ideological reaction, or a political one, they did not coincide chronologically with what has been supposed to be the social reaction of the later eighteenth century. Even accepting that these various different phenomena did occur, the single broad 'aristocratic reaction' has been synthesised only at the cost of glossing over many such obstinate difficulties.

Meanwhile it seems increasingly doubtful whether even the particular reactions can be substantiated. In political terms, the only irrefutable reaction was confined to the years of the Regency, and that was short-

---

[125] Aulard, *Féodalité*, pp. 51-3; Davies, 'The Origins', p. 36.

[126] See Cobban, *Social Interpretation*, pp. 48-50; Forster, *House of Saulx-Tavanes*, pp. 94-104.

[127] On these grounds Cobban, *Social Interpretation*, goes so far as to call the 'feudal reaction' a misnomer.

[128] E.g., M. Reinhard, 'Sur l'histoire de la Révolution Française', *Annales, ESC*, 14 (1959), pp. 568-9; Cobban, *Social Interpretation*, ch. 4, passim; Furet, 'Le catéchisme', p. 264.

[129] Which incidentally ignores the fact that as often as not the landlords or farmers concerned were bourgeois.

lived. Nothing after it appears unambiguous enough to deserve the name reaction, at least until the sudden emergence of the social question in 1787-88, which is rather a different problem. In ideological terms, there was no unanimity among theorists on anything more precise or less superficial than increased power for aristocrats, a theme which seems to peter out, or at least petrify, between about 1750 and 1787. In social terms, most institutions in France seem to have become less, not more exclusive in their recruitment as the century went on. Although a hostile awareness of this trend seems to have been spreading among certain noblemen, it had made little impact on the trend by the time of the Revolution. In the countryside, the burden of the seigneurial property structure may have grown more heavy, but in most areas this had little to do with any reaction. Over-exclusive study of the years immediately preceding the Revolution seems to have produced a historian's illusion. But the ship has now sunk. Not without trace; a few masts obstinately protrude above the surface to mark where the wreck lies. But wreck it remains. Can anything be salvaged?

Little remains for the supposed reaction under Louis XVI, at least prior to the collapse of the government's reform plans in the summer of 1788. There were those who felt that the barriers of privilege should be strengthened, if only to help the petty nobility. There were moves, like the Ségur ordinance, in that direction. But they had little to do with the collapse of the established political order which produced the real reaction, in the form of moves to capture control of the political machinery of the future for the provincial nobility. Perhaps, with no revolution, the moves towards exclusivism would have snowballed: the new army regulations of 1788, for example, would have had the effect of closing many of the loopholes which the Ségur ordinance had left open.[130] But, however much they inflamed a public opinion whose hostility was perhaps growing,[131] the practical impact of exclusivist sentiment remained small. Wealth, rather than privilege, remained the key to social success before 1789.[132] Such 'reactionary' tendencies as there were, were precisely directed at altering this state of affairs. But no reaction was necessary to ripen conditions for a revolution; all that was

---

[130] See J. Egret, *La Pré-Révolution Française (1787-1788)* (Paris, 1962), pp. 87-94; and Mousnier, *La société*, pp. 128-9.

[131] Carré, *Noblesse de France*, p. 313.

[132] See J. McManners, 'France' in Goodwin (ed.), *European Nobility*, for the most elegant expression of this view.

needed was a growing consciousness among those whom the old regime had always excluded from honour of the injustice of their exclusion.

Some historians, seeing the limitations of the idea of a reaction under Louis XVI alone, have preferred to speak of a longer process, of a century or more. This certainly lessens the chronological difficulties in synthesising such a movement, and outflanks many of the arguments which demonstrate that things were much the same under Louis XVI as under Louis XIV. Noble pressure for the revival in the early and mid seventeenth century of the long-dormant law against *dérogeance* might suggest that such a long-term reaction may have been beginning then.[133] This may be so; but it is doubtful whether, thus extended, the concept has much meaning, especially when considered as a factor in the origins of the Revolution. By the later eighteenth century it would be important as a structural characteristic of the old order, but hardly by then a development peculiarly significant in precipitating the revolution which overthrew that order. Nor would anything, except some element of dramatic contrast, be lost by such a disappearance. There is still more than enough in the circumstances of Louis XVI's reign to explain the outbreak of revolution.

Besides, behind the idea of a long, secular reaction would still lie the assumption of a different order in previous centuries, a less aristocratic France in the fifteenth, sixteenth, or early seventeenth centuries. Such assumptions may prove justified but, until their truth is demonstrated, we should beware of them. A critical examination of the supposed 'reaction' on the eve of the Revolution justifies such reservations. Historical clichés invite confirmation by research as much as they stimulate criticism, and most scholars have set out to explain and illustrate the aristocratic reaction. Yet by looking beyond the period characterised by the supposed reaction we find plenty of justification for questioning it. Perhaps future research will still show that institutions did become more aristocratic, or that more terriers were remade, in the later eighteenth century. But that research is essential if we are to establish beyond doubt that such things did take place. In the meantime much of the evidence points in quite the opposite direction.

[133] Grassby, 'Social Status', p. 19.

3

The Price of Ennobling Offices in Eighteenth-Century Bordeaux

There has been much talk of the fall in the price of offices in the eighteenth-century parlements. A number of general explanations have been put forward, without perhaps taking sufficient account of local conditions. My own research on the parlement of Bordeaux under Louis XVI has led to a wider examination of the question of ennobling offices in this city over the eighteenth century. A source of the first importance kept at the departmental archives of the Gironde provides enough information to suggest several general conclusions. This is the *Minutes notariales retirées des fonds en exécution et décret du 9 brumaire An II, portant suppression des offices: Inventaire Alphabétique.*[1]

There can be no doubt that the parlement stood at the summit of Bordeaux society in the eighteenth century. Its judicial, administrative and political powers gave it an unequalled social prestige in a province without local estates. Even so, its local prestige had perhaps never been lower than at the beginning of this century. Although it was still considered the local 'senate', it had been exiled for fifteen years by Louis XIV and, finally allowed to return to Bordeaux, it subsequently remained completely subservient to royal authority. It was a humiliation which could only diminish the court's prestige, and this was reflected in a fall in the price of its offices. The intendant Bazin de Bezons, in his account of the province in 1698, noted that an office of president *à mortier* had just been sold for 72,000 *livres*. Offices of counsellor, Bezons reported, were hardly reaching 25,000 *livres*, whereas around 1690, when the parlement had just returned from exile, they had gone for as

[1] In two typewritten volumes, répertoire numérique, 100. See too the royal declaration of 22 March 1773 ordering reimbursement of the offices suppressed by Chancellor Maupeou. Copy in AM, Bordeaux, fonds ancien, 77/5b.

much as 40,000.[2] This difference could doubtless be explained by a revival in 1690 of the parlement's prestige after so many years of exile; but, the intendant added, in 1698 there were suddenly plenty of offices for sale and even more likely to fall vacant soon, at a time when the novelty had worn off. And so appeared one of the foremost characteristics of the market for offices in the eighteenth century: wide variations in price over quite short periods. The complexity of the reasons behind these variations can also be glimpsed.

Prices for the office of counseller were not high under Louis XIV. In 1710 Monsieur de Pontac bought his for only 20,000 *livres*, and none went for more than 27,000 before 1715. But with the minority of Louis XV, when the Regent made important political concessions to the parlements, prices began to rise. They were over 30,000 *livres* by 1716. Henceforth, their average level went steadily up until the 1740s. There were of course fluctuations from year to year: if in 1734 Counsellor Duhamel managed to sell his office for 40,000 *livres*, two years later Montesquieu bought one for his son for only 27,000. Nevertheless, for all these fluctuations, there was a clear rise in the price of offices of counsellor at Bordeaux, which does not accord with the usual conclusion of historians that prices of *parlementaire* offices were falling everywhere at this time.[3]

Why was it happening? For one thing, no doubt, the parlement under Louis XV recovered some of the prestige which it had lost under the heavy hand of his great grandfather. The court once more enjoyed the right to remonstrate, the essential source of its political importance. Additionally, the parlement was successful in its conflicts with the local *cour des aides*.[4] But there were even more important reasons. During this time much more money was available among the groups from which the parlement normally recruited for the purchase of offices. Bordeaux's great eighteenth-century commercial expansion had begun, an expansion that would make it one of the richest towns in Europe. Merchants and their families, enriched by trade, could easily achieve social advancement by purchasing ennobling offices. Thus the merchant Jean Pellet, who had bought himself the office of *secrétaire du roi* in 1738 and 1742 bought for his sons two offices in the parlement at 39,000 and

[2] Archives des Affaires Estrangères, Paris, mémoires et documents, France, 1587, pp. 107-8.

[3] See F.L. Ford, *Robe and Sword: The Regrouping of the French Aristocracy after Louis XIV* (Cambridge, MA, 1953) pp. 148-9: P. Sagnac, *La formation de la société française moderne*, 2 vols (Paris, 1946), ii, p. 55.

[4] S. Quet, 'La cour des aides de Guienne: ses rapports avec le parlement de Bordeaux', *Revue historique de Bordeaux et du département de la Gironde* (1939-40).

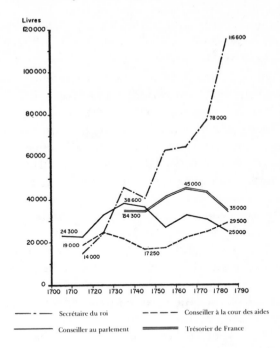

Fig. 3.1 Average price by decade of some ennobling offices in eighteenth-century Bordeaux

43,000 *livres*.[5] Nor were merchants the only ones to profit from commercial expansion: the wine trade prospered too, and the greatest vineyard owners were members of the parlement. For thirty years of peace, therefore, families both from the traditional recruiting grounds of the parlement, and the mercantile families from which most 'new men' came, were well placed to pay good prices for offices at the very moment when the restored prestige of the parlement made them more and more sought after. The start of this period can be pinpointed very precisely, since peace was restored shortly before the basic political event: the death of Louis XIV. Price movements did not only depend on the situation of the parlement; they also reflected the economic situation of the town.

This was clearly shown during the periods of war between the 1740s and 1760s. The seaborne conflict with Great Britain curtailed the trade of Bordeaux far more completely than during the war of the Spanish Succession, and the wealth of both merchants and wine growers was damaged accordingly. Office prices fell. It is true that the fall was light

---

[5] J. Cavignac, *Jean Pellet, commerçant de gros (1694-1772): contribution à l'étude du négoce bordelais au XVIIIe siècle* (Paris, 1967) pp. 284-5.

enough initially: no office sold for less than 35,000 *livres* between 1740 and 1749 and the average price for the decade hardly fell. But between 1750 and 1759 the highest price realised was not over 36,000, and there were offices selling below 30,000. 'The price at which the most recent offices have sold', noted Counsellor de Lamontaigne in 1758, 'is none too brilliant; they have gone for 25,000 or 27,000 *livres* but given the unfortunate times we live in, it is not surprising; no doubt they will recover if peace came to restore trade and affluence'.[6] Once the wars ended, prosperity soon returned and the price of offices began to climb again. The average price over the 1760s did not reach the level of the 1730s and 1740s, but some comparable prices were achieved. Around 1770, 40,000 was a good price, and normal enough.

Then, out of the blue, came the 'Maupeou Revolution'. Venal offices were abolished for three and a half years, an event whose importance can hardly be exaggerated. Louis XVI restored the parlement in 1775, but prices scarcely stopped falling from 1776 right down to the Revolution: in 1782, an office was sold for a mere 20,000 *livres*. The Maupeou Revolution, by the overthrow of the parlements and slow reimbursement of their offices, had brutally shaken the previous confidence in the security of these offices. What had been done once could be done again, as Lamoignon was to show in 1788 and the National Assembly a year later. Careers in the parlement, therefore, seemed less secure after 1775; besides, there were other reasons in those years for their shrinking appeal. Quarrels within the body between the 'remainers' and 'returners' of 1771 brought justice to a standstill and outraged the public.[7] Judicial strikes over the question of the reception of President Dupaty damaged the prestige of the parlement yet further, and these internecine clashes were not offset in the public mind by the resounding victories over the government in defence of provincial traditions and privileges.[8] To all this should perhaps be added the parlement's decision in 1780 to admit only noblemen in future; but it would be too simple to explain the fall in the price of office in the parlement by this restriction of the market. It might have been the case elsewhere, but at Bordeaux prices were already in decline before the ruling. Besides, from 1782, as the worst internal disputes died away, prices began to rise again and in 1786 one office changed hands for 26,000 *livres*. At Toulouse, moreover, one of the most aristocratic

---

[6] BM, Bordeaux, MS 1698 (fonds Lamontaigne), correspondence, no. 90, 28 Nov. 1758.

[7] See W. Doyle, *The Parlement of Bordeaux and the End of the Old Regime, 1771-1790* (London, 1974), chs 11 and 12.

[8] Ibid., chs 15 and 16.

parlements in the kingdom, prices recovered vigorously after 1775 and kept up well until the Revolution.[9] Exclusivism was not therefore alone responsible for the general fall in prices. Analysis of the price of other ennobling offices in Bordeaux suggests other reasons for the way they moved.

The parlement itself offers examples. The dearest offices were those of president *à mortier*, of which there were only nine. This is not enough to establish a graph, but the broad trend is clear enough. The 72,000 *livres* mentioned by Bazin de Bezons in 1698 was the lowest price ever; it never fell so low again. In 1739 the going price was 120,000, rising to 153,000 by 1753. Here again the Seven Years War brought a slight fall. 114,000 was paid in 1760. By 1770 prices were back to 120,000, and even after Maupeou they kept up, with 126,000 in 1778, and 123,000 a year later. Yet none of this diminishes the importance of the Maupeou Revolution as a factor in prices; these were very rare offices, often passed on from father to son, and they came onto the open market only occasionally. The one sold in 1779 was the last in Bordeaux before the Revolution.

As for presidencies in the lower chamber of *enquêtes*, after rising rapidly from 22,000 to 30,000 *livres* between 1708 and 1721, prices kept up throughout the century between 33,000 and 37,000 *livres*. The two offices of advocate-general were more and more in demand, doubtless because of the opportunities they gave to shine. In 1760 and 1767 both sold at 84,000; in 1778 at 91,200 and 92,400. It was the same, even more so, for the two offices of chief clerk, where it was possible, unlike other offices in the parlement, to make a good profit; selling at 65,000 in 1728, by 1777 they fetched 80,000 *livres*.

Offices of clerical counsellor, six in number, had a limited recruitment by definition. For this reason, and doubtless too because of the lack of appeal of a legal career to the clergy, and perhaps above all because those thinking of it were younger sons with only a small inheritance, these offices sold cheaply. Thus in 1729, when lay counsellorships were selling at 35,000 or 40,000, clerical ones were going for less than 20,000. In 1787 they were down to a mere 16,000 *livres*, having fallen to 14,000 in 1775.

Offices of counsellor-commissioner in the *requêtes du palais* were altogether special. Because the judgements of this chamber were subject to appeal, its prestige was very modest and offices there cost less than those of counsellor. To buy one was therefore an easy way of getting into

[9] P. de Peguilhan de Larboust, 'Les magistrats du parlement de Toulouse à la fin de l'ancien régime, 1775-1790' (Mémoire de diplôme, University of Toulouse, 1965), p. 65.

the parlement. They were always in demand among those who feared that they might not be acceptable as full counsellors. Moreover, because they were cheap, they were always much more in demand than others when a candidate's means precluded him, however temporarily, from buying a counsellorship. During the general rise in prices, from 1715 to 1750, the prices of offices in the *requêtes* went down; between 1720 and 1729 they wavered between 19,000 and 25,000, but in 1751 they were to be had at 13,000 *livres*. From 1757 onwards, as the price of counsellor-ships dropped, offices in the *requêtes* revived somewhat, to 14,000, 16,000 and even 19,000 *livres*. Peace brought a new fall, but a short one, since in 1768 20,000 *livres* was being paid. There are no further examples after 1775; but when, in 1786, the office of Counsellor Roche de Lamothe came on the market, he asked 18,500 *livres* and his potential buyer refused, on the grounds that this price was 'exorbitant', – a reaction reasonable enough at a moment when offices of full counseller were fetching only 7,000 or 8,000 more than that.[10]

Along with the parlement, ennoblement was also conferred by member-ship of the *cour des aides*, the *bureau des finances*, and the companies of *secrétaire du roi* attached to the two sovereign courts. The prestige of the *cour des aides* never equalled that of the parlement. 'If that company', wrote the intendant Tourny in 1749, 'from the scant business it has, from the mediocrity of most of its officers, from some of them dwelling on their estates and others engaging in things quite divorced from their functions, and last from the shade cast upon it by the Parlement, has not fallen here into public contempt, 'tis a close-run thing'.[11] And towards the end of the old regime the local diarist Pierre Bernadau was still observing that, 'these gentry in the Aides, who would ape the parlement in all things, have not a hundredth of the wisdom and energy of this latter body. They are the object of derision and contempt with the public, who call them the court of asses. Those who wish to get their sons into the Senate go there to wipe out their ignoble birth.'[12] Even so, there were around fifty offices in the court conferring nobility on their holders, when few people in the century got into the parlement without being already noble. Several of the latter's members were sons of counsellors at the *cour des aides*: it was indeed, as Bernadau observed, a way-station between low birth and full robe nobility. Duties in the court

[10] AD, Gironde, 2E 1213[5] (Titres de famille: Filhot de Chimbaud, correspondance), Mazières to Filhot, 2 March 1786.

[11] M. Lhéritier, *Tourny*, 2 vols (Paris, 1920), ii, pp. 442-3.

[12] BM, Bordeaux, MS 713 (1st series), 5, *Tablettes* of Pierre Bernadau, i, p. 338, 2 Oct. 1788.

were not heavy, and its jurisdiction, which was purely fiscal, was fairly narrow. It only commanded attention, in fact, when the parlement was not there, as during its exile in 1787-88. These offices, therefore, enjoyed esteem low enough to be cheap, yet were in enough demand not to be given away.

At the beginning of Louis XV's reign their value was rising. Soon it had exceeded that reached by offices in the parlement during the last years of the reign of Louis XIV. No doubt this rise resulted from the same growing prosperity whose influence on the price of offices in the parlement has already been noted. At this time, too, the *cour des aides* was challenging the pre-eminence of the parlement, which no doubt gave it a certain prestige; but in 1734 these disputes were resolved in the parlement's favour, and even before this the price of offices in the *aides* was failing to keep up. The relationship between the two sorts of office seems to have been comparable to that found between offices within the parlement. When money was abundant, dearer offices rose in price; when it became scarce, they fell and cheaper ones recovered. Thus until the 1760s the movement of average prices in the *cour des aides* was very similar to that of offices in the *requêtes*, even if *cour des aides* prices were always somewhat higher. The low point came in 1747, when an office there sold for a mere 14,000 *livres*. During the Seven Years war, their value began to climb again whilst those in the parlement fell. The rise went on, though less markedly, afterwards, even though offices in the parlement went up again. When around 1775 the final decline in prices in the parlement began, the rise in *cour des aides* prices speeded up, and around 1780 the parlement was overtaken. Amazingly but significantly, between 1780 and 1790 it cost more to become a counsellor at the *cour des aides* than at the parlement. Some offices reached 30,000 *livres*, which only happened once in the parlement during this time.

The nine presidencies in the *cour des aides* maintained a fairly constant level throughout the century, between 38,000 and 46,500 *livres*. Their fluctuations were too small and too short-term to have much significance. As in the parlement, offices of advocate-general fell between those of president and counsellor, at between 23,000 and 28,000 *livres*. For all these offices, the highest prices are explicable in terms of their greater scarcity and the greater dignity attached to them. But how was it that towards the end of the century prices in the *cour des aides* generally exceeded those in the parlement? In the first place it was certainly true that the *cour des aides* was easier to get into in terms both of family origins and technical competence. It was a much less demanding career: as Tourny had noted, there was not much to do since fiscal administration had been more and more taken over by the intendant. These reasons operated throughout the century, it is true, but after 1771 another came into play. Maupeou had not abolished the Bordeaux *cour des aides*. Nothing, therefore, threatened the security of its offices at a moment when those of the parlement were suppressed. Even more important, perhaps, was the fact that at the same time, alongside its administrative and judicial activity the political role of the *cour des aides* revived, bringing renewed prestige. It sent in remonstrances of considerable impact on the subject of revising the *vingtième* rolls, the *corvée*, and the exile of the parlement in 1787. All this provides a simple explanation of the remarkable rise in the value of its offices: under Louis XVI, it was easy to get into the court, safer, and not without political prestige, while duties there were less burdensome: and of course these offices enno-bled, too. Yet contemporaries seem to have been struck above all by how little these officers had to do. Thus Joseph Sébastien de Laroze, lieutenant-general at the *sénéchaussée* of Guyenne, counsellor at the parlement and father of a president in the *cour des aides*, could write in 1789: 'There is at Bordeaux a superior Court of Aides and Finances. The intendants have largely deprived this tribunal of almost all its functions. It would be easy to give these magistrates something to do; a Chamber of Accounts could be joined to it, to which the Treasurers of France established at Bordeaux could be associated.'[13]

The *trésoriers de France*, who made up the *bureau des finances* of Bordeaux, had even less to do in 1789 than the officers of the *cour des aides*. There were only about twenty of them, enjoying gradual ennoblement. It was not a sovereign jurisdiction, but an intermediary stage on the scale of special courts. It heard appeals from the *elections*, which could then go on up, sometimes to the parlement, sometimes to the *cour des aides*, sometimes to the *grand conseil* depending on the substance of the case. The president-treasurers of France checked tax rolls and oversaw highways and the royal domain. In mid century the government, acting in concert with the *grand conseil* and the intendants, began to encourage their pretensions in fiscal and domainial matters as a way of evading obstruction by the parlements. The treasurers lent their support to this campaign. In any case, their importance was enhanced in time of war, with increased tax demands. In Bordeaux, this policy took shape in a dispute over the royal terrier between 1752 and 1758 which brought the *bureau* into conflict with the parlement. The latter did not scruple, in the heat of the conflict, to describe the treasurers as 'talentless people,

---

[13] AN, B III, 34, pp. 979-80. Laroze to *Garde des Sceaux*, 14 Apr. 1789.

without wisdom, rectitude and feelings, essentially ignorant . . . incapable of acquiring the knowledge necessary to do their job'.[14] Several members of the parlement, however, were sons or relatives of these 'people', and in fact bitterness lasted only as long as the government was prepared to support the treasurers against the parlement. After 1760 this phase of the struggle with the parlements was forgotten. In 1763 the third *vingtième* ended with the war and the *bureaux des finances* fell back into relative obscurity. Lamoignon destroyed them in 1788, but within a few months they were restored. According to Laroze, they had so little to do that they could have been absorbed by other tribunals with no loss.

This brief survey of the *bureaux des finances* explains, partially at least, movements in the price of their offices. At the start of the century, they were well above those of the parlement. Three factors might explain this: the lack of business of the treasurers; the fact that their offices ennobled without qualifications or examination; and, above all, their small number. Between 1730 and 1750, while not falling, these prices were overtaken by those of the parlement. But, from 1750 down to 1770 they rose quite markedly. Whereas all other offices fell, the war had no effect on them. This contrast can only be explained by the government's campaign to restore their prestige and jurisdiction, and by their special importance in time of war. Even so, the rise was sustained long after the government abandoned its efforts to boost them. It was not until after 1775 that their prices began to fall once more; they were falling still when the Revolution began. Since prices in the parlement were falling too, their paths did not cross again. It can thus be said that the general level of their prices can be explained first by the nature and the number of these offices; but the drift corresponds exactly to their political fortunes, and on the eve of the Revolution they had fallen very low, as the treasurers themselves made clear:

> How many successive blows have tormented our existence? Loss of privileges, loss of jurisdiction, heavy fees, our best-established rights impugned, we have borne them all. Created to administer the domain, and for the levy of the *taille* and other taxes, we have seen the intendants take away our functions by surreptitious infringements. If we do not get back the whole of the functions to which we remain entitled, we have at least grounds for hoping that we can be reconstituted on invariable lines, and that, restored to useful functions, we may no longer be reduced to eating ourselves up with painful complaints.[15]

[14] Quoted by Lhéritier, *Tourny*, ii, p. 462, in a useful, if not always accurate, account of the terrier affair.

[15] Letter to Necker from the Bordeaux treasurers, 14 Nov. 1788, quoted in M. Marion, *Dictionnaire des institutions de la France aux XVIIe et XVIIIe siècles* (Paris, 1923), p. 62.

The final ennobling offices were those of *secrétaire du roi*, the notorious 'soap for scum' (*savonnettes à vilains*). Candidates needed no qualifications. In Bordeaux, their main function was to seal and expedite judicial documents in the chanceries of the parlement and the *cour des aides*. In reality, they had practically nothing to do. Yet these offices conferred complete and immediate nobility, which was transmissible too and brought all the usual privileges. In this way, a merchant could buy himself nobility very easily without encumbering himself with duties distracting from commercial activity, which was impossible with offices in the parlement and the *cour des aides*, and theoretically, the *bureau des finances*. A score of offices of *secrétaire du roi* were therefore much in demand in a city full of rich merchants. This was very clearly visible from the movement of their prices.[16]

During the last years of the reign of Louis XIV they sold quite cheaply: in 1713 Bernard de Lamolère-Sibirol bought one for 17,750 *livres*; and in 1717 they were to be had even at 10,000 *livres*. But from then on began an ever-accelerating rise. Between 1720 and 1730 they cost from 20,000-26,000 *livres*, and in 1730 an exceptional buyer paid as much as 52,000 *livres*. Between 1730 and 1740 no office fell below 25,000, with a maximum of 61,000. During this decade their prices outstripped all others paid in Bordeaux for ennobling offices, with the exception of the 'Grand Bench' (presidents) and the *gens du roi* in the parlement. This remained the case until the end of the old order: whilst other prices fluctuated markedly according to particular circumstances, those of *secrétaire du roi* simply reflected the sustained growth of the port of Bordeaux.

Of course, war did influence these prices. There was a slight fall in the average price during the war of the Austrian Succession, but it did not last. The Seven Years War, though it limited the rise, failed to stop it, and once it was over the rise in value accelerated. Around 1775 over 70,000 was being paid, and the American War of Independence had no impact at all. By 1780 prices were beyond 100,000 *livres* and 125,000, the highest price of the century, was paid in 1785. These were therefore the most valuable offices in the city, worth more even than presidencies in the parlement, which in 1778 and 1779 brought only 126,000 and 123,000 *livres* We should note, however, that there were considerable variations in individual contracts of sale. If 120,000 and 125,000 *livres* were paid in 1785, other offices only brought 80,000 *livres* in 1784 and

[16] I found much information on the secretaries in the manuscript notes of M. Alain d'Anglade, 'Recherches sur la compagnie des conseillers secrétaires du roi: maison et couronne de France à Bordeaux (XVIIe et XVIIIe siècles), kindly lent to me by the author.

77,298 *livres* in 1789. Average prices are, therefore, an arbitrary measure; but the general long-term rise is clear enough. Those who bought in mid century made enormous profits when they sold later.[17] Morel, who bought an office for 52,000 *livres* in 1730 sold it for 95,000 in 1767; Collingwood, who bought in 1746 for 34,000 sold in 1767 for 61,000; Giac, paying 55,000 *livres* in 1735, realised 85,000 for the same office twenty years later. Between 1769 and 1782 alone Maccarthy saw his charge go from 95,000 to 120,000. Such profits were an extra incentive for merchants to buy these offices; unlike most others, it was almost impossible to lose on them. This, too, helped to explain the rise in their value.

This, then, is the overall picture of the price of the 200 or so ennobling offices in Bordeaux in the eighteenth century. It is now worth looking at the general factors behind their fluctuations. Fundamental were the amazing fortunes of the port of Bordeaux. The monetary resources of the two groups who bought these offices – the great merchants and the great wine-growers – depended ultimately on the city's trade. War at sea damaged both equally, and their diminished means at these times was reflected in falls in the value of the dearest offices and, in proportion, a relative rise in the less expensive ones – showing that offices influenced one another. Overall, it was the prosperity of Bordeaux which kept the general price level of all these offices so high throughout the century.

Another factor was the number of offices. It is obvious that the high price of presidencies, and the offices of *trésorier de France* and *secrétaire du roi* was largely the result of their small number. Yet matters were not quite that simple: there was also a ratio between privileges and work which modified the equation. Those which realised the highest prices were mostly those requiring least work and conferring most noble privileges: the offices of *secrétaire du roi*. Less dear, but requiring more commitment and slower ennoblement, were the offices of *trésorier de France*. The least attractive ratio between privileges and occupation was that of counsellor at the parlement.

Also important, however, was the prestige attached to the office itself. It was because of the prestige of the 'Bordeaux Senate' that those in the parlement cost more than those in the *cour des aides*, except in the last years before the Revolution. Presidencies *à mortier* cost more for the

---

[17] But it has been pointed out by a later reader of this essay that successive increases in the nominal capital of these offices by the government, in the form of *augmentations de gages* or *de finance* would have much diminished any profit calculated on private market prices alone: J.F. Solnon, *215 bourgeois gentilhommes au XVIIIe siècle: les secrétaires du roi à Besançon* (Paris, 1980), p. 90.

same reason. On the other hand, this same prestige meant that many of those rich enough to aspire to the parlement, but feeling themselves unqualified in other ways, sought their ennoblement elsewhere. All this explains the position of office in the parlement in relation to other ennobling offices. Here, once again, we come back to the conclusion that the appeal of an office depended closely on the quantity, the quality and finally the security of comparable offices available on the local market. There were many ennobling offices in Bordeaux, which explains many of the fluctuations in their price.

The most striking feature of this general picture is that there was no uniform fall in prices. Some went up. Ennoblement by office was in demand in Bordeaux, even on the eve of the Revolution. Nobility had not lost its prestige. But the offices whose prices went up most steadily, those of the two chanceries and the *cour des aides*, were ones which demanded little effort of their acquirers but ennobled nonetheless. It seems as if the rights of nobility were more and more in demand but that less and less thought was being given to its duties. Where duties might be heavy, as in the parlement, prices tended to go down.

Obviously this was not the only reason for the fall in *parlementaire* offices. None of the trends followed here had a single cause. What cannot be accepted is the view that the decline in the price of offices in the parlements was the result of deliberate policies to restrict recruitment to nobles. This played no more than a limited part in Bordeaux: not only was office in the parlement more and more demanding but, as the century went on, so were the social credentials demanded of candidates. Doubtless the effect was to push many towards offices less exacting in every respect. Parlementary exclusivism was therefore of some importance in the market both for the court's own offices and for others. The political prestige of any court acted in the same way. But other things were more important. The decline in the price of offices in the parlement was merely one aspect of a much broader market for ennobling offices, whose most important variations resulted from a wide range of localised circumstances.

4

Venality and Society in Eighteenth-Century Bordeaux

The study of seventeenth-century French society was transformed in 1945 by the publication of Roland Mousnier's great thesis on the venality of offices under Henry IV and Louis XIII.[1] In view of the impact which Mousnier's work made, it is surprising that nobody followed his lead for periods later in the seventeenth century, or indeed the eighteenth. The problem of venality under the old regime remains largely unexplored territory, especially in respect of the lower offices in the venal hierarchy. And yet at the same time, the lower office holders have come to occupy a central place in the controversies of recent years about the origins of the French Revolution. For Alfred Cobban, in fact, they were the key to the revolutionary bourgeoisie. 'A section of society', he wrote, 'which was definitely not rising in wealth, and was barely holding its own in social status, was that of the *officiers*. The test of this is the decline in the value of venal offices and the failure to find purchasers for them. The decline seems to have been general, from the parlements downwards, though until the end of the eighteenth century it was much less marked in the offices of the parlements than in those of the *présidiaux, élections, maréchaussées* and other local courts.'[2] Cobban goes on to suggest that it was just such officers as these who provided the Third Estate in 1789 with its revolutionary driving force – their fervour derived from the fact that they were a declining class. While not all subsequent writers have accepted this argument, few have disputed that the petty office holders were in a declining position.[3] Nor are the upholders of more traditional

[1] R. Mousnier, *La vénalité des offices sous Henri IV et Louis XIII* (Rouen, 1945).
[2] A. Cobban, *The Social Interpretation of the French Revolution* (Cambridge, 1964), p. 59.
[3] See, for example, C. Lucas, 'Nobles, Bourgeois, and the Origins of the French Revolution', *Past and Present*, 60 (1973), pp. 113-14.

views about the revolutionary bourgeoisie likely to dispute this assertion of Cobban's, at least, for a bourgeoisie disgusted by the traditional attractions of office fits in very well with their own view, of a revolutionary class convinced of the superior merits of capitalism.

But doubts arise if one considers the evidence upon which the claim that offices were declining in value, is based. For non-ennobling offices, Cobban cited complaints made by the *cahiers* of two judicial companies in Rouen in 1789, and a page in Franklin Ford's *Robe and Sword*. When we follow up this reference in Ford, we find that *his* evidence for a decline in value is based on a letter written by Chancellor d'Aguesseau to subordinates in Brittany in 1740.[4] Such straws in the wind might well give a true impression, but we should be unwise to assume that they do until we have a rather fuller body of evidence. I do not by this mean to minimise the effort that would be required to amass such evidence. We are talking about no less than 51,000 venal offices, many of them changing hands several times over the eighteenth century.[5] The records of these transactions are buried for the most part in the enormous labyrinth of the notarial archives, and are only to be unearthed at the cost of years of tedious and frustrating labour. The task is daunting – and yet only if it is done can we be sure once and for all whether the value of petty offices really was on the decline. The one historian who has recently suggested that, at least in the case of magistrates in *bailliages* and *sénéchaussées*, they were *not* declining, also admits that his claim is only based on what he calls 'scattered indications',[6] hardly more numerous than those cited by Cobban.

There may, however, be a way round this problem. In Brumaire Year II, in connection with the final liquidation of venal offices by the Revolution, it was decreed that all contracts for the sale of such offices should be removed from notarial records. In certain cases, these contracts have surfaced as separate collections in departmental archives. And in the case of one such archive, that of the Gironde, the contents of the collection have been carefully inventoried in a document which gives, between two covers, the prices of the vast majority of venal offices

[4] F.L. Ford, *Robe and Sword: The Regrouping of the French Aristocracy after Louis XIV* (Cambridge, MA, 1953), p. 149 n.7.

[5] For a sketch of the venal system, its scale and its significance, see G.V. Taylor, 'Noncapitalist Wealth and the Origins of the French Revolution', *American Historical Review* (1967), p. 477-9.

[6] P. Dawson, *Provincial Magistrates and Revolutionary Politics in France, 1789-1795* (Cambridge, MA, 1972), p. 341.

which changed hands in Bordeaux over the eighteenth century.[7] For Bordeaux, therefore, we can actually draw up century-long series of figures which enable us to reach rather firmer conclusions about the movement of office prices. In 1968 I used this source to trace the movement for ennobling offices[8]; I was able to show that not all of them were decreasing in value and that, even in the case of those that were, the decrease was far from spectacular and straightforward. Some offices indeed, notably those of *secrétaire du roi*, were increasing phenomenally in value, and at no time faster than on the eve of the Revolution. I now want to turn my attention, using the same source, to *non*-ennobling offices – to test the Cobban thesis by a well-documented regional example.

Even here there are still severe methodological problems. The range of information is, if anything, *too* abundant. There were less than 300 ennobling offices in Bordeaux; but ordinary, non-ennobling offices numbered in all well over a thousand. Nor do they all fall into neat, large categories for which we can draw up long series of figures. Many of them were isolated, not strictly comparable to any others, and not subject to enough changes of ownership over the century to provide evidence of a general evolution of prices. Particularly disappointing, for example, is the case of *sénéchaussée*, the civil and criminal court of first instance for the city and a wide area around; or the *élection*, its fiscal counterpart. Only ten sales, covering five different offices, are recorded for the whole century in the *sénéchaussée*, the last one in 1776. Only twenty-two sales, covering four different offices, are recorded for the *élection*. Such small samples can only yield the 'scattered' indications that I have already stigmatised as inadequate, but for what they are worth, they suggest rather different conclusions. The picture for the *sénéchaussée* is one of stagnation – no fall in prices but certainly no rise. By the 1760s most of the ordinary offices were vacant, largely on account of a peculiar local regulation which prohibited officers from transmitting their charges to their sons while there were other offices not occupied in the court. In any case the lieutenant-général de Laroze (who was also a counsellor at the parlement) thought that eight or ten officers would be more than

---

[7] AD, Gironde, répertoire numérique, 100. Cessions d'offices: minutes notariales retirées des fonds, en exécution du décret, du 9 brumaire an II, portant suppression des offices: inventaire alphabétique (2 vols, typewritten).

[8] See above, pp. 75-86.

Fig. 4.1 Average price of offices in eighteenth-century Bordeaux: *notaires*

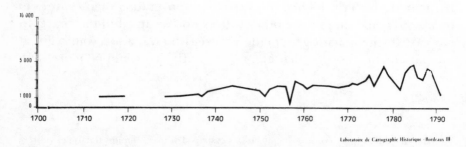

Fig. 4.2 Average price of offices in eighteenth-century Bordeaux: *perruquiers, barbiers, baigneurs, étuvistes.*

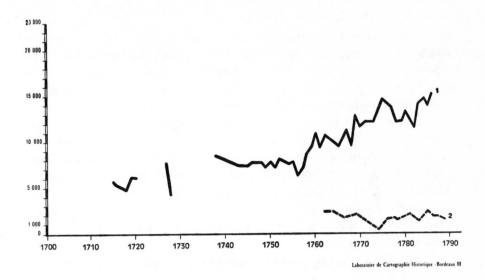

Fig. 4.3 Average price of offices in eighteenth-century Bordeaux: *courtiers.*
 1. *Courtier royal*   2. *Courtier breveté*

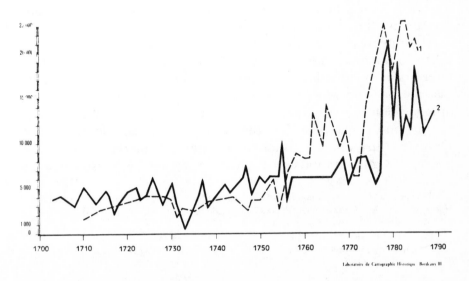

Fig. 4.4 Average price of offices in eighteenth-century Bordeaux: *procureurs.*
 1. *Procureurs à la sénéchausée*   2. *Procureurs au parlement*

enough to dispatch all the business there was.[9] Competition from the court of the *Jurade* in criminal matters, and the *chambre des requêtes* of the parlement in civil matters concerning nobles (and so the most lucrative cases) had robbed the court of much business. 'So there are no longer any litigants coming before the seneschal . . . other than townsfolk, petty tradesmen, artisans, that countless multitude of poor inhabitants who earn their living by their industry or by the work of their hands.'[10] Laroze was constantly petitioning the government to take measures to increase the court's business by expanding its attributions, and to make its offices more attractive by granting their holders various honorific privileges. How far these petitions reflected a real crisis in the *sénéchaussée*, and how far they reflect special pleading, we shall have to consider in a moment.[11] As to the *élection*, the evolution of prices there seems to have been slightly upwards, despite constant complaints, as in the *sénéchaussée*, of lack of business and lack of interest in buying offices.[12] Petitions and complaints, in fact, however illuminating, are no substitute for figures; and therefore I want to confine myself to those offices for which long series *do* exist.

The most numerous office for which we have a long series is that of *perruquier-barbier-baigneur-étuviste*. We can take this as an example of that rare phenomenon, an artisan's office, one at the bottom of the ladder of prestige, and not one which anybody would buy for any other reason than that of profit. The number was limited – in 1766 for example there were only ninety-nine.[13] On the other hand there was considerable pressure for the creation of more. By 1774, accordingly, there were 108, and the intendant was recommending the creation of eight more.[14] Nor did the community of *perruquiers-barbiers* oppose this expansion of their numbers in the way that we might perhaps expect; they merely asked that the price at which the government chose to sell newly-created offices should not be lower than the current price of offices already existing on the market – that, they said, merely made the new offices speculative investments rather than working additions to the complement of wigmakers and barbers. These fears were well-justified: in the

[9] AD, Gironde, C 878, intendant to vice-chancellor, 22 Mar. 1768; C 879, Laroze to intendant 19 Mar. 1767; AM, Bordeaux, Fonds Delpit 177, 'Présidiaux', undated and unsigned petition.

[10] AD, Gironde, C, 3331, petition of Laroze, 1777.

[11] See below, p. 99.

[12] AD, Gironde, C 4868, fos 10-12v, registers of the *élection*; C 3731, intendant to keeper of the seals, 19 Sept. 1780.

[13] AD, Gironde, C 876, subdelegate to intendant, 19 Sept. 1766.

[14] AD, Gironde, C 889, subdelegate to intendant, 1 July 1774; intendant to comptroller-general, 19 July 1774.

1760s Philippe Delasalle, a merchant from Lyon, bought fifteen of these offices in a block and sold most of them off between 1763 and 1765 at 2,600 *livres* each.[15] It was also common to lease them at an annual rent, which rose from 75 *livres* a year in the 1750s, to between 150 *livres* and 165 *livres* in the 1760s, and 300 *livres* and above in the 1780s. Prices rose too, as the graph shows, rarely exceeding 2,000 *livres* until the 1750s, but after that climbing slowly until in the mid 1780s these offices might sell for as much as 5,800 livres. Clearly positions of *perruquier-barbier* were in increasing demand as the century went on, and from all sorts of people. In 1766 the company petitioned for negroes or mulattoes to be forbidden to buy them, for instance.[16] Nor did the local authorities have much doubt of why there was such a demand. 'The town of Bordeaux', noted the subdelegate that same year, 'is very considerable in inhabitants and travellers and has acquired such a luxurious tone that all down to the lowest artisans have their hair dressed . . . it is difficult to be served within a quarter of an hour, which inconveniences men of business.'[17] In other words the popularity of these offices, and the rise in their price, could be mainly attributed to the phenomenal expansion of the population and wealth of Bordeaux in the later eighteenth century. Their holders were assured of making an increasingly good living, and accordingly outsiders were prepared to offer an ever-increasing price for the privilege. This explanation certainly seems the most plausible, but before we accept it completely we should also remember that the officer of wigmaker was rising in price in several other places in the eighteenth century, places as diverse in size and economic structure as Angers and Lyon.[18] In the latter, indeed, prices reached from two to three times those of Bordeaux. Only if we find rises occurring over a whole range of other offices shall we be justified in firmly attributing a role to the boom conditions prevalent in Bordeaux.

Let us then look at another office – this one firmly linked to the commercial world of the city, that of *courtier* or broker. The main job of these officials was to introduce merchants to wine-growers and vice versa in order to facilitate the sale and export of the wines of the Bordeaux region.[19] Until 1760 they were organised into a company of forty

---

[15] AD, Gironde, répertoire numérique, 100, i, p. 160.

[16] AD, Gironde, C 876.

[17] Ibid.

[18] Taylor, 'Noncapitalist Wealth', p. 477 n. 35.

[19] Their operation has been very fully analysed and described by P. Butel, 'La croissance commerciale bordelaise dans la seconde moitié du XVIIIe siècle' (thèse présentée devant l'Université de Paris I, 1973, 2 vols), i, pp. 449-55.

hereditary *courtiers royaux*, but in that year, for reasons that are not clear, the king increased their number to sixty. Apparently this did not satisfy the mercantile community. In response to their objections the king revoked this edict the next year, re-established the number of *courtiers royaux* at forty, but at the same time created 200 new offices of *courtier breveté héréditaire* at 2,000 *livres* each for Frenchmen or 4,000 *livres* for foreigners.[20] The *courtiers royaux* were hardly more satisfied; they feared the competition of the new officers, and no doubt they feared that the very number of them would devalue their own charges. At the same time they thought that merchants would buy up whole batches of the new offices in order to appoint their own employees to them so as more easily to commit fraud. The chamber of commerce expressed similar fears. Yet they seem to have been groundless, if we are to judge from the evolution of prices for these offices. In 1781 the intendant noted that only 106 of the new offices of *courtier breveté* had been taken up;[21] and prices on the open market soon fell below the official value. Those of *courtier royal* on the other hand, though once more increased to sixty in 1772, steadily rose, and in 1782 one sold for 18,500 *livres*, twice the normal price of 1761. These differences are not easy to explain unless we assume – perhaps not unreasonably – that 360 *couriters* was too high a number for the business available in the *sénéchaussée*. We might also suspect that the *courtiers royaux*, being an older and better established body, enjoyed more prestige and more trust on the part of both buyers and sellers of wines and other goods. Unlike the *courtiers brevetés*, these offices were only open to Catholic Frenchmen (as opposed to foreigners of any religion) and perhaps this added to their prestige. At any rate, it seems clear that the *courtiers royaux* cornered most of the business, at least if the price of their offices is any guide. It is striking how similar the pattern is to that of the *perruquiers-barbiers* – a fairly uneventful development until the late 1750s, when the depression brought about by the Seven Years War seems to have pulled prices down. Then a steady recovery throughout the 1760s, accelerating in the 1770s and reaching a peak in the early to mid 1780s. Perhaps then we should attribute a role to the general expansion of the Bordelais economy over this period after all?

---

[20] Copies of the edicts concerned in AD, C 3868; and AM, fonds ancien, HH 84. For the reactions of the *courtiers* and the mercantile community in general, see AD, Gironde, 6 E 50 (courtiers), where there are various legal consultations and memoranda.

[21] Butel, 'La croissance', p. 452.

This conclusion is reinforced if we turn from artisan and commercial offices to legal ones, the very hub of the system of venality. I have already lamented the absence of figures for offices on the bench and courts of first instance. But these were still only a minority of the total of venal offices in the legal system, and for two other more numerous categories we do have good series of figures: the notaries and the *procureurs*. Both are interesting categories, for they were offices occupied by just the sort of professional bourgeois who were the mainstay of the Third Estate in 1789.

First the notaries. After some fluctuations early in the century, the complement of the company of notaries of the city of Bordeaux was settled by the 1730s at thirty. The members of the company regarded this as quite adequate and opposed all attempts throughout the century to increase it.[22] No wonder: such a limited number of essential officers in a city that was expanding so rapidly could only prove extremely profitable. Offices of notary in the villages around the city, whose business was limited, seldom sold for more than a few hundred *livres*; although in rich communities, such as Pauillac, one might reach as much as 4,000 *livres* in 1764.[23] But in Bordeaux itself prices had seldom fallen as low as that at any time in the century, and by 1764 they were three times as high. Information is very fragmentary for the earlier part of the century, but it seems that prices did not fluctuate much until the late 1740s, when they began to rise markedly. The upward trend continued, though more erratically, into the 1760s, and from around 1770 the rise becomes steep and spectacular. The average price in 1782 was 900 per cent higher than in 1740 – an average rate of increase of over 21 per cent per year. By this time it cost more to become a notary than to buy any ennobling office, except a presidency in the parlement or a post of *secrétaire du roi*. The rate of rise was only exceeded by that of these latter offices, with their unrivalled social and fiscal rewards.[24] It is true that there seems to have been a downturn in the price of notarial offices in the late 1780s, but when the Revolution broke out they still cost more than they had for all but the seventeen best years of the century.[25] Here again there can surely be little doubt about the reason for the rise. Social

---

[22] J. Gaston, *La communauté des notaires de Bordeaux (1520-1791)* (Bordeaux, 1913), p. 42-4.

[23] AD, Gironde, répertoire numérique, 100, ii, p. 430.

[24] See above, pp. 83-85.

[25] This sudden drop is based on a single transaction, for 15,000 *livres* in 1787, when Antoine Alexandre Monier sold an office that he had bought in 1780 for 30,000 *livres* – AD, Gironde, répertoire numérique, 100, p. 357. This loss seems on the face of it so untypical that a clerical error or some special hidden circumstances cannot be ruled out.

historians know the value of notarial records; they know that all the most important transactions in social and economic life were made before notaries. Nothing substantial was bought, sold or agreed without their presence – a presence for which of course they also levied fees. In a town whose social and economic activity was expanding, the rewards of being a notary could also be expected to grow; and with them, the attractions of holding such an office. Contrast the situation in Besançon, a judicial centre but not noted for its growth over the eighteenth century. There the highest recorded price for notarial office of the century was only 5,000 *livres* in 1762.[26] In 1786, when Bordeaux candidates could expect to pay not less than 15,000 *livres* and probably far more, the going rate in Besançon was 3,700 *livres* – less than that for offices of *huissier* in the lowest courts of that city, and less than that paid for an office of wigmaker in Bordeaux.

The *procureurs* have the advantage, from our point of view, of being the most numerous of all judicial officers. Every lawcourt was served by a body of them and every litigant employed one to act for him before the court. In the 1780s there were sixty offices of *procureur au parlement*, twelve at the *cour des aides*, and thirty at the *sénéchaussée*; in 1749 the latter had absorbed the six offices of *procureur à l'élection*.[27] The enormous number of *procureurs* was a standard complaint made about the judicial system of the *ancien régime*, from the sixteenth century down to the *cahiers* of 1789. It was alleged that, because they were so numerous, they tended to spin out and complicate the cases they were handling in order to increase their fees.[28] The implication of this logic is that these offices were not very desirable, especially in courts with limited business. 'Of twelve offices of procurator at the Court of Aides', wrote the members of this company from Bordeaux in 1745, 'only three remain occupied, the nine others long ago having fallen vacant, as they will long remain, unsought, because they procure no profit and no other advantages. The three which are occupied are only so because their holders can find no willing acquirers . . . '[29] Nearly forty years later, in a petition to have

---

[26] M. Gresset, 'Le monde judiciaire à Besançon de la conquête par Louis XIV à la Révolution Française, 1674-1789' (unpublished thesis, University of Paris IV, 1974, 2 vols), i, p. 230.

[27] AD, Gironde, 6 E 109, 'Mémoire pour les procureurs du parlement de Bordeaux', Dec. 1788; C 3731, intendant to keeper of seals, 19 Sept. 1780.

[28] See M. Marion, *Dictionnaire des institutions de la France aux XVIIe et XVIIIe siècles* (Paris, 1923), p. 460.

[29] AD, Gironde, C 856, 'Mémoire contenant les moyens de faire payer par les procureurs de la cour des aydes de Bordeaux, la taxe de 265 l., 13 s. 4 d. à laquelle chacun d'eux est imposé'.

the business of *procureurs* before the *élection* transferred from the *procureurs* at the *sénéchaussée* to themselves, the same body of *procureurs* complained that working at the *cour des aides* alone did not give them enough to do.[30]

Yet the *cour des aides* was notorious for its lack of business: a dozen of its fifty or so magistrates were enough to keep going what business there was.[31] Far more interesting and significant are the busier courts, the *sénéchaussée* and the parlement. Here we find that, to judge from their prices, offices of *procureur* were in increasing demand as the century went on. It is true that for the first sixty or so years of the century the level of prices remained much the same, which suggests that there was no great pressure to acquire these offices. In 1732 the company of *procureurs au parlement* agreed to value their offices at 4,000 *livres* each, and undertook to buy in on behalf of the company any office that could not command this minimum price.[32] By the 1760s they had raised their valuation to 6,000 *livres* but they were still buying in offices, which suggests that selling remained difficult. In 1771, when a royal edict obliged all office holders to set a valuation on their offices for taxation purposes, they lowered their estimate to 5,000 *livres*.[33] By this time, however, prices for the less numerous office of *procureur à la sénéchaussée* had already begun to rise steeply, and in 1771 these officers valued their charges at 10,400 *livres*.[34] After a brief recession in the early 1770s, prices continued to rise steeply, and those for offices of *procureur au parlement* soon followed them. It is true that there was a downward tendency once more after the mid 1780s, but in 1789 prices were still several times higher than they had been earlier in the century. Even the offices of *procureurs* in the *cour des aides* and the *bureau des finances*, which had been notorious for their low price and lack of business earlier in the century, had doubled in value by the 1770s and 1780s.[35]

---

[30] AD, Gironde, C 4686, memorandum of 1784. The indignant response of the *procureurs* at the *sénéchaussée* is in C 887.

[31] Denise Bège, 'Une compagnie à la recherche de sa raison d'être: la cour des aides de Guyenne et ses magistrats, 1553-1790' (unpublished Ph.D. thesis, University of Paris I, 1974), 2 vols, i, pp. 329, 345, 557-9.

[32] AD, Gironde, 6 E 109, deliberation of the company of *procureurs*, 15 Dec. 1732.

[33] Ibid., quittance in the name of Pierre Disabeau, June 1780.

[34] AN, D XVII 7 n. 98, petition from former *procureurs à la sénéchaussée* to committee of judicature of National Assembly, 19 April 1791.

[35] Pascal Thibault, *procureur* at the *cour des aides*, bought his office in 1752 for 1,500 *livres*; he sold it in 1767 for 4,000 *livres*. AD, Gironde, repertoire numérique, 100, ii, 186. Louis Dalbusset, *procureur* at the *bureau des finances*, bought his office in 1773 for 1,500 *livres*, selling it in 1785 for 2,500 *livres* – ibid., i, p. 145.

Before we conclude, however, that here is yet more evidence of the influence on office prices of Bordeaux eighteenth-century expansion, we should note that in stagnant, uncommercial Besançon there was an even more spectacular rise over the century in the price of offices of *procureur* at the parlement. Created at 1,000 *livres* in 1694, these offices were selling in the twenty thousands by the 1780s and one, in 1781, reached over 30,000 *livres* which is well above anything paid in Bordeaux.[36] Offices of *procureur* at the *bailliage* of Besançon, sold at 600 *livres* in 1693, had reached between 11,000 and 12,000 *livres*, by the early 1780s – an important rise, though this time not as spectacular as that of the *procureurs* in the Bordeaux *sénéchaussée* court.[37] These movements are surprising. In the absence of studies which might show whether or not the volume of judicial business at Besançon was increasing for some reason, we can only note that in Bescançon there were only half the number of *procureurs* there were at Bordeaux – thirty at the parlement and fifteen at the *bailliage*. Lower numbers would automatically assure each *procureur* of more business, and this no doubt has something to do with the rise there.

The most surprising thing about the Bordeaux figures is the way that, from the mid 1750s, it cost more to become a *procureur* at the lower court of the *sénéchaussée* than at the parlement – another contrast with Besançon, where the situation was more what we would expect. Some of the explanation must lie in the fact that there were only half the number of the parlement's *procureurs* at the *sénéchaussée*. No doubt too the latter were busier, and therefore earned more. Even if, as the lieutenant-general complained, no large and lucrative cases were now heard before the *sénéchaussée*,[38] in an expanding town the amount of petty business must have remained substantial. Moreover, in 1749, the *procureurs* at the *sénéchal* had taken over the functions of the six offices of *procureurs* at the *élection*, which increased their business: the officers of the *élection*, petitioning for the re-establishment of the six offices on a separate basis in 1780, claimed that the increase in their activity since 1749 justified it, and that the *procureurs* at the *sénéchal* were so busy that they were

---

[36] Gresset, *Le monde judiciaire*, i, p. 223-5. But according to the Bordeaux *huissiers* (who it is true had no love for the *procureurs*) the *procureurs* of the parlement were *asking* 30,000 or 36,000 *livres* for their offices in the 1780s: AD, Gironde, 6 E 66 (Communauté des Huissiers au Parlement), memorandum of 1786.

[37] Gresset, *Le monde judiciaire*, i, p. 228.

[38] See above, at n. 9.

neglecting *élection* business.[39] At the parlement, on the other hand, to set against the prestige of serving the most important court in the province, there was the uncertainty of regular work. The last twenty years of the parlement's existence were scarred by quarrels, strikes and interruptions of sittings which had serious repercussions for the livings of the *procureurs* serving it.[40] They only worked if the magistrates worked. Claiming a discharge from taxes on 16 December 1788, they alleged that they had earned nothing substantial since 1786 owing to the disruption of the parlement's sittings by the pre-revolutionary conflicts.[41] These disruptions undoubtedly had an effect on the parlement's prestige, and no doubt helped to account for the fact that it was also more expensive by the 1780s to buy a place of counsellor in the *cour des aides* than in the parlement.[42] The *huissiers* at the parlement, who were constantly at loggerheads with the *procureurs* over the question of professional fees, also claimed in 1786 that the company of *procureurs* was so torn by internal vendettas that many people were deterred from buying an office in it – especially at the absurd prices (in the *huissiers'* view) to which the *procureurs* felt themselves entitled.[43] Such factors as these, no doubt, helped to counterbalance the threefold rise in the income of *procureurs* which the *huissiers* alleged had occurred over the century; and kept the price of their offices, though buoyant, below that for posts of *procureur* in the calmer, and more consistently busy, lower jurisdiction of the *sénéchal*.

What general conclusions can we draw from this brief survey? The first thing to note is that hardly any office prices were actually falling. In the whole of Bordeaux, indeed, the only offices whose price showed a clear downward trend over a long period – from the 1760s onwards, in fact – were ennobling ones: those of counsellor at the parlement and *trésorier de France*. I have already discussed in another essay the special circumstances that influenced these particular cases – the high relative price, the shaken prestige in the case of the parlement and the lack of business in the case of the *bureau des finances*.[44] I also noted that in the case of the

---

[39] AD, Gironde, C 3731, intendant to keeper of seals, 19 Sept. 1780, with attached memorandum from the *élection*.

[40] See W. Doyle, *The Parlement of Bordeaux and the End of the Old Regime, 1771-1790* (London, 1974), chs 11 and 12.

[41] AD, Gironde, E 109, 'Mémoire pour les procureurs du parlement de Bordeaux'.

[42] See above, p. 81.

[43] AD, Gironde, 6 E 66, cited above, n. 36.

[44] See above, pp. 77-8, 81.

ennobling offices whose price was *rising* in the later eighteenth century – offices of *secrétaire du roi* and in the *cour des aides* – the very lack of duties and business, in return for ennoblement and a whole range of other privileges, seems to have attracted buyers. In other words they were bought for prestige rather than profit. This seems to have been a powerful incentive all the way down the ladder. How else can we explain a rise in the price of notoriously under-occupied offices such as those of *procureur à la cour des aides?* 'Au moment de notre suppression' recalled the former *procureurs* at the parlement in 1791,[45]

> le capital de nos offices représentait, en nos mains, une somme de sept cent vingt mille livres au moins, et ce capital, alors dans le commerce, augmentait à chaque mutation. Alors, la santé, les talens, l'estime publique faisoient rendre, à chacun de nous un intérêt plus ou moins fort, au capital qu'il avoit déboursé; mais, en général, le fruit de notre travail étoit insuffisant pour nous procurer le nécessaire, payer les impositions et subvenir aux besoins de l'Etat.

> [At the time of our suppression, the capital of our offices represented, in our hands, a sum of seven hundred and twenty thousands at the least, and this capital was rising on the open market with every change of owner. And so health, talent, and public esteem brought in to each of us a greater or lesser interest on the capital laid out; but, in general, the fruits of our labours were insufficient to procure our necessities, pay our taxes, and come to the aid of the state.]

Similarly the *huissiers* at the parlement, petitioning in 1782 for a rise in fees, complained that their offices did not bring them a living. The *procureurs*, who would have borne the brunt of any such rise, refused to believe this, but they did note that many *huissiers* had other jobs too, and often leased their offices to merchants who were seeking certain exemptions that they conferred.[46] Clearly the financial rewards were not the primary motives of those who became *huissiers*. One factor in the buoyancy of office prices in general in Bordeaux, therefore, must have been an intense, even a growing, status consciousness among its moneyed population.

The second thing to note, above all from those prices for which it has been possible to compile graphs, is the uniformity of the movement across the whole range of offices. With the exception of the overnumerous *courtiers brevetés*, the general tendency of all prices follows a similar pattern – unspectacular and fairly level until mid century, and then a

---

[45] AD, Gironde, D XVII, 7, no. 98.
[46] AD, Gironde, 6 E 66.

strong upward movement reaching its peak in the early to mid 1780s. Between then and 1789 prices seem to be beginning to waver rather uncertainly, although we have not enough information to decide whether this was a significant movement. A uniform movement suggests a common cause; and surely this must have something to do (however many objections and special cases we can think of) with the spectacular economic expansion of Bordeaux in the eighteenth century. The pattern of this expansion is now well known.[47] We know that it was at its most spectacular from the end of the Seven Years War onwards, and that in the late 1780s signs of deceleration were beginning to appear. This matches the general evolution of the graphs for offices prices almost exactly. We know too that the population of the city probably doubled between 1715 and 1790.[48] These factors must surely have meant that offices like those of *perruquier-barbier*, *courtier royal* and notary became much more lucrative because of rapidly increasing business. This would surely account for the marked rise in their prices, for these offices were obviously very attractive investments. Not only status seeking, therefore, pushed the Bordelais into venal offices in the eighteenth century. There were plenty of opportunities for profit too. The surging prosperity of this eighteenth-century boom town affected most professions, even those not directly connected with trade or commerce; and this served not only to prevent prices from falling, but to push them up quite markedly.

So the Cobban thesis does not seem to work for Bordeaux. If the test of decline is a fall in the value of venal offices and a failure to find purchasers for them, then the office-holders of Bordeaux were certainly not declining. Nor were they showing that disenchantment with venality that comes over so strongly from the *cahiers* of 1789. We do not in fact find office-holders playing a prominent or a militant part in the elections to the estates-general in 1789. In Bordeaux, as we would perhaps expect, the *bourgeoisie* was dominated by merchants, who played the decisive role in the elections for the Third Estate.[49] Such lawyers as were

---

[47] See F. Crouzet in F.G. Pariset (ed.), *Bordeaux au XVIIIe siècle* (Bordeaux, 1968), pp. 191-323; and P. Butel, *Les négociants bordelais: l'Europe et les îles au XVIIIe siècle* (Paris, 1974), pp. 15-23.

[48] J.P. Poussou in Pariset, *Bordeaux au XVIIIe siècle*, pp. 325-8.

[49] M. Lhéritier, *La Révolution à Bordeaux*, i, *La fin de l'ancien régime et la préparation des états généraux (1787-1789)* (Paris, 1942), pp. 219-20, 232, 258-9; A. Forrest, *Society and Politics in Revolutionary Bordeaux* (Oxford, 1975), pp. 34-8.

involved in the process were advocates, who did not buy or own their offices. Their disenchantment with venality (which showed in various demands voiced by the Third Estate's *cahier*) was derived not so much from dissatisfaction with its rewards as from the fact that they were excluded by venality from public office themselves.

Unfortunately, the fact that Cobban's argument does not work for Bordeaux is no real guide to whether or not it might be valid for France as a whole. Bordeaux was, after all, an exceptional town in the eighteenth century. Only a handful of ports like Nantes, Le Havre and Marseille were expanding in the same spectacular way. Its circumstances were quite untypical of most French towns, and it seems probable that its office market was too. What we need (as usual) is much more information on this question. It would be interesting first of all to have some figures for the price of non-ennobling offices in the boom towns I have just mentioned. Jean Meyer has studied the price of ennobling offices in Nantes: in the case of the *chambre des comptes* he found a stability of price not entirely dissimilar to that found in the Bordeaux *cour des aides* – although at twice as high a level.[50] In the case of the *secrétaires du roi* he found a similar price level to Bordeaux in the 1720s and a comparable dramatic rise between the 1760s and 1780s – although prices in Nantes never reached the dizzy heights of the Bordeaux ones.[51] Perhaps therefore non-ennobling offices did as well too – but that remains to be seen. Even more interesting would be to have figures for inland towns without the commercial vigour of the ocean ports – places like Dijon, Grenoble or Toulouse. All we have so far are Gresset's figures for Besançon. There the graph for offices in the parlement – ennobling offices of course – is very close to that of Bordeaux, reaching its height in the early 1740s and then declining. But *procureurs* were doing phenomenally well, better even than at Bordeaux, commanding prices which at times approached those for a place in the parlement itself. The *huissiers* paid a steadily rising price for their offices; but the officers of the *bailliage* – at the very core of Cobban's argument – saw the price of theirs falling steadily and commanding less, from the 1750s onwards, than those of mere *huissiers*.[52] Away from the coast, we might be

[50] J. Meyer, *La noblesse bretonne au XVIIIe siècle*, 2 vols (Paris, 1966), i, pp. 179-83.

[51] Ibid., i, pp. 257-60. The highest Breton price was 106,000 *livres* in 1783. In Bordeaux the highest was 120,000 *livres* in 1782, above, pp. 84-5.

[52] Gresset, *Le monde judiciaire*, i, p. 224.

tempted to conclude, the *bailliage* officers at least fit Cobban's argument – if we did not have Philip Dawson's assurance that in the several *bailliages* which he studied, prices were rising[53]. Nor has Gresset himself studied any *non*-legal offices in Besançon. What all this amounts to is that in 1979 we had nothing like enough information to come to valid general conclusions. The market for venal offices before 1789 remained a subject little known or understood. This preliminary study of one corner of it suggested that further investigation would be well worthwhile.

[53] Dawson, *Provincial Magistrates*, p. 341.

5

The Price of Offices in Pre-Revolutionary France

One of the most distinctive features of the French *ancien régime* was the sale of offices. Several European states resorted to this method of tapping the wealth of their richer subjects in the sixteenth and seventeenth centuries,[1] but nowhere did venality spread further through society than in France, and nowhere did its importance persist so long. Although the revolutionaries of 1789 abolished it, it reappeared for certain public functions in the early nineteenth century, and has not quite vanished even today.[2] The origins and early history of the system have been authoritatively studied,[3] but its eighteenth-century history has received very little attention. This is all the more curious in that France continued to be governed largely by holders of venal offices, they constituted the backbone of opposition to the government in the form of the magistrates of the parlements, and huge amounts of capital continued to be absorbed by office buying.[4] Even so, most historians

[1] See K.W. Swart, *The Sale of Offices in the Seventeenth Century* (The Hague, 1949); J.H. Parry, *The Sale of Public Office in the Spanish Indies under the Hapsburgs* (Berkeley, CA, 1953); A.M. Birke, I. Mieck, K. Malettke (eds), *Ämterkäuflichkeit: Aspekte sozialer Mobilität im europäischen Vergleich (17. und 18. Jahrhundert)* (Berlin, 1980).

[2] Swart, *Sale of Offices*, pp. 17-18; see too P. Louis-Lucas, *Etude sur la vénalité des charges et fonctions publiques et sur celle des offices ministériels depuis l'antiquité romaine jusqu'à nos jours*, 2 vols (Paris, 1882); E. Avond, *De la vénalité des offices ministériels et de sa suppression* (Paris, 1905); T. Zeldin, *France 1848-1945*, 2 vols (Oxford, 1973-77), i, pp. 45-7.

[3] G. Pagès, 'La vénalité des offices dans l'ancienne France', *Revue historique*, 169 (1932); M. Göhring, *Die Ämterkäuflichkeit im Ancien Régime* (Berlin, 1938); and, above all, R. Mousnier, *La vénalité des offices sous Henri IV et Louis XIII* (Paris, 1945; 2nd edn, 1971).

[4] G.V. Taylor, 'Noncapitalist Wealth and the Origins of the French Revolution', *American Historical Review*, 72 (1967), esp. 477-9. Some long-term political implications of venality are examined in R.E. Giesey, 'State-Building in Early Modern France: The Role of Royal Officialdom', *Journal of Modern History*, 55 (1983).

consider that by this time the venal system was in decline. This seemed to be demonstrated by unsold offices remaining on the market, and above all by falling office prices.[5] For Alfred Cobban, indeed, these trends were symptoms of the decline of a whole class, the *officiers*. Here was 'a section of society which was definitely not rising in wealth, and was barely holding its own in social status' as falling office prices showed. 'The decline seems to have been general, from the parlements downwards, though until the end of the eighteenth century it was much less marked in the offices of the parlements than in those of the *présidiaux, élections, maréchaussées* and other local courts.'[6] Resentment at this decline explained the revolutionary fervour of the *officiers*, whom Cobban had previously shown to be the largest bourgeois group in the national assembly;[7] and 1789 was largely the work not of a rising capitalist bourgeoisie, but rather of a declining professional one.

This idea has proved influential, at least among English-speaking historians of the French Revolution, over the twenty years since it was first propounded.[8] But a glance at Cobban's footnotes shows that it was advanced on very slender evidence. Of his two examples of falling prices, one came from a parlement, where offices conferred nobility. It was, therefore, of no relevance to the non-noble office-holders with whom he was primarily concerned. The other was a minor office in Rouen. It is clear, in fact, that our whole view of the price of offices in the eighteenth century is based on isolated examples, and may prove to be mistaken. If it is, we may need to revise our view not only of the later history of French venality, but also of a number of social and political

[5] Recent examples of this view are E. Labrousse in F. Braudel and E. Labrousse (eds), *Histoire économique et sociale de la France*, 4 vols (Paris, 1970-7), ii, pp. 480-1; G. Cabourdin and G. Viard, *Lexique historique de la France d'ancien régime* (Paris, 1978), p. 236; R. Mousnier, *Les institutions de la France sous la monarchie absolue*, 2 vols (Paris, 1974-80), ii, pp. 335-8, 346, 350-3. As recently as 1983, a prominent American authority on French judicial history, James F. Traer, could write in a review (*American Historical Review*, 78, p. 129) that the sale of offices 'fell into decline in the eighteenth century as judicial offices lost value due to their increasing number and the existence of other, more attractive avenues for investment'.

[6] A. Cobban, *The Social Interpretation of the French Revolution* (Cambridge, 1964), p. 59.

[7] Idem, 'The Myth of the French Revolution', an inaugural lecture of 1954 reprinted in *Aspects of the French Revolution* (London, 1968), pp. 90-111.

[8] See C. Lucas, 'Nobles, Bourgeois and the Origins of the French Revolution', *Past and Present*, 60 (1973), p. 114; W. Doyle, *The Old European Order, 1660-1800* (Oxford, 1978), p. 148; idem, *Origins of the French Revolution* (Oxford, 1980), pp. 134-5; O. Hufton, *Europe: Privilege and Protest, 1730-1789* (London, 1980), p. 40, L. Berlanstein, 'Lawyers in Pre-Revolutionary France', in W. Prest (ed.), *Lawyers in Early Modern Europe and America* (London, 1981), p. 169; J.H. Shennan, *France before the Revolution* (London, 1983), p. 34.

developments for which the decline of office prices has been cited as evidence.

Before reviewing the evidence on prices, it may be useful to remind ourselves of the extent of the venal system and the reasons why men bought offices. In 1778 the department in charge of venality, the *bureau des parties casuelles*, estimated that there were at least 50,969 civil offices.[9] This is certainly an underestimate, however. In 1791 the wigmakers of Paris claimed, perhaps improbably, that there were 30,000 offices of wigmaker alone throughout France.[10] The survey of 1778 put a capital value on the offices it counted of 584,700,176 *livres*, but this too was an underestimate. It was based on declarations made for tax by office-holders themselves under an edict of 1771, and the committee of the national assembly entrusted with planning the liquidation of the venal system in 1790 thought that it should be raised by at least a half. Even that seems conservative. An estimate that 2 or 3 per cent of French adult males were office-holders, on the other hand, seems entirely plausible.[11]

Venality permeated every sphere of public life, from government ministers downwards.[12] The finances of the state were largely managed by receivers, payers and accountants who bought their positions.[13] Military commissions were subject to purchase. So were many municipal dignities. The entire judiciary, from the presidents of sovereign courts down to the humblest attorneys, clerks and ushers, was made up of venal offices. A number of key services were also venal monopolies, such as those of notaries, brokers, surveyors, auctioneers, and even, as we have seen, wigmakers. Ways of classifying the bewildering variety of venal offices are innumerable, but for the study of prices they are best categorised according to why they were bought. Here the basic division was threefold. Offices tended to be bought for profit, for prestige and for posterity.

The *parties casuelles* normally divided them into offices with and without *gages*. *Gages* were technically the interest payable by the crown

---

[9] BN, MS Fr. 1140, 'Mémoire sur l'état actuel des offices tant casuels qu'à survivance', pp. 468-9.

[10] AN, D XI, i, petition of August 1790.

[11] Taylor, 'Noncapitalist Wealth', p. 477.

[12] AN, D VI, ii, contains a memorandum of 1790 from four of Louis XVI's secretaries of state claiming repayment of sums paid to their predecessors.

[13] See J.F. Bosher, *French Finances 1770-1795: From Business to Bureaucracy* (Cambridge, 1970), ch. 4.

on an office's original purchasing price, so offices with *gages* yielded an automatic notional profit. Most judicial offices fell into this category. By the eighteenth century, however, the value of *gages* was extremely modest. In 1778 the 13,132 officers with *gages* had to share 13,605,911 *livres* between them.[14] Entitlement to *gages*, therefore, did not by itself put an office-holder in a different category from his fellows who were expected to seek a return on their investment from the profits of their functions. Nor was the distinction between buying an office for profit or prestige clear cut. A really profitable office was bound to attract prestige too in some sense. But there is no doubt that profit was the main reason for acquiring, for instance, the great financial offices; and the same can be said at the other end of the scale for offices like attorneys, auctioneers or wigmakers.[15] These were quite simply ways of making a living. They might, as in the case of notaries, also bring a measure of social standing,[16] but nobody bought them for that alone, or even primarily. Most of the offices in the teeming judicial hierarchy, on the other hand, could not have been bought for financial gain. The profits of office in the *bailliages* and *sénéchaussées* were notoriously slender and erratic.[17] Many higher special courts (such as the *chambres des comptes* or *cours des aides*) had very little do do, and consequently little business on which to levy fees. Even in the parlements it was already notorious under Louis XIV that the financial returns were poor,[18] and in the eighteenth century matters did not improve.[19] But in all these instances office-holders were

[14] Calculated from BN, MS Fr. 1140, pp. 420, 464, 469. See too, M. Marion, *Dictionnaire des institutions de la France aux XVIIe et XVIIIe siècles* (Paris, 1923), pp. 250-1. The average of 1,036 *livres* which this left each office-holder was in every case subject to deductions for tax, not to mention arrears of payment that often ran on for years.

[15] For wigmakers, see Taylor, 'Noncapitalist Wealth', p. 477 n. 35; and above, pp. 92-3.

[16] See J.-P. Poisson, 'Le rôle socio-économique du notariat au XVIIIe siècle: quatre offices parisiens en 1749', *Annales, ESC* (1972), pp. 758-75; M. Gresset, 'Le notariat bisontin au dernier siècle de l'ancien régime (1692-1789)', in *Les actes notariés: source de l'histoire sociale, XVIe-XIXe siècles* (Strasbourg, 1979), pp. 71-8.

[17] E. Laurain, 'Essai sur les présidiaux', *Nouvelle revue historique de droit français et étranger*, 19-20 (1895-6), pp. 533-5; P. Dawson, *Provincial Magistrates and Revolutionary Politics in France, 1789-1795* (Cambridge, MA, 1972), pp. 80-3.

[18] J.C. Paulhet, 'Les parlementaires toulousains à la fin du XVIIe siècle', *Annales du Midi*, 76 (1964), pp. 196-9; J.J. Hurt, 'Les offices au parlement de Bretagne sous le règne de Louis XIV: aspects financiers', *Revue d'histoire moderne et contemporaine*, 23 (1976), pp. 1-31.

[19] The consensus of recent work on this is unanimous. See J. Egret, *Le parlement de Dauphiné et les affaires publiques dans la deuxième moitié du XVIIIe siècle*, 2 vols (Paris, 1960), pp. 168-72; J. Meyer, *La noblesse bretonne au XVIIIe siècle*, 2 vols (Paris, 1966), ii, pp. 946-53; P. Robinne, 'Les magistrats du parlement de Normandie à la fin du XVIIIe siècle', *Annales de Normandie* (1967), p. 267; W. Doyle, *The Parlement of Bordeaux and the End of the Old Regime, 1771-1790* (London,

not dependent on their offices for an income. They bought them for reasons of prestige and social standing. The return on the investment came not in financial terms, but in social recognition. These aspirations were the true driving force behind what Charles Loyseau, the seventeenth-century authority on offices, had called 'archeomania'. As late as 1911, Ernest Lavisse saw it as a French national habit: 'We love tranquillity, a regular life, tomorrow the same as yesterday, a decent competence, a little authority, precedence, and signs of distinction. Offices conferred all this . . . '.[20] They also conferred heredity. The fundamental reason why unprofitable offices sold so readily throughout the seventeenth and eighteenth centuries was that they and the status they conferred could be passed on down the generations like real property. Admittedly this was only allowed on payment of a tax, the famous *paulette* or, as it was known in the eighteenth century, the *annuel*. But the cost of this proved no deterrent. In 1778 the *centième dernier*, which had replaced the *annuel* in 1771, was yielding revenue to the crown of 4,610, 952 *livres*.[21]

It was considered important at every level in the hierarchy of venal offices to pass on an office to one's posterity, but nowhere was it more important than in the case of ennobling offices. Ennoblement was the greatest incentive to buy an office that the crown could offer, and in the seventeenth and eighteenth centuries this was the way most families entered the nobility. In the later eighteenth century there were at least 3,700 civil ennobling offices in France,[22] and over the century anything between 5,510[23] and 7,180[24] individuals and their families entered the nobility through them. But not all ennobling offices ennobled in the same way.[25] Less than half conferred first-degree nobility, meaning

---

1974), pp. 40-2; P. Sueur, *Le conseil provincial d'Artois (1640-1790)* (Arras, 1978), pp. 257-88; M. Gresset, *Gens de justice à Besançon (1674-1789)*, 2 vols (Paris, 1978), i, pp. 326-31.

[20] E. Lavisse, *Histoire de France depuis les origines jusqu'à la Revolution*, 9 vols (Paris, 1903-11), vii, p. 368.

[21] BN, MS Fr. 1140, p. 466.

[22] J. Meyer, 'La noblesse française au XVIIIe siècle: aperçu des problèmes', *Acta Poloniae historica*, 36 (1977), pp. 9-11, suggests a total of 2,404 outside the parlements; F.L. Ford, *Robe and Sword: The Regrouping of the French Aristocracy after Louis XIV* (Cambridge, MA, 1953), p. 53, advances 1,250 for the parlements; and there are others whose classification is uncertain. In addition senior military offices also ennobled from 1750, but these are not under discussion here.

[23] Calculated from Meyer, 'La noblesse française', p. 11.

[24] G. Chaussinand-Nogaret, *La noblesse au XVIIIe siècle: de la féodalité aux lumières* (Paris, 1976), p. 46.

[25] The full rules are set out in F. Bluche and P. Durye, *L'anoblissement par charges avant 1789*, 2 vols (Paris, 1962).

nobility transmissible from the first generation. Most brought gradual, or second-degree nobility, which meant the office must be held for twenty years or until death by two consecutive generations before the family's nobility became complete and transmissible. This tended to keep such offices off the market for long periods. The fact that ennobling offices were the only ones compatible with the dignity of noblemen also immobilised large numbers in the hands of families which had achieved it, and when they did come up nobles tended to buy them. Some parlements even excluded non-nobles formally.[26] Thus the 1,250 magistrates in the parlements only produced some 150 ennoblements between 1710 and 1790, whereas the 819 offices of *secrétaire du roi*, which those already noble disdained, added between 3,000 and 3,200 individuals and their families to the ranks of the order.[27] All these nuances are vividly reflected in the movement of ennobling office prices.

Before moving on to the prices themselves, however, it should be noted that an office-buyer's outgoings did not end with the purchase. In addition to the *annuel* or *centième dernier* there were mutation fees, stamp duties on legal papers, and from 1770 buyers of ennobling offices whose nobility was not complete were required to pay a *marc d'or de noblesse*. Most offices also brought membership of a professional company, which levied reception fees. In some offices it was customary to supplement the price with an extra payment to the vendor, the so-called *pot de vin*. Thus a *lieutenant particulier* at the *sénéchaussée* of La Rochelle could pay 14,000 *livres* for his office in 1781, but a further 4,150 *livres* under twenty-two different headings.[28] Provisions (i.e. the legal documents) to a presidency in the parlement of Bordeaux that cost 126,000 *livres* in 1778 amounted to an extra 12,809 *livres* alone;[29] reception costs for a Parisian office of *secrétaire du roi* bought for 120,000 *livres* a year later came to 11,000 *livres*.[30] The actual prices paid for offices are elusive enough; tabulations of legal and reception fees are even rarer. As a result, in what follows they are never included in prices given. But we should bear in mind that sums disbursed were always more than the nominal price; and

[26] For an introduction to this question see above, pp. 62-3.

[27] Meyer, 'La noblesse française', p. 11.

[28] P. Dawson, 'Sur le prix des offices judiciairies à la fin de l'ancien régime', *Revue d'histoire économique et social*, 42 (1964), pp. 390-2.

[29] Doyle, *Parlement of Bordeaux*, p. 31.

[30] AN, D XVII, 3, Delville to president of the committee of judicature, 13 Aug. 1790.

as a general rule, the dearer the office, the higher the additional expenses.

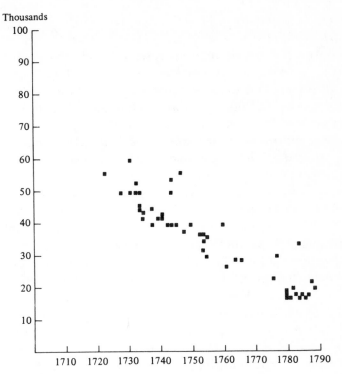

Fig. 5.1 Prices for office of *conseiller au parlement de Grenoble*

Recent research broadly confirms the traditional picture of a fall in the price of office in the parlements. The most frequently cited case is that of the parlement of Grenoble, where counsellorships went for around 60,000 *livres* in the 1720s, but around 20,000 *livres* in the 1780s.[31] A counsellor in the parlement of Paris in the early 1720s might have paid around 100,000 *livres* but by 1770 prices had fallen by half.[32] At Rennes, the more prestigious *originaire* counsellorships averaged 70,000 *livres* in the 1720s, and just under 30,000 *livres* sixty years later, while the

---

[31] See AN, D XVII, 4. Cited by Göhring, *Ämterkäuflichkeit*, p. 287; Egret, *Parlement de Dauphiné*, i, p. 18, and ii, p. 36; Cobban, *Social Interpretation*, p. 59. Further information in AN, D XVI, 14a, *Déclaration du roi concernant le remboursement . . . des offices du parlement de Grenoble*, 5 Sept. 1773. See Fig. 5.1.

[32] Bluche, *Magistrats du parlement*, p. 167.

cheaper *non-originaire* offices fell even more spectacularly.[33] At Aix, counsellorships made prices over 60,000 *livres* throughout the 1720s, but were in the 40,000 *livres* range by the late 1760s.[34] At Rouen, from a high point of 46,000 *livres* in 1729 they had fallen to levels below 20,000 *livres* in the late 1760s.[35]

Yet these overall trends in most cases conceal striking short-term fluctuations, and some parlements defied the general tendency significantly. At Bordeaux and Besançon prices rose until the 1740s, peaking then in the upper 30,000 *livres* range. Only after that did they drift downwards to levels 10,000 *livres* lower in the 1780s.[36] At Besançon there was a slight upturn in the late 1780s, and at Dijon and Toulouse the whole period 1775-89 was one of modest recovery.[37] At Douai, prices held steady at around 50,000 *livres* throughout the century, and rose markedly in the final years.[38] Presidencies and less numerous offices held up everywhere better than more commonplace ones.

Falling prices in the parlements are usually ascribed to a combination of poor profits and growing social exclusivism.[39] But it seems unlikely that these offices had ever been bought for financial gain, even when prices were much higher;[40] if exclusivism was important at all, profitability could never have been more than secondary to that. Even the importance of exclusivism has been questioned in the case of Rennes, the most socially exclusive parlement of all, on the grounds that the court had been effectively closed to outsiders and non-nobles long before the eighteenth century.[41] Nevertheless, the small number of ennoblements via the parlements over the century demonstrates that there was little bourgeois interest in this market.[42] Only those who were

---

[33] Meyer, *Noblesse bretonne*, ii, pp. 938-41.

[34] AN, AD XVI, 15[6], *Déclaration du roi concernant le remboursement . . . des offices du parlement de Provence*, 5 Sept. 1773.

[35] AN, AD XVI, 15[6], *Déclaration du roi concernant le remboursement . . . des offices du parlement de Rouen* etc., 22 Aug. 1773.

[36] See above, pp. 77-8; Gresset, *Gens de justice*, i, p. 61.

[37] A. Colombet, *Les parlementaires bourguignons à la fin du XVIIIe siècle* (Dijon, 1937), pp. 62-3; P. de Peguilhan de Larboust, 'Les magistrats du parlement de Toulouse à la fin de l'ancien régime (1775-1790)' (unpublished *mémoire de diplôme*, Toulouse, 1965), pp. 64-5.

[38] AN, H[2], 1140, *Déclaration du roi concernant la remboursement . . . des offices du parlement de Flandre*, 8 mai 1772; D, XVII, 7, anonymous memorandum of 1790 or 1791.

[39] Ford, *Robe and Sword*, p. 149; Mousnier, *Les institutions*, ii, pp. 336-7.

[40] See above, p. 109.

[41] Meyer, *Noblesse bretonne*, ii, p. 937.

[42] See above, p. 110.

already noble usually contemplated buying office in a parlement, and this limited demand considerably.

Yet except for the highest presidencies, a long noble lineage was not essential outside Brittany,[43] and this may help to explain the clear upturn in some parlements in the 1780s. The only career more socially prestigious than that of a *parlementaire* was that of an army officer. But the officer corps was effectively closed to all but those of very distinguished ancestry by the Ségur law of 1781,[44] which may have pushed a number of recently ennobled families towards the parlements.

There also seems to have been a correlation between the political turbulence of a parlement and the value of its offices. In Paris, where defiance of the crown brought national notice, prices could be boosted. The lawyer diarist Barbier noted in 1723 that offices in the parlement rose in value when it took an extreme political stance: 'They will become like shares in the Indies Company. They will rise and fall on the market according to events.'[45] Yet sustained disruption of the judicial routine eventually served to depress prices even in the capital;[46] and when, after mid century, the provincial courts became politically active,[47] the same effect was observable there. The 1760s, when clashes with the crown reached their peak, witnessed low prices almost everywhere. They continued low in the 1770s and 1780s in parlements like Bordeaux or Grenoble, where personal quarrels and vendettas kept the magistrates at each others' throats.[48] 'I and others have tried,' wrote the business manager of a Grenoble magistrate trying to sell his office in 1778, 'but no buyer has yet come forward and only the assurance of a general and stable peace in matters of the day will bring out buyers.' It took two more years to sell, at a price which the seller even then thought inadequate.[49]

Such examples suggest that local circumstances influenced prices significantly; as does the fact that levels for the same office differed from place to place. Higher prices in Paris obviously reflected the prestige of the first court in the land. The notorious political quiescence of Douai no

[43] J. Egret, 'L'aristocratie parlementaire française à la fin de l'ancien régime', *Revue historique*, 207 (1952), pp. 1-14.

[44] D.D. Bien, 'La réaction aristocratique avant 1789: l'exemple de l'armée', *Annales, ESC*, 29 (1974), pp. 23-48, 505-34.

[45] E.J.F. Barbier, *Journal historique et anecdotique du règne de Louis XV*, ed. A. de la Villegille, 4 vols (Paris, 1847-56), ii, p. 5.

[46] Bluche, *Magistrats du parlement*, pp. 167-8.

[47] J. Egret, *Louis XV et l'opposition parlementaire, 1715-1774* (Paris, 1970), pp. 45ff.

[48] Doyle, *Parlement of Bordeaux*, pp. 29-30; Egret, *Parlement de Dauphiné*, ii, pp. 27-37.

[49] Ibid., ii, pp. 36-7.

doubt helps to explain the buoyancy of prices in Flanders. Bordelais magistrates, with strong ties to the mercantile community, were convinced that the office market was linked to the vicissitudes of overseas trade.[50] Prices in Toulouse perhaps held up after 1775 because in that year the suppression of a whole chamber of the parlement diminished the number of offices available by thirty-two in a city where other ennobling offices were few.[51] The overall picture of the market for offices in the parlements is, however, a sluggish one, with values in gentle decline. It reflected a closed world of secure, vegetating noblemen unworried by meagre returns or social competition, certain of their superiority. In these doldrums, the slightest breeze had exaggerated effect. But none of this is any guide to what was happening in other parts of the venal system.

Ennobling offices outside the parlements can be divided into magistracies in various sovereign or superior courts; and offices in chanceries. The latter, largely made up of *secrétaires du roi*, are best dealt with separately. What, however, was happening to offices in the nine *chambres des comptes*, four *cours des aides*, four sovereign councils, twenty-five *bureaux des finances* and certain other courts such as the Paris and Lyons *cours des monnaies*? These bodies have been far less exhaustively studied than the parlements, but enough information is available to make the general trend clear. The salient feature is that in most of them prices were higher than in the parlements.[52]

Offices in the Paris *chambre des comptes*, uniquely, sold at a standard price between the mid-seventeenth century and the Revolution of 150,000 *livres* for a *maître des comptes*.[53] In the Nantes chamber prices were not fixed, but offices of *maître* remained in the 45,000-52,000 *livres* range for most of the century, while the less prestigious *auditeurs* went from around 30,000 *livres* in the 1720s to 40,000 *livres* on the eve of the Revolution.[54] In Rouen, 35,000 *livres* would secure an office of *maître* in the 1720s or in 1770, but more went above that price at the later date.[55] Counsellors in the court at Aix were paying around 40,000 *livres* on the

[50] Doyle, *Parlement of Bordeaux*, p. 29; see also above, p. 77.

[51] Larboust, 'Magistrats du parlement de Toulouse', p. 21; Meyer, 'Noblesse française', pp. 9-10.

[52] Not the view of Ford, *Robe and Sword*, p. 150.

[53] AN, D VIII, 'Précis sur la liquidation de la chambre des comptes de Paris' (1790 or 1791).

[54] Meyer, *Noblesse bretonne*, i, pp. 179-83, 205-8.

[55] AN, D VI, 2, above, n. 35.

eve of the Revolution, which they claimed was a third higher than two decades earlier.[56] At Montpellier, a *cour des comptes, aides et finances* all in one, counsellorships originally bought in the mid 60,000 *livres* range around 1700 were fetching much the same price in the 1780s.[57] In the Bordeaux *cour des aides* prices dipped in mid century to 14,000 *livres* but by 1789 were approaching 30,000 *livres* and had overtaken those in the local parlement.[58] A similar mid century dip, followed by recovery after 1775 to the levels approaching 30,000 *livres* seen in the 1720s, has been established for the sovereign council of Arras.[59]

All this information is very random, but most of it points in the same direction. Prices in these courts were rising. And while it is undoubtedly true that local factors – the distance from a parlement or other institution with ennobling offices, the state of the local economy, the impact of the judicial upheavals of the early 1770s[60] – played their part, there can be no real doubt about the decisive influence. It was a bourgeois desire for ennoblement.[61] Most of these courts gave only second-degree nobility, but they had light or non-existent duties, and a family could ennoble itself over two privileged, unexacting generations. Contemporaries had no illusions about it. Nobody would miss the *cour des aides* of Clermont, claimed an anonymous report,[62] for 'almost all the officers of this company are very rich and very comfortable persons who only buy an office to give themselves nobility, to exempt themselves from the duty of *franc fief* and to escape from public burdens . . . ' The members of the Bordeaux *cour des aides*, noted a local observer in 1788, 'are the object of derision and contempt among the public, who call them the court of asses. Those who wish to get their sons into the Senate

---

[56] AN, D XVII, 6, Autheman, *avocat-général*, to president of the National Assembly, 20 May 1791.

[57] P. Vialles, *Etudes historiques sur la cour des comptes, aides et finances de Montpellier* (Montpellier, 1921), pp. 77-8, 292-3.

[58] See above, pp. 80-2.

[59] Sueur, *Conseil provincial d'Artois*, pp. 220-33.

[60] For such factors in Bordeaux, see above, pp. 80-2; in Arras, Sueur, *Conseil provincial d'Artois*, pp. 230-2; in Aix, M. Cubells, 'Le recrutement de la cour des comptes, aides et finances de Provence au dix-huitième siècle', *Revue historique*, 257 (1977), pp. 14-17.

[61] See F. Bluche, *Les magistrats de la cour des monnaies de Paris au XVIIIe siècle, 1715-1790* (Paris, 1966), pp. 22-6; M. Garden, *Lyon et les Lyonnais au XVIIIe siècle* (Paris, 1970), pp. 389-90; Meyer, *Noblesse bretonne*, i, pp. 183-5.

[62] AN, K 890, 'Mémoire concernant la cour des aydes et bureau des finances de Clermont', undated, but seemingly late 1760s or early 1770s.

[parlement] go there to wipe out their ignoble birth.'[63] The social composition of these courts confirms such opinions. No less than 79 per cent of the members of the Paris *cour des monnaies* between 1771 and 1790 were ennobled by the offices they had bought,[64] although it is true that membership here conferred first-degree nobility and so gave no incentive to pass on offices to children. At the Bordeaux *cour des aides* over the same period, the figure was 66 per cent. Twenty per cent of those already noble were sons of officers in the court, completing the ascent to full nobility.[65] The court at Aix, admittedly, was much more aristocratic, ennobling only 15 per cent of its members over the century. But it fell into local discredit after co-operating with the judicial reforms of the early 1770s, and the proportion of bourgeois entrants rose to 26 per cent between then and the Revolution. Twenty-two per cent of the Aix magistrates over the century were sons of officers in the same court, a similar proportion to Bordeaux.[66]

The *bureaux des finances* and their 636 *trésoriers de France* appear at first sight to be institutions of much the same character. All except sixty of these offices (the *bureaux* of Paris and Grenoble) ennobled in the second degree, and none had onerous duties. They were traditionally thought of as a preserve of rich men, and prices were high. In Paris they cost between 60,000 and 90,000 *livres* in the middle years of the century, with a tendency to become more erratic in the 1760s.[67] In Bordeaux they rose from 34,000 *livres* in the 1730s, peaking in the 1760s at 45,000 *livres*. After that they fell back towards the levels of the 1730s by the 1780s.[68] At Moulins too prices peaked at 50,555 *livres* in 1766, falling to 38,600 *livres* five years later.[69] At Nantes, where the *bureau* was subsumed into the *cour des comptes*, prices rose to 80,000 *livres* in 1752, slipping back to the low 70s by the next decade.[70]

---

[63] Quoted above, p. 80.

[64] Bluche, *Magistrats de la cour des monnaies*, p. 22.

[65] D. Bège, 'Une compagnie à la recherche de sa raison d'être: la cour des aides de Guyenne et ses magistrats, 1553-1790', 3 vols (unpublished thesis, Université de Paris I, 1974), iii, appendix, pp. 20-9.

[66] Cubells, 'Recrutment de la cour des comptes', pp. 12-13, 16-17.

[67] F. Bluche, 'Les officiers du bureau des finances de Paris au XVIIIe siècle, 1693-1791', *Bulletin de la Société de l'Histoire de Paris et de l'Ile de France*, 90 (1970), pp. 167-212. For other figures see AN ZIf 643, procès-verbaux du bureau des finances de Paris; and AN, D XVII, 9, for liquidation figures. See Fig. 5.2

[68] See Fig. 5.2 and above, p. 83.

[69] F. Dumont, *Le bureau des finances de la généralité de Moulins (1587-1790)* (Moulins, 1923), pp. 14-15.

[70] Meyer, *Noblesse bretonne*, i, pp. 218-22.

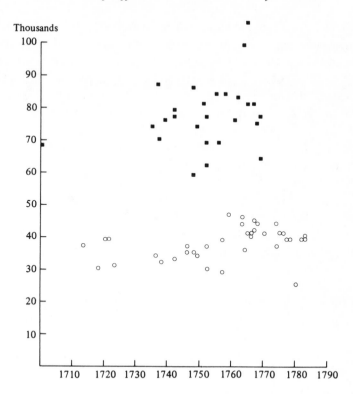

Fig. 5.2 Prices for office of *trésorier de France*.
  ○ Bordeaux   ■ Paris

Here then was another category of institution where prices were not rising. The reason, however, does not seem to have been bourgeois lack of interest or institutional exclusivism. Sixty per cent of the Paris *trésoriers* were ennobled by their offices, and their high average age on entry suggests men investing fortunes made in other fields.[71] Even the revenues, at between 2,000 and 3,000 *livres* p.a. in most *bureaux*, were quite attractive for ennobling offices.[72] But because the government too believed the *trésoriers* to be particularly rich, it continued to squeeze them financially in a way that had been normal for all office holders in the later years of Louis XIV,[73] but had been largely abandoned since. Thus in 1743, 1748 and 1770 they were forced to make disguised loans to the state in the form of *augmentations de gages*; and in 1743 and 1771 they

[71] Bluche, 'Officiers du bureau des finances', pp. 152-7.
[72] AN, K 889, Bureaux des Finances. A summary of intendants' responses to a circular letter from the *contrôleur-général* of 23 Nov. 1767.
[73] Ford, *Robe and Sword*, pp. 110-11.

were forced to repurchase the right to heredity.[74] Moreover, from the 1750s onwards the government constantly toyed with projects for a comprehensive reform of the *bureaux*. A draft declaration of 1758 intended to subject them to the parlements drew protests from all over the country.[75] Continued uncertainty led the *trésoriers* of Soissons to complain in 1762 of 'the notable prejudice which . . . our status and our offices receive' as a result. In 1769 the *bureaux* banded together in order to petition for better treatment,[76] but exactions continued and the Paris *bureau* was reorganised with the loss of a number of offices. Around 1780 there were new rumours of reform, and the *bureau* of Aix lamented: 'There is yet time . . . to give a helping hand to twenty-seven tribunals of justice which for several years have borne the brunt of all sorts of injustice and which . . . ought to be able to expect some softening of the ills which overwhelm them, which degrade offices of considerable value and have made them fall into absolute discredit.'[77] This was to exaggerate; but quite obviously the *bureaux* were in a state of crisis over the last decades of the *ancien régime*, and cautious social climbers with substantial funds to invest were well advised to look elsewhere. Fortunately for them the *secrétaires du roi* were under no such threat.

Uncertainties over the security of investment in the *bureaux des finances* may have helped to push up prices in other non-*parlementaire* courts. The *trésoriers de France*, after all, accounted for around 17 per cent of all ennobling offices. No doubt too these uncertainties gave an extra boost to the most spectacular of all rises in office prices, that of the *secrétaires du roi*.

The ostensible function of the 819 *secrétaires du roi* was to seal and expedite documents emanating from the royal chancery and the sovereign courts. No less than 300 of these offices were attached to the *Grande Chancellerie* in Paris, the rest distributed among the various courts. In practice their duties could be performed by deputies, they were not obliged to reside at the place of their appointment, and they could pursue other professions without incompatibility. Their offices

---

[74] AN, D XVII, 7, Le Telier-Vauville to National Assembly, 20 Jan. 1791; also 'Observations adressées à Monsieur le Président du comité de Judicature, au nom des officiers du Bureau des Finances de Lyon . . . ' See too Dumont, *Bureau des finances de . . . Moulins*, p. 231.

[75] AN, K 890, for letters from the *bureaux* of Caen, La Rochelle, Limoges and Soissons.

[76] Ibid., for a petition of 1770. AN, K 889, for a printed *Mémoire pour les presidents, trésoriers de France, généraux des finances, et autres officiers des bureaux des finances* presented in 1769.

[77] AN, K 889, *Bureau des finances* of Aix to Miromesnil, 4 Oct. 1780.

could be, and often were, leased. Above all, they ennobled in the first degree. They are the most notorious example of offices created and multiplied by the state entirely as a way of raising money,[78] since they offered buyers the maximum of social advantage for the minimum of obligation. The only essential prerequisite was increasing amounts of money.

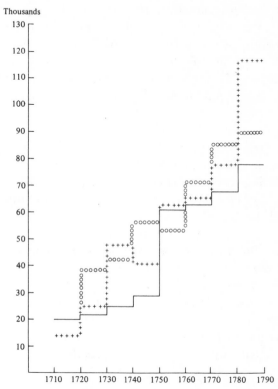

Fig. 5.3 Average price per decade for office of *secrétaire du roi*
  − Besançon   + Bordeaux   ○ Brittany

Prices for these offices rose dramatically over the century throughout the provinces. In Dijon they went from 34,000 *livres* in 1729 to 85,000 *livres* in the late 1780s.[79] In Besançon over the same period the rise was

[78] See D.D. Bien, 'The Secrétaires du Roi: Absolutism, Corps, and Privilege under the Ancien Régime', in E. Hinrichs, E. Schmitt, R. Vierhaus (eds), *Vom Ancien Régime zur Französischen Revolution* (Göttingen, 1978), pp. 158-68; and F. Bluche, 'Von Monsieur Jourdan zu Monsieur Necker: Ein Portrait des "secrétaire du Roi" (1672-1789)', in Birke, Mieck and Malettke, *Ämterkäuflichkeit*, pp. 78-86.

[79] A. Bourée, *La chancellerie près le parlement de Bourgogne de 1476 à 1790* (Dijon, 1927), p. 42.

from around 22,000 *livres* to over 77,000 *livres*;[80] in Brittany from 37,000 *livres* to 95,000 *livres*;[81] in Bordeaux from 26,000 *livres* to 125,000 *livres*.[82] The upward movement was not always continuous; in Brittany and Bordeaux for example prices dipped quite markedly in mid century. But by the 1780s they were soaring again, making these easily the most expensive ennobling offices in their respective provinces. Only in Paris was the pattern significantly different. Examples of metropolitan prices are curiously elusive, but until 1770 the movement seems to have been strongly upward. In 1729, therefore, 90,666 *livres* seemed a reasonable price;[83] by mid century upwards of 110,000 *livres* was normal,[84] and by 1770 the level was 150,000 *livres*.[85] But by 1779 they had fallen back to 120,000 *livres*[86] and it was at this level they were liquidated in 1790.[87]

The general upward movement of these prices is not difficult to explain. The attraction of the office for socially ambitious bourgeois was obvious. It is true that occasional nobles were found in the market,[88] but the overwhelming majority of buyers were financiers, merchants and industrialists.[89] In 1762, 37 per cent of the company of tax-farmers were *secrétaires*, and this was the most frequent means by which members of this increasingly aristocratic body ennobled themselves.[90] The relatively high price of the office in western seaports similarly reflects the prosperity of their merchants, who sometimes sought the same office at inland centres where it was cheaper.[91] The mid century deceleration in its price in Bordeaux or Nantes echoes the uncertainties of overseas trading profits at a time of war with Great Britain. Even if we did not know that buyers of these offices were bourgeois seeking ennoblement, the fact that hardly any fathers were succeeded in them by their sons

[80] J.F. Solnon, *215 bourgeois gentilshommes au XVIIIe siècle: les secrétaires du roi à Besançon* (Paris, 1980), p. 80. See Fig. 5.3.

[81] Meyer, *Noblesse bretonne*, i, pp. 257-60. See Fig. 5.3.

[82] See Fig. 5.3, and above, p. 84.

[83] Y. Durand, *Les fermiers-généraux au XVIIIe siècle* (Paris, 1971), p. 138.

[84] V. Bazoche, 'La vénalité des offices à Paris, 1748-1750' (unpublished *mémoire de diplôme*, Université de Paris X, Nanterre, 1971), p. 61.

[85] Solnon, *215 bourgeois gentilshommes*, p. 81; Durand, *Fermiers-généraux*, p. 138.

[86] AN, D XVII, 3, Deville to president of committee of judicature, 13 Aug. 1790.

[87] P. Robin, *La compagnie des secrétaires du roi (1351-1791)* (Paris, 1933), p. 30.

[88] E.g. 7.4 per cent over the century at Besançon: Solnon, *215 bourgeois gentilshommes*, p. 97.

[89] Ibid. pp. 97-130; Bien, 'Secrétaires du roi', p. 155; Garden, *Lyon*, pp. 387-8.

[90] Durand, *Fermiers-généraux*, pp. 296-9.

[91] Meyer, *Noblesse bretonne*, i, pp. 242-4.

would indicate that first-degree nobility was their great attraction.[92] All this makes the buoyant market for these offices eloquent testimony to the growing wealth and unchanging social ambitions of the eighteenth-century French commercial bourgeoisie.

Why, however, did the market in Paris begin to falter after 1770? No doubt the high number of Parisian offices played some role. No doubt the availability of provincial offices conferring the same benefits at lower prices was also important – and helped to sustain the uninterrupted rise of provincial prices, too. Above all, however, after 1770 the government appears to have been squeezing the Paris *secrétaires* too hard as a source of money. Ministers knew that, like the *trésoriers de France*,[93] most *secrétaires* were wealthy *parvenus* who would seemingly pay any price for instant nobility. Over the century all the companies of *secrétaires du roi* were repeatedly forced to increase the *finance* (legal price charged by the government) of their offices, buy *augmentations de gages*, and pay for confirmation of privileges. Like the *trésoriers*, they were tapped in one or other of these ways in 1743, 1755, 1758 and 1770. 'I am exempt from the *taille* and billeting through the attributes of the office of criminal lieutenant', grumbled a Besançon *secrétaire* at the time of the first demand.[94] 'Ennoblement is proving useless to me with only one remaining son whose only child is a daughter; not seeing myself in any position to enjoy any of the privileges of the office of *secrétaire du roi*, it would be more advantageous for me to have the price reimbursed than to raise it by such a considerable amount.' In practice, officers tended to raise these extra sums by borrowing as a company rather than dipping into their own pockets. In this way the crown tapped sources of credit not usually open to it.[95] But the Paris *secrétaires* were always expected to raise more than the others, and make up any shortfalls out of their own resources. This happened at the time of the great credit crisis of 1770,[96] when the *finance* of each office was raised by 40,000 *livres*. Each officer was required to find at least 10,000 *livres* of this from his own capital, and as a result the company almost went bankrupt. It was, it is true, authorised to begin amortising its debts in 1771 by levying a 3,000 *livres* entrance fee on each new member, but that plus the new *marc d'or de*

---

[92] Bien, '*Secrétaires du roi*', p. 155.
[93] See above, pp. 117-8.
[94] Quoted in Solnon, *215 bourgeois gentilshommes*, p. 90.
[95] See Bien, '*Secrétaires du roi*', passim.
[96] Robin, *Compagnie des secrétaires*, pp. 114-17; J.F. Bosher, 'The French Crisis of 1770', *History* (1972), pp. 17-30.

noblesse became a deterrent to recruitment.[97] 'Since then', noted a memorial of 1786, 'these offices have only sold at a loss of one-sixth of capital. They are still being affected today by the company's discredit.'[98] In its eagerness to exploit the ambitions of rich social climbers, the government had gone too far. When in 1782 it was proposed to raise a further 300,000 *livres* from the *secrétaires* for the war effort, there were stormy meetings.

> Our offices [wrote one][99] are not financial, their honourable functions are not lucrative, the annual product . . . is well below the interest on their purchasing price . . . The first third of the company is made up of millionaires, another third of people living nobly in comfort, the third, in fact, of people in straitened circumstances. So it will be easy for the first class to give all that is required, the second will make it a duty and a point of honour to follow this example, but the third, which I think is the most numerous, will have trouble in meeting this object.

It was perhaps more prudent not to get involved, especially when ennoblement was more cheaply available in provincial chanceries or other less noticeable institutions.

Ennobling offices commanded great prestige and were relatively few in number. Their prices are recorded in so many sources that to ascertain them is not difficult. The volume and variety of non-ennobling offices, however, is of an altogether different order; and their prices must largely be sought in notarial archives which few foreigners have the time to consult in any depth. Happily, as we shall see, non-notarial sources can also yield reliable results in certain cases. But in two important areas information is particularly elusive.

The first is financial offices, comprising perhaps 1,500 receivers, payers, treasurers and comptrollers who together kept the financial wheels of *ancien régime* government turning.[100] A fair proportion of these offices never reached the open market.[101] When their holders

---

[97] See above, p. 110.

[98] AN, VI, 55, 'Délibérations de la Compagnie des Secrétaries du Roi de la Grande Chancellerie'.

[99] Ibid., letter of Guérard, 12 June 1782.

[100] Bosher, *French Finances*, is the standard authority on this area. He lists 1,302 financial offices but points out that they fluctuated constantly in number and are impossible to tabulate completely, ibid., pp. 77-91 passim.

[101] Of the 276 office holders listed by Bosher on pp. 319-42, eighty-four inherited them from relatives.

went bankrupt, moreover, as they often did, they reverted to the state. And in the last two decades of the old order repeated government attempts to rationalise the financial system brought suppression of many financial offices. Even when they were recreated their future remained uncertain. All this means that there is a good deal of information on the official *finance* of such offices, but little on their private market value. It is at least clear, however, that the greater financial offices were among the most expensive in the country. Receiver-generalships averaged 500,000 *livres*; particular receiverships averaged 100,000 *livres*.[102] In 1775 the two *trésoriers de l'extraordinaire des guerres* held offices each worth 1,640,000 *livres* and those of the two *trésoriers de la marine et des colonies* were valued at 1,200,000 *livres*.[103] Nor is there any doubt why such offices commanded such prices. They were extremely lucrative business propositions, acquired for the most part by professional financiers in order to gain access to public funds which they could then employ for their own profit.[104] Of sixty-three major financial offices listed in 1775, only eight yielded an annual profit on their *finance* of less than 4 per cent, and six brought in 10 per cent.[105] When we consider that these *finances* ran into six and seven figures, the rewards look impressive. It would be surprising in these circumstances if private prices had fallen. *Finances* were certainly raised when suppressed offices were recreated. In 1782, 370 offices of receiver of the *tailles* were recreated after suppression by Necker, and 308 had their *finances* raised above those assigned them in 1771.[106] So perhaps the four offices of *receveur des émoluments du sceau de la chancellerie établie près le parlement de Paris* are typical enough. One of them sold in 1741 for 48,000 *livres*. By 1785 the same office was worth 57,000 *livres* and by 1787 another could bring 72,000 *livres*.[107]

The second poorly-documented category of non-ennobling offices is that of the magistrates of the lower courts in the judicial hierarchy – the *bailliages*, *sénéchaussées* and *présidiaux*. This is doubly unfortunate, for not only was this an important category, numbering over 2,600 persons,[108] it is also the core of Alfred Cobban's supposed declining bourgeoisie.

---

[102] Ibid, p. 79.

[103] AN, K 892, 'Tableau général des finances, évaluations frais de provisions et de réception et de différents offices de trésoriers et de leurs controlleurs'.

[104] See Bosher, *French Finances*, ch. 5, passim.

[105] Ibid., ch. 5, n. 103.

[106] AN, F4 2022, *arrêt du conseil*, 18 May 1782, printed schedule. A further thirty offices had no comparable figures.

[107] AN, D XVII, 3, undated memorandum of the early 1790s.

[108] Dawson, *Provincial Magistrates*, p. 37.

There is plenty of evidence that the members of these courts, and outside observers too, perceived a crisis of recruitment in mid-century.[109] Many offices remained unfilled, and those that changed hands often did so without sales. 'The fall of the lower courts . . . and distaste for the magistracy are facts of public notoriety', complained the *présidial* of Tours in 1740, 'Several seats [of justice] in the province of Touraine are threatened with total desertion, and judicial offices that once were regarded as a solid and precious family asset are now looked upon as a distinct liability.'[110] 'Three-quarters of these offices', wrote an observer at Riom in 1758, 'are in the *parties casuelles*, and the others are only occupied because their owners are unable to dispose of them.'[111] From the 1750s onwards certain *présidiaux* began to concert measures to remedy their plight. In petitions to ministers they argued that the financial ceiling of their jurisdiction, unchanged since the sixteenth century, should be raised in order to swell their business and consequently their fees. Some argued too that their offices should confer nobility or at least other tangible or visible privileges.[112] Most of these proposals were ignored, but from the 1760s the number of established offices in these courts was reduced somewhat, and in 1774 the financial limits of *présidial* jurisdiction were raised. These courts also came much more into the public eye through involvement in the judicial reforms of the early 1770s and 1788. Whether for these or other reasons, the fortunes of some certainly seem to have revived, and this revival was reflected in office prices. The 'scattered indications' found by the historian of the provincial magistracy as a whole suggest that they were tending to rise.[113] At the *Châtelet* of Paris, admittedly rather a special *bailliage*, it was common knowledge that the price of counsellorships doubled between 1772 and 1788.[114] At Tours, the subject of mid century lamentation, most prices were certainly going up by the 1770s and

---

[109] Cobban's authority is Ford, *Robe and Sword*, who takes it in turn from a letter of d'Aguesseau in 1740 quoted in A.E. Giffard, *Les justices seigneuriales en Bretagne* (Paris, 1903), p. 214. But see too Laurain, 'Essai sur les présidiaux', pp. 532-63; A. Macé, *La réforme des présidiaux au XVIIIe siècle* (Vannes, 1890); E. Everat, *La sénéchaussée d'Auvergne et siège présidial de Riom* (Paris, 1886), pp. 52-69; J.A. Tournerie, *Recherches sur la crise judiciaire en province à la fin de l'ancien régime: le présidial de Tours de 1740 à 1790* (Tours, 1975), pp. 2, 8-25.

[110] Quoted in Tournerie, *Recherches*, p. 2.

[111] Quoted in Everat, *Sénéchaussée d'Auvergne*, p. 53.

[112] Dawson, *Provincial Magistrates*, pp. 58-64.

[113] Ibid., p. 341.

[114] AN, D VI, 11, *Considérations sur l'état actuel des notaires au Châtelet de Paris* (Paris, 1791), p. 8.

1780s,[115] and they appeared buoyant too at Riom and Clermont.[116] At Bordeaux, on the other hand, they were stagnant,[117] and at Besançon they were in clear decline.[118] These variations underline once again the importance of local circumstances in the office market. Where, as in Touraine or Auvergne, there were no sovereign courts to overshadow them and attract the socially ambitious, the *bailliage* and *présidial* magistrates dominated local society. In the great provincial capitals they wilted in the shadow of mightier institutions which offered greater rewards for less effort.[119] But nowhere were prices notably high, except for senior magistrates such as the *lieutenants-généraux*, who in the 1770s or 1780s might pay 60,000 *livres* in Riom or Clermont, 90,000 *livres* in Tours. The more ordinary position of *assesseur* might go for 8,000-10,000 *livres* in the courts of Auvergne, 10,000 *livres* in Bordeaux, or a mere 2,400 *livres* in Besançon. And whether their prices were high or low, rising or falling, offices seldom seem to have been the main source of income for *bailliage* or *sénéchaussée* magistrates.[120] What was happening to the value of their offices, therefore, seems unlikely to have been their overriding concern when the procedures chosen for electing the Estates-General in 1789 thrust so many of them into the forefront of politics.

When in 1790 the National Assembly's committee of judicature set about implementing the decision of 4 August 1789 to abolish venality of offices, it was immediately faced with the problem of compensation.[121] It recommended that in most cases compensation should be paid on the basis of valuations made by office-holders themselves under an edict of 1771. The 1771 valuations, however, had been required for tax, with the result that many offices had been deliberately undervalued. The committee was now inundated with letters of protest from office-holders threatened with receiving compensation far below their offices' market value.

[115] Tournerie, *Recherches*, pp. 16-18.

[116] Everat, *Sénéchaussée d'Auvergne*, pp. 66-70, 380.

[117] Doyle, 'Venality and Society', above, pp. 91-2.

[118] Gresset, *Gens de justice*, i, p. 62.

[119] See Dawson, *Provincial Magistrates*, pp. 104-6, for a comparison between the status of *bailliage* magistrates in Auvergne and Dijon; for similar considerations, see also L.A. Hunt, *Revolution and Urban Politics in Provincial France: Troyes and Reims, 1786-1790* (Stanford, CA, 1978), pp. 27-9.

[120] Dawson, *Provincial Magistrates*, pp. 80-100; see too Mousnier, *Les institutions*, ii, p. 349.

[121] Dawson, *Provincial Magistrates*, pp. 255-62, offers a clear account of this process.

Among the most vocal of these protesters were notaries,[122] who claimed not only that their offices had been undervalued in 1771, but also that their value had risen substantially in the intervening years. In the 1760s, claimed the notaries of Paris, their offices had been worth 120,000 *livres* but by the late 1780s they had reached over 300,000 *livres*.[123] The notaries of Bordeaux claimed a tripling of their offices' value since 1771, with 40,000 *livres* being a typical price since 1784.[124] Their fellows in Toulouse claimed a rise from 10,000 *livres* in the 1760s to at least 20,000 *livres* twenty years later.[125] Similar claims came from small provincial towns as well as capitals. In twenty years, said the notaries of Barjols in Provence, prices had doubled.[126] Rises were also reported over the same period from places as far apart as Nevers, Cahors and Blois.[127]

All these petitions, of course, are partial documents. They were protesting against under-compensation, and those whose offices had not risen in value since 1771 were unlikely to complain. So claims that prices had risen need to be corroborated by other evidence before they can be accepted. In some cases, however, this is possible. The soaring price of notarial office in Paris, for example, was common public knowledge.[128] An analysis of sale contracts in Bordeaux confirms that notarial office there had risen by 900 per cent, or 21 per cent per year, between 1740 and 1782.[129] And when we consider what notaries did, we can see every reason for prices to go up. Notarial acts were required for most transfers of property, and notaries levied fees on them all. In a country without proper banks, they handled most cash deposits and investments by individuals. The twenty notaries of Riom, noted the magistrates of the

---

[122] J.L. Magnan, *Le notariat et la Révolution* (Montauban, 1952), pp. 51-3.

[123] AN, D VI, 2, 'Projet de représentations à faire et d'arrangements à proposer à l'Assemblée Nationale'.

[124] AN, D III, 378, petition received 3 Nov. 17[91].

[125] Ibid., 'Adresse des Notaires de la ville de Toulouse à l'Assemblée Législative de France' (received 12 Dec. 1791).

[126] AN, D XVII, 4, 'Réflexions des notaires de la viguerie de Barjols sur la suppression de la vénalité des offices de notaires'; also printed in Magnan, *Le notariat*, pp. 160-7.

[127] AN, DIII, 378, *Adresse des notaires royaux de la ville de Nevers, à l'Assemblée Nationale Législative* (Nevers, 1792), p. 5; petition from Cahors, received 21 Jan. 1792; AN, D XVII, 8, petition of Jousselin, notary at Blois, 1791.

[128] E.g., it was alluded to in great detail in *Adresse à l'Assemblée Nationale Législative, par les notaires de la ville de Moulins, chef-lieu du département de l'Allier* (Moulins, 1791), p. 2. Copy in AN, D III, 378. See too, ibid., the petition of Bordeaux notaries received on 3 Nov. 1791. The publications of the Parisian notaries themselves sought to explain the fact away, which suggests embarrassment at its notoriety. See J.P. Poisson, 'Le notariat parisien à la fin du XVIIIe siècle', *Dix-huitième siècle*, 7 (1975), pp. 107-8.

[129] See above, pp. 95-6.

local *présidial* in 1731, were 'depositaries of the fortune of almost all the families in the province'.[130] In Paris they handled huge sums, taking percentage commission, and resisted all attempts to establish a common reserve fund to protect depositors whose notaries got into difficulties.[131] All this meant that in towns which were flourishing economically notaries could make substantial profits, and their offices were in increasing demand. But not all towns in eighteenth-century France were prosperous, and in those that were not the office of notary was far less desirable. In shrinking Tours the number of notaries fell from twenty-seven in 1737 to twelve in 1789, when they were still complaining about their situation.[132] Their counterparts in Rennes lamented that 'the office of notary, though honourable in itself, is in a state removed from that in other towns of the kingdom; here it is quite without lustre, has no distinction, and enjoys no consideration; here the estate of notary is regarded as the most slender of employments and is undertaken to provide diversion from other occupations'.[133] Besançon was similar. Prices there actually fell, from a peak of 5,000 *livres* in 1762 to 3,700 *livres* in 1786, a contemptible level compared with those already cited.[134] Once again, therefore, office prices seem to have been much affected by local circumstance. In towns which tapped the economic expansion of the century, however modestly, notarial office was a good investment, and its price went up, especially in the two decades before 1789. Whether this was a majority of towns is still impossible to say. But it would be surprising if the predominant trend was downwards; for the pattern of other petty legal offices was all the opposite way.

The most spectacular example is that of the *procureurs. Procureurs* were attorneys or solicitors who initiated and channelled all litigation. It was only in the course of the early eighteenth century that they became entirely distinct from notaries, and many of them continued like notaries to function as bankers.[135] A number of *procureurs* were attached

---

[130] Quoted in Everat, *Sénéchaussée d'Auvergne*, p. 92.

[131] AN, F4, 1938, for proposals to establish a state depository in 1780; see too Poisson, 'Le rôle socio-économique du notariat', pp. 758-75.

[132] L. Langlois, *La communauté des notaires de Tours de 1512 à 1791* (Paris, 1911), pp. 63, 468-70.

[133] Quoted in V.N. de Kérangué, *Essai sur la communauté des notaires royaux et apostoliques de Rennes au XVIIIe siècle* (Rennes, 1904), p. 61.

[134] Gresset, 'Le notariat bisontin', pp. 71-2, 79.

[135] 'In Marseilles' (claimed that city's *procureurs* in January 1790) 'more than in any other town, *procureurs* are the depositaries of the fortune of individuals. Merchants, men of substance [*bourgeois*] and citizens of all classes entrust them with original insurance policies whose value often exceeds 300,000 *livres* and they are payable to the bearer . . . Every day they are entrusted with notes and letters of exchange of considerable value', AN, D XVII, 3.

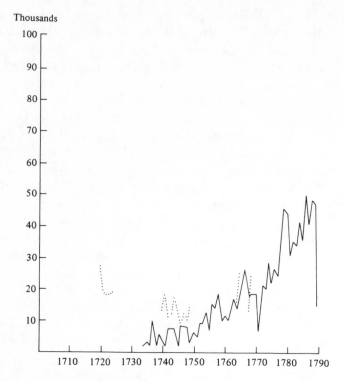

Fig. 5.4 Average annual price for office of *procureur* in Paris.
...... *Procureur au parlement*
—— *Procureur au Châtelet*

to every court in the land, and in France as a whole there must have been
thousands.[136] They too felt cheated by the liquidation of their offices in
the 1790s at 1771 valuations. Their protests to the committee of
judicature were more voluminous than those from any other category,
and they were practically unanimous in claiming that the value of their
offices had risen markedly over the preceding two decades. In Lyons
over that period they were said to have gone from 15,000 or 18,000 *livres*
to 80,000 *livres*.[137] The *procureurs* at the *chambre des comptes* of Dauphiné

---

[136] The *procureurs* at the *présidial* of Rennes estimated in 1790 that there were over 60,000 –
doubtless something of an exaggeration, AN, D XVII, 3, petition received 14 May 17[90]. C.
Bataillard and E. Nusse, *Histoire des procureurs et des avoués, 1483-1816*, 2 vols (Paris, 1882), ii, p.
264, suggests more probably that there were 12,000 in 1789.

[137] AN, D XVII, 2, *Mémoire à consulter, et consultation sur les abus qui se commettent depuis près
d'un siècle à Lyon, dans l'instruction des procédures judiciaires; sur la nécessité et moyens d'y rémédier*
(Paris, 1786), p. 59.

claimed that their offices, worth 12,000 *livres* each, had at least doubled in value since 1769.[138] In Colmar, *procureurs* at the sovereign council of Alsace had paid 24,000 *livres* in 1770 for an office which reached between 36,000 and 42,300 *livres* in 1787.[139] Even from small towns without major courts the story was the same. At Auch prices were said to have tripled or quadrupled since 1771, to reach 12,000 *livres*.[140] In forty years the price of a *procureur*'s office at Grasse had gone from 5,550 *livres* to 25,000 *livres*; it had already reached 9,000-12,000 *livres* in 1771, when it had been officially valued at only 3,000 *livres*.[141] Claims like these, of course, must be just as suspect as those of notaries unless they can be independently confirmed, but there is plenty of evidence from other sources to corroborate them. In Bordeaux, where there were five courts with *procureurs*, prices for all categories began to drift upwards from a low point in the 1730s, and by the late 1770s they had begun to soar. At both the parlement and the *sénéchaussée* they had reached levels in the low 20,000 *livres* range, and asking prices were higher still.[142] In Besançon, where there were fewer offices, prices rose even higher. Offices of *procureur* at the parlement of Franche Comté increased tenfold over the century, peaking at 30,630 *livres* in 1781 and averaging 25,000 *livres* over the rest of the decade. This was a level not far below magistracies in the parlement itself.[143] It is also possible to construct price curves for certain Parisian offices. Fragmentary information for the *procureurs au parlement* certainly suggests that prices were moving up, and makes claims of the 1790s that by 1789 prices had exceeded 50,000 or even reached 60,000 *livres* seem quite credible.[144] And a complete collection of contracts detailing prices for the 236 *procureurs au Châtelet* shows a clear rise over the century, from averages of 2,000-3,000 *livres* in the 1740s to the mid 40,000 *livres* range in the 1780s, with some reaching

[138] AN, D XVII, 4, 'Mémoire pour les procureurs de la chambre des comptes de la cy-devant province de Dauphiné', received 6 Apr. 1791.

[139] Ibid., undated petition of 1790; see too AN, D XVII, 7, petition of June 1791 from J.F.X. Jacquot, *procureur*.

[140] Ibid., petition received 14 May 1791.

[141] AD, D XVII, 3, three undated petitions.

[142] See above, pp. 96-9.

[143] Gresset, *Gens de justice*, i, pp. 61-3.

[144] AN, X 56, collection of transfer contracts. See too AD, D XVII, 7, petitions from *procureurs* Prudhomme and Brunetière, undated; D XVII, 9, 'Mémoire concernant les officiers ministériels de justice'; Bataillard and Nusse, *Histoire des procureurs*, ii, pp. 75-6, speak of the highest prices in the 1780s in the 120,000-125,000 *livres* range, and the lowest between 35,000 and 40,000 *livres*. See Fig. 5.4.

over 70,000 *livres*.[145] A final well-documented example is that of the *avocats aux conseils du Roi*, who as well as pleading cases before the privy council acted as *procureurs* for them.[146] In mid century these offices sold for around 20,000 *livres*. By the late 1780s they were fetching around 90,000 *livres*; and the 78,000 *livres* paid by Danton in 1787, often considered suspiciously exorbitant, was in fact on the cheap side.[147]

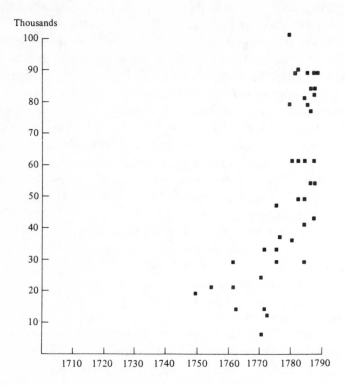

Fig. 5.5 Prices for office of *avocat aux conseils aux roi*

There seems to be no doubt, therefore, that prices for the office of *procureur* were moving up everywhere. The rate of rise varied widely from place to place, as usual according to local circumstances. The profits to be made, the number of offices available and the scale of work

---

[145] AN, Y, 5207-8; see too Bataillard and Nusse, ii, pp. 77-8. See Fig. 5.4.

[146] M. Antoine, *Le conseil du roi sous le règne de Louis XV* (Paris and Geneva, 1970), pp. 244-6. See too E. Bos, *Les avocats aux conseils du roi: étude sur l'ancien régime judiciaire en France* (Paris, 1888), esp. pp. 495 and 515.

[147] AN, D XVII, 3, 'Analyse des contrats d'acquisition des offices d'avocats aux conseils du roi'. See too Göhring, *Ämterkäuflichkeit*, p. 286; and N. Hampson, *Danton* (London, 1978), pp. 22-3. See Fig. 5.5.

involved all influenced the price. The universality of the rise is harder to explain. The volume of litigation does not appear to have been increasing – quite the reverse.[148] At Bordeaux the price of *procureurs'* offices rose even in courts notorious for their lack of business.[149] A more probable explanation, therefore, is rising demand among well-educated bourgeois for legal careers. There is clear evidence for this in rising enrolments in law faculties,[150] and although it was not necessary to be a graduate in order to become a notary or *procureur*, a good level of literacy was essential, and ambitious school leavers may have seen these offices as a safer route to status and fortune than the more precarious, though more prestigious, all-graduate world of the bar.[151] This would doubtless also help to explain rises in the price of offices that were still lower on the ladder of public esteem – what have been termed the 'small change of venality'.[152]

Anyone who consults the papers of the committee of judicature of the National Assembly cannot fail to be struck by the range and variety of occupations affected by the suppression of venality. It would take whole volumes to do justice to the prices obtained for the thousands of offices represented by civic dignitaries, clerks of courts, ushers, tipstaffs, process-servers, sack-keepers, hammer-keepers, auctioneers, valuers, surveyors, salt-measurers, salt-fish counters, salt-fish packers, barbers, surgeons, wigmakers, various sorts of policeman, and many others. Only a few examples can be given to illustrate what was happening to prices in the teeming petty office market. What is striking is that the vast majority support the same conclusion.

[148] C. Kaiser, 'The Deflation in the Volume of Litigation at Paris in the Eighteenth Century and the Waning of the Old Judicial Order', *European Studies Review* (1980). Contemporaries were well aware of the trend too. The *huissiers* of Paris complained in 1780 of 'the great diminution of business in all the courts of Paris over a number of years' and a 'new diminution in business at the Palace [of Justice] which has happened again since the revolutions of 1771, as is publicly notorious', *Mémoire à consulter et consultation en faveur des huissiers-audienciers des cours et jurisdictions de Paris* (Paris, 1780), pp. 4-5. Copies in BN, Joly de Fleury, 2134; and AN, D XVII, 2.

[149] Doyle, 'Venality and Society', above, p. 96-7. The courts were the *cour des aides* and the *bureau des finances*.

[150] R.L. Kagan, 'Law Students and Legal Careers in Eighteenth-Century France', *Past and Present*, 68 (1975), pp. 62-7.

[151] On the nuances of status between advocates and *procureurs* see L.R. Berlanstein, *The Barristers of Toulouse in the Eighteenth Century (1740-1793)* (Baltimore and London, 1975), pp. 5-6, 38-9.

[152] Taylor, 'Noncapitalist Wealth', p. 477 n.35.

Ushers and process-servers (*huissiers*) everywhere, for instance, echoed the protestations of those with whom they dealt most, *procureurs*. The twenty-six *huissiers* at the parlement of Paris listed all sales between 1770 and 1787 which showed a rise from 46,000 *livres* to almost 80,000 *livres*.[153] A similar list for the *huissiers à la Bourse* of Bordeaux ran from 10,500 *livres* in 1764 to 36,000 *livres* twenty-one years later.[154] At Besançon rises over twenty-five years were more modest, but most still rose.[155]   Lack of business, as the Paris case shows,[156] did not prevent rises in price. Nor did it do so in more obviously commercial offices. The forty *agents de change* of Lyon, a city whose manufacturers were in serious trouble in the 1780s, declared it common knowledge that their offices had experienced *une progression sensible* since the 1770s.[157] But where business was good or expanding the situation was even more promising. The auctioneers of Paris thought that 'luxury in furniture' had helped to raise their offices' value.[158] The forty *courtiers royaux* or brokers of flourishing Bordeaux, who played a role in the city's economy analogous to that of the Lyons *agents de change*, saw theirs rise steadily too. The less prestigious office of *courtier breveté*, however, created in too great abundance in 1760, failed to take off.[159] Broking was a precarious business in which confidence was everything. When it was lost, the system no longer worked and had to be dismantled, as at Marseilles in 1774.[160] The Bordelais trusted the familiar, established royal brokers. Against them, 200 lower-grade officers had little chance of winning prestige or attracting buyers.

---

[153] AN, D XVII, 8,'Etat et situation des huissiers du ci-devant parlement de Paris, extrait de leurs titres pièces et mémoires'. See too AN, U, 1398, deliberation of the *huissiers*, 9 Aug. 1772.

[154] AN, D XVII, 7, letter of 3 Feb. 1791.

[155] AN, D XVII, 3, a petition sent on 2 March 1790 lists the difference as follows (in *livres*):

	1765	1780s
Huissier ordinaire au parlement	12,000	15,800
Huissier à la chancellerie	4,000	5,000
Huissier aux requêtes du palais	10,000	10,000

Gresset, *Gens de justice*, i, pp. 63-4, confirms a general rise in prices for offices of *huissier*.

[156] See above, n. 148.

[157] AN, D XVII, 8, petition received 20 Aug. 1791. See too L. Trenard, 'La crise sociale lyonnaise à la veille de la Révolution', *Revue d'histoire moderne et contemporaine*, 6 (1959), pp. 5-10.

[158] AN, D XVII, 4, memorandum of 1790 from the *huissiers, commissaires priseurs vendeurs de biens et meubles*.

[159] See above, pp. 93-5.

[160] F.X. Emmanuelli, *La crise marseillaise de 1774 et la chute des courtiers: contribution à l'histoire du commerce du Levant et de la banque* (Paris, 1979).

Perhaps the most abundant business office of all was that of wigmaker, in a century where no man of any means wore his own hair. The bottom was soon to drop dramatically out of this trade, but in 1789 it was still booming, and prices for the office reflected that trend. So did rising rents, since whole batches of these offices were often bought up *en bloc* by entrepreneurs who then leased them out piecemeal.[161] In Bordeaux, prices almost trebled between the 1750s and the 1780s.[162] There were also rises in Lyon, Angers,[163] Sedan and Paris.[164]

No doubt examples could be multiplied, as they could for most of the offices appearing in this brief survey. Further investigation, however, seems unlikely seriously to modify the general conclusion about office prices to which most of the present evidence points. It is not true that there was a general decline in the value of venal offices. In a few cases prices undeniably did decline, but that can invariably be ascribed to special circumstances. The overall trend was for office prices to rise. And although, as we have seen, special circumstances can often be invoked to explain rises as well, so general a movement seems likely to have had at least some general causes, to which we must now turn.

Many of those who claimed in the 1790s that the value of their offices had risen were also prepared to speculate on why it had happened. 'Offices have risen progressively in price,' declared the *procureurs* of Grasse, 'like all other real estate (*immeubles*).'[165] The *expéditionnaires de la cour de Rome* also invoked 'the progressive increase which all real estate has undergone'.[166] 'You know better than anyone', argued the municipal officers of Douai, ' . . . that our offices were marketable, and that their value constantly followed the progressive augmentation of money and the price of other things which are marketable objects.'[167] Admitting that the value of their offices had undergone a *surhaussement*, the notaries of Paris pointed out that this had happened to others in the capital,[168] and it was 'perhaps rather the result of the common impulsion

---

[161] AN, D XI, 'Pétition pour les locateurs d'office de perruquiers de la ville de Lyon', received 31 July 1791. See also above, pp. 92-3.

[162] Ibid.

[163] Taylor, 'Noncapitalist Wealth', p. 477 n.35.

[164] AN, D XII, undated petition from Sedan; August 1791 from Paris; see too D VI, 2, 'exposé des maîtres perruquiers', undated.

[165] AN, D XVII, 3, cited above, n. 138.

[166] AN, D XVII, 8, undated petition.

[167] AN, D XVII, 4, 'Pièces relatives à la liquidation des offices de la municipalité de la ville de Douay'.

[168] AN, D VI, 2, *Considérations sur l'état actuel des notaires au Châtelet de Paris et sur le droit qu'ils ont à un remboursement entier du prix réel de leurs offices* (Paris, 1791), p. 8.

which pushed up the price of all manner of goods and properties in general, than of an effective, real extension of value'. Their Bordeaux colleagues agreed: 'All this proves much less a greater real value in things, than an abundance of money which no longer presents the price it had when it was rarer.'[169] In other words, they blamed inflation.

Historians have been familiar with inflation in eighteenth-century France for half a century.[170] The price of basic commodities went up by two-thirds between the 1730s and the 1780s. Rents for land doubled or tripled.[171] In these circumstances it would have been quite extra-ordinary if the value of an investment field as large as that of offices had fallen. Land and office, after all, attracted the same sort of capital and conferred the same sort of benefits.[172] There is in fact a striking similarity between the movements of rents and that of office prices. Regional and local differences were important in both cases, but there was an overall twofold or threefold rise; it began sluggishly in mid century, but accelerated quite markedly from around 1770. And since this rise was far steeper than that of basic commodities, the real as well as the nominal value of both types of property must have been increasing. Like large landowners, office-holders were therefore getting richer. In this light, the proposition that *officiers* were a class in decline seems untenable.[173]

Office-holders were therefore right when they attributed price rises to inflation; but most of them did not see it as the sole cause. More typical was the complex explanation advanced by two city councillors of Lille for their own offices' increased value:

> This progression in any case has followed that of other offices in the province, and that of other offices in the same body. Their small number having regard to the population; the consideration attached to them which was once less esteemed; public opinion, education, the multiplication of money, all this combined to make them sought after, and the great competition between aspirants must naturally have raised their price considerably.[174]

---

[169] AN, D XVII, 8, petition to the parlement of Bordeaux, 1785.

[170] C.E. Labrousse, *Esquisse du mouvement des prix et des revenues en France au XVIIIe siècle*, 2 vols (Paris, 1933).

[171] Labrousse in *Histoire économique et sociale de la France*, ii, pp. 454-6.

[172] Taylor, 'Noncapitalist Wealth', pp. 471-3.

[173] Cobban, *Social Interpretation*, p. 59.

[174] AN, D XVII, 4, 'Mémoire sur les offices de second et troisième conseiller pensionnaire de la ville de Lille'.

Inflation – the 'multiplication of money' – came low on this list. The emphasis was much more on competition, and this was an important theme in other petitions. Price increases, argued the Paris auctioneers, had 'arisen, as in all offices, from the difficulty of finding a situation (*état*)'.[175] Jean Doussault, president of the *grenier à sel* at Craon, attributed the dearness of his own office in 1783 to 'two causes. The first is that his colleagues were provided at a time when it was easier to find situations and when offices were consequently less sought after and less dear. The second is that [he] had competitors and in this respect it is essential to observe that his office was knocked down to him as the highest bidder . . .'[176] 'Everyone' observed the always-eloquent notaries of Bordeaux, 'is trying to establish themselves, and this engenders a competition which has added to the cause of the amazing surge found in the price of notaries' offices.'[177] The appearance of 'several buyers looking for a situation' had had the same effect on *procureurs*' prices at Dijon.[178] Instances where competition was not increasing, as demonstrated by stagnant or falling prices, can be convincingly explained by circumstances peculiar to the offices in question such as traditions of exclusivism, excessive fiscal pressure, or over-creation of posts. The general trend at almost every level was all the other way. On the eve of the Revolution, 'archeomania' was intensifying.

Some companies thought it resulted from diminishing the number of offices available,[179] and doubtless in a local context this sometimes had a stimulating effect. But in general, offices could only be suppressed in a company if holders of those to remain agreed to buy them out. This increased the financial burdens borne by the offices left, since funds for buying out were usually borrowed on the collective credit of the company. Besides, most companies already had important debts going back to ruthless exploitation of venal office-holders during the last years of Louis XIV, and a diminution of offices meant that fewer members had to share that burden.[180] Altogether, reducing numbers created as many problems as it solved, and in fact the overall total of venal offices

---

[175] AN, D XVII, 7, letter of 3 Feb. 1791.

[176] AN, D XVII, 7, petition received 18 Aug. 1791.

[177] AN, D XVII, 7, petition to the parlement of Bordeaux, 1785.

[178] AN, K 663, 'Mémoire des procureurs au parlement de Dijon', undated, but from internal evidence after 1783.

[179] AN, D III, 378, *Adresse des notaires royaux de la ville de Nevers à l'Assemblée Nationale Législative* (Nevers, 1792), p. 5.

[180] On these problems, see *Second rapport du comité de judicature, sur les dettes des compagnies supprimées* (Paris, n.d.), delivered by Gossin on 2 September 1790.

does not appear to have fallen over the century before 1789. If anything it rose.[181] Major suppressions, like Laverdy's introduction of election into municipal offices,[182] or Maupeou's remodelling of the parlements, proved transitory, and do not appear to have shaken the public's faith in the long-term future of venality. Competition was not therefore evidence of a shrinking system. It reflected increasing numbers of competitors.

For artisans' offices a simple increase in the general population was enough to make them more sought after.[183] All that was required, beside ability to raise the purchasing price, was a measure of manual skill to make the office pay. Most of the offices under discussion, however, had no manual involvement. That indeed was part of their attraction. What they did require was a high level of literacy and considerable capital; and this made them the preserve of the bourgeoisie. Estimating the size of the bourgeoisie is as difficult as defining it, but all historians would agree that bourgeois numbers expanded dramatically over the eighteenth century. A reasonable guess would be that they trebled,[184] and in that case the supply of offices quite obviously failed to keep pace. Ambitious bourgeois did not react by attempting to break into areas traditionally beyond them, like the parlements. That is one reason why prices there declined. But in all categories which had always attracted bourgeois capital, from ennobling dignities at the top to petty clerkships at the base of the system, bourgeois pursuit of offices increased as the century went on. They were never more in demand than on the eve of their abolition.

The market for office, then, offers no evidence for the existence of a declining bourgeoisie in late eighteenth-century France. Quite the reverse: rising prices are evidence of a bourgeoisie expanding in numbers, wealth, education and ambitions. But the ambitions they reflected were traditional ones. So far from rejecting the structures and

---

[181] Enquiries made by Colbert in 1664 reached a total of 45,780 offices, 11 per cent less than the 51,000 counted in 1778. See P. Véron de Forbonnais, *Recherches et considérations sur les finances de France*, 2 vols (Basle, 1758), i, pp. 327-9, and above, n.9. Both these figures are probably underestimates, and between 1664 and 1778 fell the massive expansion of venality produced by efforts to finance Louis XIV's last two wars. Much of this was transitory, but a net rise in the overall number of venal offices seems certain to have resulted.

[182] M. Bordes, *La réforme municipale du contrôleur général Laverdy et son application (1764-1771)* (Toulouse, 1967).

[183] For the example of the wigmakers of Bordeaux see J.P. Poussou, *Bordeaux et le sud-ouest au XVIIIe siècle: croissance économique et attraction urbaine* (Paris, 1983), pp. 31 and 124.

[184] P. Léon, in Braudel and Labrousse (eds), *Histoire économique et social*, ii, p. 607.

values of old regime society, the French bourgeoisie in the 1780s seemed intent on behaving as they had for two centuries. They were prepared to pay ever-increasing prices for the privilege of abandoning the inferior world of trade and manufacture as soon as they could muster enough capital to buy their way into the secure and respectable ranks of proprietary wealth.[185]

Many failed to achieve this ambition, of course. Increasing competition and rising prices must have meant that more were failing than ever. No less than 4,000 young hopefuls, wrote Mercier in the early 1780s, dreamed of 113 notarial offices in Paris.[186] Those who failed to achieve such dreams certainly had ample grounds for resentment against the old order. The Revolution's ideal of careers open to the talents had an obvious appeal to men of ambition who found that most public careers seemed open increasingly only to riches. One of Alfred Cobban's most perceptive insights was that much of the reforming thrust of the Revolution was against the power of money.[187] The evidence on office prices, which destroys his idea of a declining bourgeoisie, lends added support to this other suggestion. Yet concrete evidence that frustrated office seekers did play a significant part in the movement of 1789 is not easy to find. The fact that the third estate *cahiers* drafted that spring expressed considerable hostility to venality proves nothing by itself:[188] noble *cahiers* too condemned the sale of offices.[189] In any case, men who held office were equally involved in the elections and *cahier* drafting.[190]

It is therefore impossible to prove one way or another whether frustration at failure to afford increasingly expensive offices turned men revolutionary. What is certain is that the abolition of venality itself was not the work of such men. Cobban's most enduring achievement in this field was his demonstration that office-holders were the largest socio-professional group in the assembly which decreed abolition.[191] The committee which elaborated procedures for the liquidation of the

---

[185] Taylor, 'Noncapitalist Wealth', passim.

[186] Quoted in Poisson, 'Notariat parisien', p. 107.

[187] Cobban, *Social Interpretation*, pp. 147-53, 168, 171-2.

[188] E. Champion, *La France d'après les cahiers de 1789* (Paris, 1897), p. 124; G.V. Taylor, 'Revolutionary and Non-Revolutionary Content in the *Cahiers* of 1789: An Interim Report', *French Historical Studies* (1972), p. 498.

[189] See Chaussinand-Nogaret, *Noblesse au XVIIIe siècle*, p. 210.

[190] For new evidence on the Paris electorate see R.B. Rose, *The Making of the Sans-Culottes: Democratic Ideas and Institutions in Paris, 1789-92* (Manchester, 1983), pp. 31-6.

[191] Cobban, 'The Myth', pp. 100-2, 110. More recent calculations have shown the proportion to be even higher than he thought. See below, p. 141.

system was dominated by office-holders too.[192] At first sight Cobban found this quite baffling. But then, with visible relief, he noted that they voted themselves compensation, and that solved the problem. By reinvesting their compensation money in confiscated church lands they merely shifted their investments and lost nothing.[193] Now, it is certainly true that many did buy national lands;[194] but many too had borrowed the price of their offices, and their compensation went towards repayment rather than reinvestment. Above all, Cobban overlooked the basis of the compensation recommended by the committee of judicature. By choosing declarations for tax that pre-dated two decades of spectacular inflation in office prices, the committee denied thousands of office-holders (themselves included) the true value of their investment. Very few office-holders can have emerged from the liquidation of venality with their fortunes intact. Many could have echoed the lament of Moreau, *huissier audiencier* at the *présidial* of Bourg-en-Bresse, who had paid 7,000 *livres* in 1785, with half still owing in 1791. His compensation at 1771 rates amounted to 2,400 *livres*:

> In order therefore that my vendor shall lose nothing on the price of his sale, he must sell all the furniture and effects that I possess and that are my last resource; by this means I shall find myself not only deprived of my office which was hardly sufficient for my existence and that of my family, but also deprived of my fortune which I sacrificed for the acquisition of this office, and which not being enough, a beloved wife also contributed her dowry, which can only now be lost to her, since I have nothing left.[195]

The abolition of venality by an assembly full of office-buyers cannot then be explained in terms of calculated self-interest. It seems to possess very little social or economic rationale. Much the same could be said of a lot that went on in 1789. Perhaps therefore the time has come to lay greater emphasis on factors that recent generations of historians have been reluctant to confront.

Is it, for instance, so preposterous to allow that many of the men of 1789 acted out of intellectual conviction? That, after all, is what they claimed; and it is odd to see historians, who earn their living by the intellect, minimising the importance of professed

---

[192] Dawson, *Provincial Magistrates*, p. 255.
[193] Ibid., p. 255 n. 191.
[194] Ibid., pp. 259-74.
[195] AN, D XVIII, 3, letter received 3 Sept. 1790.

principles.[196] Most eighteenth-century writers who discussed the subject (though not all) condemned venality,[197] and at the time of Maupeou the government itself had taken a lead in arguing that to sell posts of public responsibility was wrong. The frequency with which this idea recurs in the *cahiers* of all orders in 1789 suggests that much of educated opinion had been won over to it. It was doubtless incongruous that many of those who were doing well out of venality found it intellectually indefensible, but such situations are not uncommon in human affairs. So long as radical changes in the state or society remained inconceivable, venality could be accepted, as Diderot had accepted it,[198] as a necessary evil. When, in 1789, the prospect opened up to change on a scale hitherto undreamed of, then venality was bound to seem an obvious abuse to remedy, and nobody was surprised when it was thrown on to the bonfire of privileges on 4 August. Very few people protested, either. They had long since ceased to believe it worth defending.

Protest, when it came, was over the principle adopted for compensation rather than abolition. Even then little enough was heard within the assembly itself, The petitions on whose evidence this article has relied so much show that a gap had opened between the great body of office-holders and their fellows in the assembly. In the heady atmosphere of revolutionary politics on the national stage, the deputies' perceptions of what might and what ought to be done developed with astonishing speed. Measures far more radical than most of the *cahiers* had envisaged a few short months before were soon being carried by deputies radicalised by the view from the centre and the experience of forming the national assembly.[199] This radicalisation took two forms. In the first place many deputies were fired by a genuine idealism. Cobban refused to believe this on the grounds that idealism and self-sacrifice were 'rarely to be predicated of the average political man'.[200] But even if this is true, 4

---

[196] There are however signs that the intellectual origins of the Revolution are once more attracting attention. See K.M. Baker, 'French Political Thought at the Accession of Louis XVI', *Journal of Modern History*, (1978), pp. 278-303; idem, 'On the Problem of the Ideological Origins of the French Revolution', in D. La Capra and S.L. Kaplan (eds), *Modern European Intellectual History: Reappraisals and New Perspectives* (Ithaca and London, 1983), pp. 197-219; or N. Hampson, *Will and Circumstance: Montesquieu, Rousseau and the French Revolution* (London, 1983).

[197] For brief surveys see Göhring, *Ämterkäuflichkeit*, pp. 299-304; Swart, *Sale of Offices*, pp. 123-5; J. Lough, *The Philosophes and Post-Revolutionary France* (Oxford, 1982), pp. 95-7. See also below, pp. 141-53.

[198] Lough, *The Philosophes*, p. 36.

[199] Taylor, 'Revolutionary and Nonrevolutionary Content', pp. 500-2.

[200] 'The Myth', p. 102.

August 1789 was a rare moment, and it can scarcely be understood unless we recognise that a spirit of genuine altruism was present, however fleetingly. Secondly, radicalism bred practicality. Liquidation of venality on the basis of the 1771 valuation was certainly inequitable. But unlike their indignant fellows outside, office-holders in the assembly recognised that liquidation had to be swift, effective and final. This made them accept that any other basis might take forever, might be 'a terrible burden for the Nation',[201] and might fatally retard the Revolution's reforming impetus. They recognised that the interests of the national revolution they had helped to make transcended their own sectional ones. It is perhaps time historians gave them credit for that.

---

[201] *Premier rapport à l'Assemblée Nationale par le Comité de Judicature sur le remboursement des offices.*

6

4 August 1789: The Intellectual Background to the Abolition of Venality of Offices

The moment came late, when the session was already several hours old. We do not even know who proposed it, except that he came from Franche-Comté. What we do know is that the proposal was greeted, as the *procès-verbal* puts it, *avec transport*.[1] The excited deputies clearly thought that it was a marvellous idea to abolish the sale of offices. Thus the night of 4 August 1789, as well as bringing the end of French feudalism, also witnessed the end of a practice which went back almost as far, and had been one of the kingdom's central institutions for almost three centuries.

Why did it happen? It seems such an improbable thing for an assembly such as this to have done. Of the 1,315 deputies who sat in the national assembly between 1789 and 1791, 483 either held, or had some direct experience of venal office.[2] Among lay members, the proportion was almost half (49 per cent), with 294 out of 654 Third Estate deputies (44.95 per cent) having such experience, and no fewer than 189 out of 311 nobles, almost 61 per cent. Still more had relatives who knew or had known venality from the inside. Thus the sale of offices was abolished by an assembly dominated by its beneficiaries. Moreover, the value of most venal offices had been rising strongly since mid century.[3]

Was this, then, something that had never occurred to them, and which they welcomed, in a famous phrase, because it seemed like a good idea at

---

[1] *Moniteur*, 5, 5 Aug. 1789, reprinting the *procès-verbal*.

[2] Calculated from E.H. Lemay, *Dictionnaire des constituants, 1789-1791*, 2 vols (Paris, 1991).

[3] See W. Doyle, 'Myth for Myth: The Rise and Fall of the Declining Bourgeoisie', *Proceedings of the Consortium on Revolutionary Europe*, 13 (1983), pp. 306-19.

the time? Or had there been a significant intellectual and cultural preparation for such a radical step, so that whoever proposed it was merely seizing the moment to do what he knew everybody wanted, and would have got round to, sooner or later? Had there been a significant debate about venality over the eighteenth century, in which, after the arguments had been weighed on both sides, the balance had come decisively down against it?

I have spent the last few years looking into this and related matters; and I think I can now confidently report that the answer is no. The eighteenth century witnessed no significant or extensive debate about venality. In whatever intellectual discussion took place about public affairs, the question of venality scarcely figured. This makes the eighteenth century very different from the seventeenth, when the first great expansion of the system was marked by fierce public exchanges about the merits of funding the government's ambitions through the sale of offices. The issue dominated the estates-general of 1614, and was prominent in all discussions of public affairs down to the Fronde – which of course began mainly as a revolt of office holders.[4] Subsequently the efforts of Colbert to curb the system kept its merits and demerits in the public mind. But by the eighteenth century public discussion of the matter had dwindled away. No works of any importance were devoted to it; while in the essay competitions set by provincial academies, those peculiarly eighteenth-century barometers of the problems preoccupying men of leisure and education, none was ever devoted to venality.[5] As far as I know only one academy, that of Metz, even considered it as a suitable topic; and that was only in the 1780s. It is true that, in 1750, a paper was read to the Académie des Inscriptions in Paris which defended venality;[6] but when we follow up the author, a certain M. Bertin, we find that he had a special interest in the matter since for the whole century he and his family ran the office of *Parties Casuelles*, which administered the venal system.[7] In any case, what he had to say, like I

[4] Roland Mousnier, *La vénalité des offices sous Henri IV et Louis XIII* (Paris, 1971), pp. 579-665; A. Lloyd Moote, *The Revolt of the Judges: The Parlement of Paris and the Fronde, 1643-1652* (Princeton, 1971).

[5] See AF. Delandine, *Couronnes académiques: ou recueil des prix proposés par les sociétés savantes, avec les noms de ceux que les ont obtenus*, 2 vols (Paris, 1787).

[6] *Histoire de l'Académie Royale des Inscriptions et Belles Lettres avec les memoires de littérature tirés des registres de cette académie depuis l'année MDCCXLIX jusques et compris l'année MDCCLI*, 23 (1756), pp. 278-83.

[7] See J.F. Bosher, *French Finances, 1770-1795: From Business to Bureaucracy* (Cambridge, 1970), pp. 86-87, 321.

suspect most of the somewhat esoteric transactions of the Académie des Inscriptions, seems to have aroused no comment, whether favourable or adverse, at all.

Apart from this, I have found only two other defences of venality in the eighteenth century, both of them incidental rather than central to the works in which they are found. Both, it is true, are from figures for one reason or another of the first rank. Even then, one of them was not a contemporary. It was Cardinal Richelieu, who in chapter 4 of his *Testament politique* defended the sale of offices as a system which had destroyed the power of aristocratic clientage, eliminated corruption by its publicity, given the rich a vested interest in supporting the government, and made them more easily manageable. It was better than most alternative ways of recruiting royal servants, and in any case was already too deeply rooted to be easily or safely abolished. Until the *Testament politique* was published in 1688, Richelieu's only publicised views on venality had been those he had expressed at the estates-general of 1614, when as spokesman for the clergy he had condemned it:[8] this belated defence, half a century after his death, was shocking. So was a lot else, however, in the *Testament politique*, and for over half a century after it first appeared its very authenticity was disputed in a debate that aroused far more passion than any discussion of venality. Among those who refused to believe that it was really written by Richelieu was Voltaire, and his confident dismissal of it (as what he called a '*mensonge littéraire*') did much to postpone general acceptance of its authenticity until the 1760s.[9] But careful scholars had already proved conclusively that it was genuine by 1750, and Bertin gleefully inserted the great cardinal's mature endorsement of venality into his own defence of the system at the Académie des Inscriptions.

The other great defender of venality was of course Montesquieu; of whom however it could be said (and duly was) that he also had a vested interest in it, having held a venal presidency in the parlement of Bordeaux. But he had long given that up by the time the *Esprit des lois* was published in 1748. What he had to say about venality in this great work was little enough – a few throwaway lines, really.[10] It was good in monarchical states, he mused, because it made the administration of justice a family craft and sustained commitment to an ordered state. It

[8] Mousnier, *Vénalité*, p. 645.
[9] Richelieu, *Testament politique*, ed. Louis André (Paris, 1947). See introduction, pp. 50-56.
[10] Montesquieu, *Esprit des lois*, v, ch. 19.

also avoided corruption and restrained the ambitious. In his notebooks he went on to say that it was an incentive to wealth creation, and ensured that only those who could afford a good education, and who having a lot to lose had a commitment to the established order, would attain public office – but these additional reflections were not published in the eighteenth century.[11] As it was, those few lines in the *Esprit des lois* were in effect the only significant attempt to defend venality made in the eighteenth century in France; and those who attacked it later in the century seldom failed to single them out for refutation.

Attacked it? So there *was* a debate after all? It is certainly true that in 1788-90 there were a number of pamphlets published both for and against venality, some before it was actually abolished and some after. Even then there were not many and, as before, discussion was often tangential rather than central to the writer's purpose. I have found eight largely devoted to attacking it and two more or less defending it in the period 1789-92. By then of course the whole context of the issue had changed and people were debating everything. Before 1789 it remains true that there was no debate. Why? Not because the issue was not important, and not because contemporaries did not perceive that very clearly. The reason there was no debate was that there was no argument. Everybody though venality was wrong.

Even Montesquieu admitted that. In the same notebook mentioned above he noted frankly: 'Il n'y a guère d'homme de bons sens en France qui ne crie contre la vénalité des charges, et qui n'en soit scandalisé.' [There is scarcely a man of good sense in France who does not cry out against the venality of offices, and is not scandalised by it.'] The editor of Bertin's paper at the Académie des Inscriptions, too, recognised that opposition to venality was 'une opinion que le nombre de ses partisans et les apparences du bien public sur lequel elle se fonde, semble avoir mis hors de toute atteinte'. ['an opinion that the number of its adherents and the appearances of public welfare on which it is founded, seems to have placed beyond all questioning'.] Even Richelieu, venality's posthumous defender, recognised that most people thought it the chief defect of the kingdom's judicial system.

The fact is that, throughout its whole history, venality of office had always been condemned by the vast majority of French people who thought about it. The first concrete evidence we have for its existence in the middle ages comes from denunciations of it by the medieval estates.

[11] B. Grasset (ed.), *Montesquieu, cahiers, 1716-1765* (Paris, 1941), pp. 126-7.

Every Estates-General denounced the sale of judicial office, which they never failed to equate with the sale of justice itself. Kings themselves, whenever they created new offices to sell, invariably invoked financial necessity as their motive rather than any intrinsic virtue in the system. It was always depicted as a necessary evil, which steps would be taken to eradicate just as soon as the emergency which had provoked each new extension of the system had been overcome. On the one occasion when this attempt was actually made, under Colbert, naturally the exercise was justified by even more forthright condemnations of the evils of selling offices. The king, who created the system, and kept it going, never pretended at any time that he thought it a good thing – and this continued throughout the eighteenth century. The reigns of Louis XV and Louis XVI saw much tinkering with the system, and a number of determined efforts to make venality yield more revenue to the treasury; but they also saw some spectacular cuts in certain categories of venal office, most notably with Laverdy's municipal reforms between 1764 and 1771, Maupeou's remodelling of the parlements between 1771 and 1774, and Saint-Germain's phased abolition of military purchase that began in 1776. Whenever this happened, venality was invariably denounced in the preambles to edicts, as an abuse to be eradicated, a burden on the public, the corruption of justice, socially and economically mischievous, and so on. If there was an attack on the sale of offices before the Revolution, it could be said that the king who sold them led it.

It was also articulated from time to time by a number of leading writers. Their motives were very various. Noble ideologists like Boulainvilliers condemned above all the sort of venality that ennobled, because it opened a group defined by blood and lineage to the adulterating power of wealth.[12] Clerics like Fénelon thought venality a disguised tax which added to the burdens on the people by the perpetual public debt that sold offices represented, and the depredations which the buyers committed against the king's defenceless subjects once they took up their functions.[13] Writers on the public finances, such as Forbonnais in the 1750s, or Necker[14] in the 1780s,[15] denounced venality's social effects. In the obverse of the argument against diluting the nobility, they criticised

---

[12] *Essais sur la noblesse de France, contenant une dissertation sur son origine et abaissement* (Amsterdam, 1732), pp. 241-52, 298-300.

[13] C. Urbain (ed.), *Fénelon: écrits et lettres politiques* (Paris, 1920), pp. 48-9, 117-122.

[14] *Recherches et considérations sur les finances de France*, 2 vols (Basle, 1758), pp. 140-1, 161, 284-5.

[15] *De l'administration des finances de la France*, 3 vols (Paris, 1784), iii, pp. 146-57.

the way venality siphoned productive capital and energies off into vanities and prestigious idleness. They also echoed Colbert in lamenting how privileges bought in this way meant a loss in tax revenue to the king. But, as always, it was the idea of selling judicial office, the right to dispose of the goods and lives of one's fellow citizens, which aroused the most, and the most general, indignation. This was the essence of Voltaire's opposition to venality, for instance. At one point indeed, in middle life, Voltaire seemed almost disposed to tolerate venality. In *Le monde comme il va*, written in 1746, he seemed to say that, though an abuse, venality also had its strong points, and perhaps ought to be tolerated. But after the appearance of the *Esprit des lois*, two years later (a book he never liked) his mind seems to have set against this abuse which Montesquieu defended. One reason why he was so reluctant to accept the authenticity of Richelieu's *Testament politique* seems to have been that it defended venality, which Voltaire could not bring himself to believe such a great architect of absolute monarchy could honestly do. Certainly, most of Voltaire's attacks on venality are linked with attacks on the *Testament* as a forgery. To come down from the highest literary level, while no provincial academies set essay competitions on venality, some did set them on how best to reform or improve the laws, and this gave the entrants plenty of opportunity to strike venality some glancing blows. Entrants for the competition at Châlons-sur-Marne in 1783 picked it out as one of the obvious abuses to remedy;[16] while those hoping to win a prize for an *éloge* of Montesquieu at Bordeaux a few years later noted his defence of venality as one of those few instances where he was wrong.[17]

Only one thing redeemed venality for a generation obsessed by the fear of despotism: a body of tenured magistrates whom it was too expensive to buy out were the surest bulwark against an over-mighty monarch. For Voltaire even that was no advantage. He admired strong and decisive rulers and he hated the *parlementaires* who were their most formidable opponents and the most prominent beneficiaries of venal offices. That was why he applauded Maupeou, who of course abolished venality, in the sovereign courts at least.[18] But for Diderot, and most of the other *philosophes*, Maupeou was a despot who threatened what slender form of liberty existed in France. His abolition of venality showed that he understood only too well what stood in his way. So for

---

[16] AD, Marne, 1J 49, report of 25 February 1783.
[17] Bibliothèque de la Ville de Bordeaux, MSS 828, xcvi, pp. 35-6; xcvii, pp. 49-50.
[18] P. Gay, *Voltaire's Politics: The Poet as Realist* (Princeton, 1959), pp. 317-30.

Diderot, who was as opposed to the selling of justice as anyone, venality had its advantages as a preservative of public liberties. It was an evil, but a necessary one.[19] This, I suspect, was quite a common view down to 1788. When, in the latter year, Lamoignon struck his own blow against the parlements and like Maupeou coupled it with a promise to abolish venality, the link between it and public liberty was re-emphasised. Lamoignon of course failed. His reforms did not even get as far as the Maupeouan ones with which they were often compared before absolute monarchy collapsed – and with it the danger of despotism. Now venality could not even be defended on the grounds of protecting public liberties. No longer necessary, it now stood forth as an evil which nothing redeemed.

This was shown very clearly in the *cahiers* of the following spring, which tell us in some detail what French public opinion thought of this central institution in national life on the eve of its abolition. Of the 523 extant general *cahiers*, five-sixths of all *cahiers* ever made, I have looked at 492: 150 clerical ones, 153 noble, and 189 Third Estate.[20] I think this is more than enough to draw some viable general conclusions. Of these, only four, all noble, defend venality. One of those does so on the grounds that it is the least bad way of recruiting officials; another on precisely the grounds just discussed – as a barrier to despotism. A larger proportion, it is true, thirty-four *cahiers* distributed across all three orders or just under 7 per cent in all, envisaged or would tolerate some sort of partial retention, either for certain specific functions or because of the likely difficulty of buying the whole system out. And 109 *cahiers*, or 22 per cent (of which by far the greatest number, fifty-nine, were from the Third Estate) insisted that when venality was abolished, just compensation should be paid to those who lost the offices in which they had invested. This does not detract from the essential point that comes out clearly from this analysis, and which confirms my earlier one: hardly anybody in France thought that venality was defensible, and such defences as there were, even, were grudging and conditional.

This shows up even more clearly if we turn to the other side of the picture, the attack on venality in the *cahiers*. Condemnation of the general principle, it is true, is found in only 11 per cent of the *cahiers*, or fifty-four, reasonably evenly distributed across the orders. But when we

---

[19] J. Lough, *The Philosophes and Post-Revolutionary France* (Oxford, 1982), p. 36.
[20] Following the guidelines laid down in B.F. Hyslop, *A Guide to the General Cahiers of 1789* (New York, 1968).

move to specifics the figures rise dramatically. Venality in the judiciary is condemned by almost 31 per cent of all *cahiers*, and over 46 per cent of Third Estate ones. Clergy and nobles both condemned it in around a fifth of their *cahiers*. The figures for ennoblement by venal office are particularly interesting. While only 7 per cent of clerical *cahiers* condemn it, a quarter of Third Estate ones do so, and – no surprise – almost 52 per cent of noble ones.

The grounds on which these demands were made were not new. Some were as old as the critique of venality. Aristotle, in his critique of Carthage, had declared that magistracy should be the reward of virtue, not wealth.[21] That had been Montesquieu's implication, too: although both thought that in practice rich magistrates were a good idea, because they had more leisure to devote to their duties, and were more likely to resist corruption. Plato argued that talent, not wealth, should be the criterion for public office; using the analogy of a ship, which requires skill to steer.[22] These arguments fill the *cahiers*, and a few samples give the flavour. Venality, says the *Tiers* of Amiens, 'a éloigné des places de judicature la science et le mérite, pour les assigner exclusivement à l'argent. Ceux qui exercent sur leurs semblables le plus saint, le plus auguste des ministères, n'y ayant plus été appelés par la confiance et la vénération de leurs concitoyens, plusieurs se sont crus dispensés de les mériter.' ['kept knowledge and merit out of judicial appointments, so as to give them exclusively to money. Those who exercise over their fellow men the holiest and most august of ministries no longer being called by the confidence and veneration of their fellow citizens, several have thought themselves excused from deserving them. . . .'] 'Les richesses, presque partout', says the clergy of Loudun, 'tenant lieu de lumières et quelquefois de probité, nous voyons avec douleur que les charges de magistrature pour la plupart sont acquises par des hommes qui n'ont d'autre mérite qu'assez d'argent pour acheter le droit de juger leurs concitoyens.' ['Riches, almost everywhere, having taken the place of wisdom and sometimes of probity, we see with grief that offices on the bench for the most part are acquired by men with no merit other than enough money to buy the right of judging their fellow citizens.'] The message is the classic one of 1789: careers open to the talents, equality of opportunity.

[21] Aristotle, *Politics*, ii, ch. 11.
[22] Plato, *Republic*, viii, section 4.

Matters become more complex when we turn to venal ennoblement. The noble argument against this was already classic, as we have seen. Nobility was a quality that could not be bought. Accordingly it should not be bought. But many nobles in 1789, as Guy Chaussinand-Nogaret has shown,[23] thought it should not be buyable, not in order to preserve their order as a closed caste but because they thought it should be open solely to virtue and talent. So did some Third Estate *cahiers*. The whole argument here, in fact, was perhaps best expressed by a Third Estate group, the advocates of Orleans, in their individual *cahier*.[24] 'L'argent', they said, 'dans un gouvernement bien constitué, ne doit pas être la source de la régénération de la noblesse. En conséquence, on demande la suppression de la noblesse transmissible par charge et office tant de judicature que de finance. Les talents, le mérite, les bonnes moeurs et les services rendus à l'état doivent seuls servir de degrés pour parvenir à cet ordre distingué.' ['Money . . . in a well constituted government, ought not to be the source of the regeneration of the nobility. Consequently, we call for the suppression of nobility transmissible through charges or offices, whether judicial or financial. Talents, merit, good conduct and service to the state should alone serve as steps up into this distinguished order.']

Nor does condemnation of specific aspects of venality end there. Certain types of offices come in for special criticism. Thirteen per cent of noble *cahiers* and 12 per cent of Third Estate ones condemn financial offices. An even spread across all three orders, amounting to a total of almost 9 per cent of all *cahiers*, denounces the Water and Forest tribunals as a major scourge of rural life. Special courts, most of them with fiscal jurisdiction, attracted the hostility of over a quarter of all *cahiers*, and 40 per cent of Third Estate ones. This was to condemn huge numbers of venal officials, from the humble clerks of the salt tribunals, all the way up to the lofty presidents of the *Chambres des Comptes* or the *Grand Conseil*. Most hated of all in terms of grievance, denounced in 32 per cent of all *cahiers*, or 19 per cent of clerical ones, 27 per cent of noble and 44 per cent of Third Estate, were a group that took me rather by surprise: auctioneers.

There is, however, no doubt about it; and if we go beyond the general *cahiers* to those of towns and villages the message comes through even

[23] G. Chaussinand-Nogaret, *The French Nobility in the Eighteenth Century: From Feudalism to Enlightenment* (Cambridge, 1985), p. 150.
[24] C. Bloch, *Cahiers de doléances du bailliage d'Orléans* (Orléans, 1907), p. 73.

more clearly. If ordinary French people hated venality in 1789, it was the auctioneers who had been the last straw. It would take a whole separate essay, and more, to go into this matter thoroughly. Suffice it to say that making auctioneering a venal monopoly had been a favourite ploy of governments in search of extra funds ever since the sixteenth century; but that monopoly had never been as tightly drawn as it finally was in the early 1780s. It is becoming increasingly clear that, contrary to a common impression, the government still saw venality as a way of raising money in times of special need right down to the end of the old regime.[25] The exploitation of the system was certainly on nothing like the scale of Louis XIV's last years; but it was determined enough, and one of the expedients adopted to pay for the American war in 1782 was to sell something like 5,000 offices of *juré-priseur* with exclusive rights to value and sell all movable goods throughout the kingdom and levy a range of hefty fees for doing so. By this means the treasury raised something like 7,500,000 *livres*, and from mutation fees and other taxes on these offices an annual addition to revenue of perhaps 175,000 *livres*.[26] In order to achieve this it had let loose on the country a swarm of new office-holders determined to exercise their rights and recoup their outlay to the full by the rigorous exercise of their rights and privileges. Soon everybody was outraged. Noble lords found that their seigneurial officials, who had tended to do the job in their fiefs, were dispossessed. Bailiffs and notaries, who had traditionally handled sales of estates, were also pushed out; while hapless peasants found themselves unable to dispose of any movable property without incurring fees which often amounted to more than the sales brought in. The extent of the dissatisfaction is shown, paradoxically, by the complaints of the auctioneers themselves – for even they drew up *cahiers*. Their profits were being eaten up, they complained, by the lawsuits they had to undertake in order to uphold their rights.[27] But these complaints were dwarfed by the volume of protest against them. They were denounced as bloodsuckers, public scourges, a burden on the poor, merciless profiteers and generally useless. All these complaints make perfectly clear that the reason for the creation of these new offices was well understood. It was simply to make

[25] See D. Bien, 'Offices, Corps and a System of State Credit: The Uses of Privilege under the Ancien Regime', in K.M. Baker (ed.), *The French Revolution and the Creation of Modern Political Culture*, i, *The Political Culture of the Ancien Régime* (Oxford, 1987), pp. 89-114.

[26] *Mémoire à l'Assemblée Nationale pour les jurés-priseurs de royaume* (Paris, 1789).

[27] See J.J. Vernier (ed.), *Cahiers de doléances du bailliage de Troyes*, 2 vols (Troyes, 1909), pp. 50-4.

the king some money; and to do so he was perfectly prepared to inflict on his subjects all the charges, depredations and hardships which the *cahiers* described in such graphic detail. The French had lived with, and grumbled about, venality for longer than anyone could remember. If they needed reminding, in the 1780s, of just how iniquitous it was, for people of every social level, nothing could have been more calculated to do so than this latest refinement.

The background, therefore, to the abolition of venality of 4 August 1789 is that hardly anybody was in favour of it, or had been for generations. No wonder the national assembly received the abolition proposal 'with transports'. The deputies knew that it was one of those things which everybody wanted to be rid of. If it still seems surprising that an assembly comprising so many venal office-holders should commit itself so happily to such an abolition, we do not need to postulate, as some historians have, that they all made quick calculations of how much compensation they would receive from the liquidation of this rising asset; and how much national property they could exchange it for. National property did not exist in August 1789; and anyway, when they came to make arrangements for compensation, they did so at penal rates far below the market value of most abolished offices.[28] The fact is that many venal officials themselves shared the view that venality was wrong: that calls for its abolition got into so many of the general *cahiers* suggests that; otherwise they would surely have used their well-documented influential position in the electoral assemblies to strain the attack on venality out or at least play it down.[29] Some companies of venal officials drew up separate *cahiers* calling for their own abolition.[30]

The problem was that venality seemed to everybody before 1789 too deeply rooted in the nature of things for anything to be done about it. Listen to Felix Faulcon, another office-holder who welcomed the abolition of venality when it came. But in 1781 matters were very different. Everyone was pressing him, he confided to his journal,[31] to buy an office in the *présidial* of Poitiers. 'En bonne conscience', he wrote,

[28] See above, pp. 125, 138-40.

[29] See P. Dawson, *Provincial Magistrates and Revolutionary Politics in France, 1789-1795* (Cambridge, MA, 1972).

[30] *Sénéchaussée* of Grasse, Provence, *Archives Parlementaires*, iii, p. 277. See also P Dawson, 'The Bourgeoisie de Robe in 1789', *French Historical Studies*, 4 (1965), pp. 16-18.

[31] G. Debien, (ed.), *Correspondance de Félix Faulcon*, 2 vols (Poitiers, 1939-1953), Société des archives historiques du Poitou, i, p. 93.

ce sont toujours bien des farces ridicules, que ces usages de se procurer des emplois à prix d'argent, mais puisqu'ils sont en vogue et qu'on est presque nu dans la société sans une charge ainsi acquise il faut bien que je fasse comme les autres . . . Hélas! ne serait-ce donc pas possible d'être utile à ses semblables sans un pareil emploi? Est-ce précisément une charge de conseiller, qui rend un être intéressant et fixe son degré de mérite? . . . Mais à quoi bon toutes ces récriminations, puisque je n'ai pas de moyen pour détruire tous les abus qui existent, tolérons donc ce qu'il n'est pas possible d'empêcher.

['In good conscience . . . they are always very ridiculous farces, these customs of getting positions for money, but since they are in fashion, and one is almost naked in society without an office got in this way, I shall just have to do as others do . . . . Alas! isn't it then possible to be useful to one's fellow men without such employment? Is it really an office of counsellor which makes someone interesting and fixes his degree of merit? . . . . But what good are all these recriminations, since I have no means of destroying all the abuses which exist, so let's tolerate what it's not possible to prevent.']

Here, I suggest, is the authentic voice of 1789. Faulcon was not someone who planned for a revolution, or thought one possible, or thought that much in society could ever be radically changed. That did not make him unaware of what was wrong about the way things were. There was just nothing you could do about it.

Then came 1789; and suddenly there was. Suddenly the old authority that had sustained all the abuses, and all the anomalies, and all the injustices of life had collapsed, and a new authority with *carte blanche* was taking over. Now was the time to cleanse the Augean Stables. Dreams so utopian that most people had not even thought them worth discussing could suddenly be realised; and when Frenchmen found that there was something they could do to change things, venality was one of the things they were most eager to change. Faulcon again sums it up. Writing to a friend late in August 1789,[32] on hearing of what had happened on the 4th, he declared:

Quant à moi, quels que soient les préjugés que je puisse éprouver, à quelque rang et dans quelle classe que je sois rejeté, je déclare ici bien formellement que j'applaudis de toutes mes facultés aux décrets de l'assemblée et que je suis intérieurement très disposé à faire tous les sacrifices possibles de fortune et de dignités pourvu que je ne vois plus l'or du pauvre passer dans les mains rapaces des maltôtiers et des gens de robe.

'As for me, whatever private prejudices I might have, whatever rank and whatever class I might be put in, I declare here in open court that deep down I am ready to make all possible sacrifices of fortune and dignities provided that I

[32] Ibid., ii, p. 108.

no longer see the poor man's gold passing into the grasping hands of extortioners and people in gowns.]

When it came to the small print, of course, it was not so easy. The second thoughts which followed the night of 4 August were not just a matter of withdrawing offers that seemed too generous in the cold clear light of dawn. They were also a recognition of the genuine difficulty and complexity of winding up the vast shapeless systems and institutions that had been abolished. It took half a dozen years and innumerable special and separate pieces of legislation finally to abolish venality; and even then it did not disappear in all cases. By 1815 it had reappeared openly, and was spreading again. But the unconditional abolition of the night of 4 August was without doubt a recognition, and an expression, of one of the deepest and most long-standing dissatisfactions that Frenchmen had about their society – their silence about it during the century before 1789 was not indifference. As Mercier put it in 1784: 'La vénalité des charges a entraîné des abus si bizarres qu'ils vous ôtent la force de les combattre. On demeure muet d'étonnement.'[33] ['Venality of offices has entailed abuses so bizarre that they leave you powerless to contend against them. One is struck dumb with astonishment.']

[33] *Tableau de Paris*, ii (Paris, 1784), pp. 154-5.

7

Reforming the French Criminal Law at the End of the Old Régime: The Example of President Dupaty

One of the most striking aspects of the late Enlightenment in France is the movement for reforming the criminal law. Taking flight in the 1760s owing to the efforts of Voltaire and Beccaria, by 1780 the movement had become a whole sub-branch of philosophic activity.[1] Yet the practical results were disappointing. The government remained largely indifferent to the proposals of literary men, and reforms that did occur (such as the abolition of the *question préparatoire*) owed nothing to their efforts.[2] Nor is it clear that the public was won over. Literary men formed the bulk of their own audience, at least down to 1789.

Between 1786 and 1788, however, all this changed. The government began to take a serious interest in criminal law reform, and so did the public. The reason seems to be twofold. First, the movement began to attract the interest not only of literary men, but also of magistrates, noblemen, the well-connected and influential. Secondly, a new generation of reformers launched a more concerted and emotional appeal to public opinion which finally won it over. Probably the most important figure in both developments was President Dupaty.

Unlike most reformers, Dupaty was a magistrate, serving as advocate-general, and subsequently president, in the parlement of Bordeaux between 1768 and 1783. Among other magistrates, only President de Lamoignon, of the Paris parlement, and Servan, advocate-general at

---

[1] D. Mornet, *Les origines intellectuelles de la Révolution Française* (Paris, 1933), pp. 249-50.
[2] J.H. Langbein, *Torture and the Law of Proof: Europe and England in the Ancien Régime* (Chicago, 1977), chs 3 and 4.

Grenoble, were well known as advocates of reform. But their impor-tance was out of all proportion to their numbers, since unlike literary men their criticisms of the law sprang from practical experience in administering it, giving them added authority. Dupaty's fame as a magistrate was boosted by his clashes with Maupeou, and it was during his exile at Maupeou's hands that he began a systematic study of criminal law reform. Between 1778 and 1782 he became even better known through his struggle to be admitted to the presidential bench in the parlement against the opposition of many of his colleagues.[3] Subse-quently he spent a year presiding over the *Tournelle* or criminal chamber of the parlement, and his first frontal attack on the law arose out of cases he tried there. It was a denunciation of the death penalty for burglary (*vol domestique avec effraction*), which he claimed had been intended to be optional rather than mandatory. Published in the *Journal encyclopédique*, in 1784, it created a sensation in judicial circles: certain young Parisian magistrates began to remit the death penalty in burglary cases, and the government was moved to prohibit further publication on such matters. This experience taught Dupaty the value of a well-judged appeal to public opinion.[4]

By this time he had ceased to be a practising magistrate, driven out of Bordeaux by continued harassment. But now his reputation was based not only on his professional position. From the very outset of his adult life he had sought to establish a literary reputation by cultivating the acquaintance of famous writers and publicists. His old schoolmaster Thomas introduced him to the Necker circle and kept him informed of all the latest literary news. In 1768 Dupaty wrote to Voltaire about his exploits in the academy of La Rochelle, they corresponded in effusive terms, and in 1771 he visited Ferney. Dupaty also knew d'Alembert, Diderot and Helvétius, and his marriage in 1769 to the sister of Fréteau de Saint-Just, a leading counsellor at the parlement of Paris, introduced him to the judicial world of the capital. In the 1770s he got to know Turgot and Condorcet, who married his niece Sophie de Grouchy in 1786. Lesser literary figures including the poet Roucher, François de Neufchâteau, Beaumarchais and Brissot also came into Dupaty's circle during this decade. He was very well connected indeed, as well as a

[3] W. Doyle, *The Parlement of Bordeaux and the End of the Old Régime, 1771-90* (London, 1974), pp. 144-5, 177-90.
[4] *Journal encyclopédique*, 15 Oct. 1784, pp. 318-25; Bachaumont, *Mémoires* (1785), xxvii, pp. 66-7; Métra, *Correspondance secrète* (1785), xviii, pp. 38-9.

famous magistrate, when he finally left Bordeaux for Paris in 1783.[5] From 1778 onwards, in fact, he had been an increasingly regular visitor to the capital in his attempts to win government backing in his struggle to become a president. These visits enabled him to frequent *salons*, meet fellow magistrates, and not least to involve himself in freemasonry. He had become a mason in Bordeaux in the late 1770s, and in 1779 he joined the most famous lodge in Paris, the *Neuf Soeurs*. His role there was an active one, and in 1784 he was elected *Vénérable*. Subsequently the lodge gave active support to his judicial crusades.[6]

Through his fame as a magistrate, his experience as a publicist, and his wide range of important contacts, Dupaty was well placed by the mid 1780s for conducting an influential reform campaign. All he now needed was an incentive and an occasion. The incentive no doubt came from his failure to interest the government in various practical proposals for studying the problem of reform. The struggle with the parlement had brought him into regular contact with the head of the judiciary, Miromesnil. Emboldened by this familiarity, in 1782 he began to send Miromesnil a series of projects which he hoped the government would agree to support and subsidise.[7] They all involved travel and the comparison of the criminal codes of the various European nations with a view to formulating universal sound principles. Miromesnil, however, consistently refused financial support, claiming that he had reform projects of his own in hand.[8] The prohibition of public discussion of criminal law reform following Dupaty's notorious letter of 1784 can only have confirmed his conviction that the government had no real interest in the question. In 1785 he began researching at his own expense with a tour of Italy, which three years later were recorded in his celebrated *Lettres sur l'Italie*. But no sooner had he returned to France than a perfect

[5] E. Micard, *Un écrivain académique au XVIIIe siécle: Antoine Léonard Thomas (1732-1785)* (Paris, 1924), p. 22; Voltaire, *Correspondence and Related Documents*, ed. T. Besterman (Geneva and Banbury, 1968-77), Best. D15445, D15538, D15540, D16304, D16743, D16802, D16824, D16847, D16859, D16979, D17035, D17043, D17205; Dupaty de Clam papers (hereafter DPC), d'Alembert to Dupaty, 6 Sept. 1769; Denis Diderot, *Correspondance*, ed. G. Roth (Paris, 1963), ix, p. 147; DPC, Helvétius to Dupaty, 3 Jan. 1771; A. Guillois, *La marquise de Condorcet, 1764-1822* (Paris, 1897), p. 94; A. Guillois, *Pendant la Terreur: le poète Roucher, 1745-1794* (Paris, 1890), p. 33; J. Lhomer, *Un homme politique lorrain: François de Neufchâteau (1750-1828)* (Paris, 1900), pp. 17-18; DPC, Beaumarchais to Dupaty, 9 May 1779; *Mémoires de Brissot*, ed. M. de Lescure (Paris, 1877), pp. 204-5.

[6] L'Amiable, *Une loge maçonnique d'avant 1789: la R ∴ L ∴ des Neuf Soeurs* (Paris, 1897), pp. 125, 135.

[7] AN, K874; Archives des Affaires Etrangères, mémoires et documents, France 1395, fos 231-2.

[8] DPC, Miromesnil to Dupaty, 7 Feb. 1784.

occasion arose for him to deploy in the case of reform all the skills and resources that he had accumulated throughout his adult life.

This was the famous *affaire des trois roués*, which began in August 1785 when the *bailliage* of Chaumont sentenced three convicted burglars to the galleys.[9] On appeal to the parlement of Paris the sentence was raised to death. But among the judges who had doubts about this was Fréteau, and he communicated them to his brother-in-law. Together they appealed to the government for a stay of execution, which was granted. Dupaty profited from this delay to examine, with Fréteau's connivance, the documents in the case. He was convinced there had been a miscarriage of justice and that the three were innocent, and in February 1786 he proclaimed this conviction in a direct appeal to public opinion to take up the case, the *Mémoire justificatif pour trois hommes condamnés à la roue*. Published anonymously, it contained a formal endorsement by Legrand de Laleu, a young advocate who was also a member of the *Neuf Soeurs*; but from the start it was an open secret that Dupaty was the author.[10] Three features stand out from the *Mémoire*. First there is Dupaty's passionate (though we may think ill-judged) conviction of the accused's innocence. Secondly, there is a far more convincing survey of the procedural faults committed by judges at every stage of the case. Thirdly, there is the use made by Dupaty of the case's circumstances to condemn the whole structure of the criminal law. As matters stood, he argued, even impeccable conduct by the judges could not have guaranteed the accused a fair trial, since the law itself was fundamentally flawed. The final peroration was a direct personal appeal to the king to decree a wholesale reform.

This was not the only case of miscarriage of justice to engage public attention in 1786,[11] but all the diaries and news sheets show it to have been by far the most important. So does the outraged response of the parlement to Dupaty's *Mémoire*. In April 1787 the royal council agreed to hear an appeal from the *roués*, and Dupaty began to write a new justification; but the parlement launched an enquiry into the first one, and Legrand de Laleu was suspended from the bar. The findings of the parlement's enquiry were reported in August by the advocate-general

---

[9] A. Wattine, *L'affaire des trois roués* (Mâcon, 1921); see too E. Seligman, *La justice en France pendant la Révolution* (Paris, 1901), pp. 98-106; and M. Marion, *Le garde des sçeaux Lamoignon et la réforme judicaire de 1788* (Paris, 1905), pp. 33-7.

[10] *Correspondance secrète inédite sur Louis XVI, Marie Antoinette, la cour et la ville de 1777 à 1792*, ed. M. de Lescure (Paris, 1866), ii, p. 26.

[11] Dupaty, *Mémoire justicatif*, pp. 250, 263, 269; Marion, *Lamoignon*, pp. 37-42.

Séguier, an academician and a renowned conservative. His *réquisitoire* was perhaps the last great defence of the *ancien régime*, its laws, and the habits and ways of thinking that underlay them, to be heard before all these things were swept away.[12] In it he chose to combat the still formally anonymous author of the *Mémoire* head-on. He denied the innocence of the accused, the alleged irregularities and, above all the supposed need for general reform in the criminal law. A minority of magistrates disputed these conclusions – in itself a minor victory for Dupaty – but they were overridden and the *Mémoire* was condemned. When Dupaty declared himself to be the author, his arrest was decreed, and he was only saved by the onset of the vacation.

Meanwhile the case had provoked a storm of publicity, and Condorcet joined his new relative-by-marriage in producing further pamphlets in the *roués'* favour. Attention was now directed to the appeal before the royal council, but Miromesnil was deliberately holding matters up. Not until he fell from office in April 1787, during the Assembly of Notables, was the way clear for quicker action. He was replaced by Lamoignon, a known advocate of reform; and Dupaty, sensing a change in the atmosphere, redoubled his efforts to keep public interest in the *roués* alive by writing no less than four pamphlets in their favour in the course of the early summer. So public opinion was well prepared, and expectant, when on 30 July 1787 the royal council reviewed the case and decided that procedural flaws had nullified the conviction. It was referred for retrial to the *bailliage* of Rouen, with appeal to the parlement of Normandy. The *roués* were not declared innocent, but the council's decision was nevertheless a triumph for Dupaty and his campaign, Lamoignon used the occasion to hint that reforms were on the way.

Meanwhile, Dupaty evidently felt the need to maintain public interest, and he now intervened in a new case concerning seven Germans from Lorraine who in 1769 had been condemned for robbery by the parlement of Metz.[13] In 1786, two brigands arrested in Zweibrücken had confessed to this crime, and the families of the seven had asked Dupaty to vindicate them. The case had several similarities to that of the *roués*, and so provided a perfect occasion for Dupaty to re-emphasise the urgent need for general reform. It certainly helped to keep the issue

---

[12] Appended to *Arrest de la cour de parlement . . . du II août 1786* (Paris, 1786).

[13] Dupaty, *Justification de sept hommes condamnés par le parlement de Metz en 1769* (Paris, 1787).

alive pending the decision at Rouen, which eventually came in November. The *roués* were exonerated and, although the parlement reviewed this decision, Dupaty was permitted to plead in person for his clients. The result was almost a foregone conclusion: on 18 December, after almost five years in custody, two of them under sentence of death, the *trois roués* were exonerated.

It was an enormous personal victory for Dupaty; and it also heralded the victory of the greater cause for which he had undertaken the campaign. Early in 1788 Lamoignon set up a commission of jurisconsults to draft reforms in the criminal law, and soon after the end of the *roués* case (although six years after he had first offered his services to Miromesnil) Dupaty was invited to join it. The results of its labours were to appear as the criminal ordinance of 1 May 1788, and the influence of the *trois roués* case on its drafters is clear. More than anything else the case had defined the areas of the law in most urgent need of reform, and Dupaty was rumoured to have drafted the preamble. Abolition of the *sellette*, greater majorities for capital sentences, longer delays between sentence and execution, announcement of sentence to the accused, indemnities for those acquitted, and motivation of verdicts, all remedied shortcomings highlighted by Dupaty.[14]

A final paradox, however, is that Dupaty did not support the final promulgation of this edict. This occurred at the same *lit de justice* at which the powers of the parlements were drastically curtailed on 8 May. Rather than identify himself with such 'despotism', Dupaty resigned from the commission, and so political circumstances deprived him of his ultimate triumph.[15] He continued in the public eye, since in August the *Lettres sur l'Italie* were published, but his sudden death on 18 September abruptly ended a career which otherwise would surely have been far from over.

It was the Revolution, not the old monarchy, which finally brought radical and comprehensive reform of the criminal law. Nevertheless, the monarchy had been brought to the brink of action, and the reforms it proposed would certainly have been widely welcomed if they had been

[14] Seligman, *La justice en France*, p. 114; Lescure, *Correspondance secrète*, ii, p. 232; J.N. Moreau, *Mes souvenirs* (Paris, 1898-1901), ii, p. 366; H. Swinburne, *The Courts of Europe at the Close of the Last Century* (London, 1841), ii, pp. 56-7.

[15] Lescure, ed., *Correspondance secrète*, ii, p. 258. Marion, *Lamoignon*, p. 103, finds this difficult to believe, noting (which is true) that no other contemporary source mentions Dupaty's resignation. But for his hostility to 'despotism' in the summer of 1788, see Guillois, *Marquise de Condorcet*, p. 83.

introduced at a less controversial moment. Public opinion had been won over to the case for reform, and so had significant elements in the government and the magistracy. Many people had contributed to this, but few were of more importance than Dupaty.

8

The Principles of the French Revolution

Even the most bitter and determined opponents of the French Revolution were prepared to admit that it had principles; even if all these amounted to, in the words of Tolstoy's vicomte de Mortemart, were 'robbery, murder and regicide'. But most of us, I suspect, when we think of the principles of the Revolution, would tend to adopt the response of the vicomte's opponent in that exchange at the start of *War and Peace*, Pierre Bezukhov: 'Those were extremes, no doubt, but they are not what is most important. What is important are the rights of man, emancipation from prejudices, and equality of citizenship.' But I wonder whether it was any of these things that, in July 1789, turned Kant into a news fanatic; or gave Caroline Böhmer hot flushes; or made Wordsworth feel that it was bliss to be alive? These were feelings stirred by news of the fall of the Bastille: but nobody knew, or could foresee, in the last fortnight of July 1789, what that even was to lead to, or how the next few years were likely to develop.

Even the Rights of Man had not been proclaimed on 14 July. It was to be another six weeks before the declaration embodying them was promulgated, and even then its precise content was far from a foregone conclusion. Nor did the French revolutionaries remain content with it. It survived as the preamble to the constitution of 1791, but in 1793 it was absorbed into a much longer and more far-reaching document adopted to begin the constitution of that year; and in 1795 it was swamped again in an even more long-winded statement of rights and duties. Which Rights of Man, then, might Pierre Bezukhov have had in mind? He had a number of different versions to choose from, emanating from France; without considering those proposed by France's fellow travellers elsewhere, such as Tom Paine. Or take the slogan every schoolboy knows to be that of the French Revolution: *Liberty, Equality, Fraternity*. That, too, had not emerged as a revolutionary battle-cry when the Bastille was stormed . There had been much talk of liberty and liberties during the 'pre-revolutionary' struggles between 1787 and 1789; and of course the struggle to unite the three orders in the estates-general, and ensure that deputies voted by head, was about a sort of equality. But Liberty:Equality, as shorthand for what the Revolution was all about, did not begin to be used until very late in 1789; and Fraternity was only added much later, in 1793, when arguably fraternity was one of the last things the Revolution seemed to be all about.

Or take symbols. Of course the Phrygian cap of liberty, the headgear of the freed slave, had always been associated with the idea of liberty, and was much used in eighteenth-century iconography – particularly in countries like Great Britain, where the rhetoric of freedom was well entrenched and its emblems instantly recognisable. But French revolutionaries only began to *wear* red caps in the winter of 1791/2. Anacharsis Clootz, the self-styled orator of the human race, first tried to launch the fashion in the autumn, to general derision; and although it eventually caught on in the Jacobin Club in March 1792, amid the patriotic euphoria which carried the nation into war a month later, the fashion was always condemned as cheap and demeaning by serious-minded revolutionaries such as Robespierre. Even that most emotive and terrifying of all revolutionary symbols, the guillotine, was not perfected until three years after the Bastille fell. The deputies to the Constituent Assembly, who took themselves extremely seriously on the whole, were thrown into a rare fit of mirth when, late in 1789, Dr Guillotin expounded his idea of a machine of execution that would make heads fly off in the twinkling of an eye. It was another two and a half years before such a device was accepted and came into use.

It would be easy to think of other examples. What they would all suggest is that the principles, ideas, style and habits of the French Revolution did not emerge all of a piece right from the start. Much that came to be indelibly associated with it was not present at the beginning, or often for some years after the beginning. What it meant, and what it was to mean to subsequent generations looking back on what seemed like a complete, integrated occurrence, largely developed as the Revolution went along, and usually in ways quite unforeseen. So far from being part of some rational, thought-out, or premeditated purpose, in fact, some of the most momentous things the Revolution came to stand for look very much like the product of accident, mischance or miscalculation.

For instance, the Revolution represented probably the greatest attack on, and challenge to, the Catholic Church since the Reformation. It stripped the French church of its wealth, reorganised its hierarchy, dissolved its monasteries. It stopped Peter's Pence and annexed papal territories unilaterally. Eventually it prohibited Catholic practice and deported or executed priests and religious in their thousands. By the late 1790s the pope was at the mercy of its armies. Yet none of this was intended, or dreamed of, at the outset. Everyone in 1789, even the clergy, thought the church needed reform, and expected changes that would make it less wasteful, better organised, and more responsible to the spiritual and pastoral needs of French citizens. There was certainly a good deal of less well-intentioned anti-clericalism in the air, as any reading of the *cahiers* of 1789 makes clear. But there was no desire to destroy the role that Catholicism played in national life: if anything, most people dreamed of strengthening it. Things began to go wrong not so much when tithe was abolished or Peter's Pence renounced, on 4 August 1789; or when church lands were confiscated two months later; or even when regular orders were dissolved the following spring. The turning point was the attempt, with the Civil Constitution of the Clergy in the summer of 1790, to bring the organisation and government of the church into line with the organisation and government of the country at large, now being envisaged in the constitution being prepared. At one level, of course, such an aspiration seemed rational enough. But again, even these constitutional principles had not been foreseen, except in the most general terms, in the summer of 1789. They were hammered out after that, and only then was it decided to bring the church into conformity with them. Who, in 1789, would have thought of trying to exclude the pope as completely from the affairs of the Catholic Church in France as the Civil Constitution of 1790 tried to do? Who would have dreamed of clergy being elected by the laity? The attempt to make beneficed clergy accept these and other principles as a prerequisite for exercising cure of souls, through the imposition of an oath, was the first great divide of the French Revolution; and although even then almost half the French clergy were still prepared to accept the new order, the pope certainly was not, and nor were Catholic clergy anywhere else. From then on Rome and Revolution were deadly enemies; and however much that quarrel was later patched up, the suspicions it aroused were never again fully allayed, and the position and pretensions of the Catholic Church in France never went unchallenged again. The example, moreover, meant that that challenge would be echoed, more or less vehemently, in almost every country where Catholicism held sway.

An equally unpredictable chapter of accidents and miscalculations led to the second great trauma of the Revolution, the destruction of monarchy. Few things moved European onlookers more than the fate of Louis XVI and his family – whether in the ignominious failure of the Flight to Varennes, the mutinous and degrading scenes at the Tuileries on 20 June 1792 or, above all, the king's trial and execution. Even Tom Paine, who had denounced monarchy root and branch in the *Rights of Man* and fully believed the king to be guilty, pleaded with the Convention not to execute him; and Wolfe Tone, founder of Irish republicanism, confided to his diary that he was sorry the execution was necessary. Only Frenchmen (and then of course by no means all of them) seemed to welcome regicide. Yet no such thought was in any Frenchman's mind, so far as we can tell, in 1789. There seems to have been hardly any overt republicanism, but rather the opposite: an almost boundless credulity about the extent of the king's good intentions. Men were still willing to believe that despotism was ministerial; that a monarch not misled by wicked or self-serving advisers would always wish for and work to bring about his subjects' wellbeing; that Louis XVI was happy to be redesignated king of the French, and accepted his loss of sovereignty. The constitution the assembly put together in those first two years was a monarchical one, even if that monarchy was now to be limited; and even after widespread republicanism took hold, after Varennes, a majority still seem to have believed that there was no alternative to a king at the head of the state; and that the king they had would accept the Revolution provided its popular excesses could be controlled. Here again, events, accidents and miscalculations eroded faith in monarchy, and paved the way to the first French Republic; but only slowly, and at a very uneven pace. The other monarchs of Europe did not really feel threatened on their thrones by the French example until French armies began to win victories in the autumn of 1792, and the French declared that they intended to export the principles of their revolution to whatever peoples asked for their fraternity and help. Not, then, until (in Danton's phrase) France threw down its gauntlet to Europe, and that gauntlet was the head of a king, did republicanism become an unequivocal identifying principle of the French Revolution – a good four years after it had begun.

Not, in fact, until the revolutionaries had become armed missionaries: but this, too, was an inconceivable idea in 1789. Of course, from a very early stage the French revolutionaries considered themselves an example to the world – and there were from the start, too, enough admirers abroad to confirm to them that they were. Even in self-satisfied Great

Britain, soaked in the rhetoric of liberty, Richard Price and the Revolution Society were proclaiming before the end of 1789 that the French had caught up with and overtaken the English in the science of freedom in the space of a few months. But equally, the men of 1789 never dreamed of exporting the Rights of Man beyond French borders by force. They thought it self-evident that many abroad would wish to follow their glorious example, and assumed that others in revolt around the same time, such as the Belgians or the Poles, were engaged in doing so. But they themselves, they proclaimed, threatened nobody's sovereignty. They wished to live at peace with all who were content to live at peace with them; and in the famous Nootka Sound debates in May 1790 they brushed aside obligations assumed under the old dynastic diplomacy and declared that they would henceforth only make war in self-defence. Only eighteen months later did they begin to rattle the sabre, and even then they could just about plausibly claim a defensive motive in that those against whom they were exercised were Rhenish princes sheltering the belligerent *émigrés* who threatened French security. Not until after the end of 1791 was all pretence of defensive war cast aside with the series of ultimatums issued to the Austrians; and even then it was another six months before the French became the armed missionaries who in the later 1790s would sweep across central Europe and Italy, destroying the established regimes there and setting up their own puppet states. Most people who experienced the French Revolution directly did so in the form of French soldiers conquering, marauding, extorting and requisitioning – yet these invaders were doing so in the name of a movement whose first thoughts about foreign affairs had been to offer peace to all and respect for the rights and integrity of other peoples.

A final, though somewhat different, example of how the Revolution's principles evolved, rather than burst all of a piece on Europe, is the case of popular power. Here at least was something that the Revolution began with. The fall of the Bastille witnessed the people in action, and the Parisian insurrection of which it was the culmination saved the National Assembly from dissolution by armed force. The people of Paris had saved the Revolution, and they knew they had. From then on they regarded it as their privileged role to be the Revolution's watchdogs – a role they first re-enacted in the October Days of 1789, and which attained its classic peak in the great *sans-culotte journées* of 1792 and 1793. These were the scenes which so appalled most of the educated classes of Europe – the heads on pikes, the stringings-up on the street lanterns, the September massacres and the jubilation of the crowds around the guillotine. Yet these scenes were equally deplored by the vast majority of the educated classes of France, too; and by none more so than the deputies of the National Assembly whom popular action saved in July 1789. They deeply deplored the fact that they had had to be rescued from despotism on the streets. That was why they rushed to endorse the setting up of the National Guard by people just like themselves; why immediately after the October Days they passed the martial law decree to prevent future tumults; why most of them applauded the way this decree was invoked at the Champ de Mars in July 1791; and why they gave France a constitution in which only those with certain property qualifications were admitted as active citizens.

In other words the men of 1789, the men who produced the original principles of the French Revolution, had no desire to see popular power established as one of those principles. They believed in equality before the law, before the tax-collector, and of opportunity, but they never believed that power and authority should be allowed to fall into the hands of the uneducated or the unpropertied. Neither did the vast majority of their successors in the Legislative, the Convention, or the Directorial Councils. The popular role in the Revolution, at whatever stage, was at best a regrettable, and always transient, necessity. Establishing popular power was not what the Revolution was about, or intended to be about; and as soon as the Convention's deputies had the means at their disposal to break the grip of the *sans-culottes* on their proceedings, they seized it. Their legacy to France, the Constitution of the Year III, for all its manhood suffrage, fixed qualifications for public office at a level far beyond what had been thought adequate by the men of 1789. Experience since that time had taught that those early safeguards had been nothing like enough. When further experience, over the next four years, showed that even these new safeguards were not enough either (as repeated Jacobin scares in 1796, 1797 and 1798 proved), the political class threw in their lot with a dictator who made no secret of his determination to rule with the co-operation of solid men of property. To the vast majority of those who governed, or attempted to govern, France in the revolutionary decade, in other words, popular power was not one of the Revolution's principles: it had been a totally regrettable by-product which in the end it became the Revolution's first priority to eliminate.

The principles of the French Revolution, then, were not static, cut in stone and invariable. They emerged uncertainly, reflected and were moulded by the play of events, and changed as the Revolution went on. Not only that: before the decade was out many of them, and by the time the Napoleonic episode was over practically all of them, had been stood on their heads by the French and yet were still being vaunted as the authentic principles of the Revolution. It began as a revolt against despotism and centralisation; yet by as early as 1794 France had a more uniform, centralised government than she had ever had before – although it proclaimed itself a temporary, emergency regime designed to last no longer than the war. By the time another five years had elapsed the man who wrote the most cogent manifesto of 1789, Sieyès, had engineered the accession to power of a ruler beside whose power the so-called despotism of the *ancien régime* seemed effetely patriarchal, and whose rigid pattern of centralised authority made the rule of the intendants look like benign neglect.

In 1789 the revolutionaries proclaimed the natural and imprescript-ible rights of man as liberty, property, security, and resistance to oppression, all of which were to be guaranteed by the rule of law. Yet within weeks one tenth of the property in France, the lands of the church, had been confiscated and then sold off (to underwrite a national debt, incidentally, which was proclaimed sacred and yet was completely written off by 1797). Security likewise was thrown to the winds in 1789 owing to the revolutionaries' deep mistrust of all existing public forces: a decade of spectacular lawlessness ensued, whose extraordinary realities Richard Cobb has spent a scholarly lifetime introducing us to, and which was only brought to an end by the military efficiency of Napoleon. As to resistance to oppression and the supremacy of the rule of law, the Terror of 1793-4 had gone down as one of history's classic regimes of oppression; and the justice by which many of its victims were con-demned as a mockery. In defence of it Saint-Just defined humanity as the extermination of one's enemies; and Robespierre, who in the early days of the Revolution had denounced capital punishment, ended up seemingly threatening a large proportion of the Convention with the guillotine. Proclaiming equal opportunities and an end to privileges based on birth, in the end the Revolution produced what its leaders consciously sought from the earliest stage, a society dominated by, and governed in the interests of, rich landowners. The only talents post-revolutionary careers were open to were those honed by the sort of education that inherited wealth alone could buy.

Or consider freedom of thought and expression, the key to Pierre Bezukhov's 'emancipation from prejudices'. Initially, it is true, the press flourished as never before. But intimidation of those with unpopular opinions was a feature of the Revolution right from the start, as the woman publicly spanked in the Palais Royal on 9 July 1789 after she had spat on a portrait of Necker found out. Once the religious schism emerged the atmosphere grew far worse; popular pressure has now been clearly identified as a major factor in whether the clergy took the oath to the constitution or not. By the summer of 1791 special laws were being passed to curb the press, and within a year most right-wing journals had been harried out of business. Another year brought all the excesses of dechristianisation; and even after the dismantling of the Terror governments never gave up the power, or the practice, of regulating both the press and religious observance. With the advent of Napoleon, both became a central feature of government activity.

Take, finally, revolutionary France's relationship with other peoples. Even as the Constituent Assembly was proclaiming that it threatened nobody it was happily cancelling the rights of imperial princes in Alsace and lending a sympathetic ear to those papal subjects in Avignon and the Comtat Venaissin who were asking to be incorporated into France. Almost the last public act of this assembly, even though it plainly realised by then that its religious policy had been mistaken, was to annex these papal territories. The decree offering fraternity and help to all peoples seeking to recover their liberty, it is often forgotten, was revoked within five months for the quite impractical promise it was. But before that was done something far more ominous had been proclaimed: the doctrine of natural frontiers, which warned all Belgians, some Dutch and many Germans that they would be turned into French citizens whether they liked it or not. Sooner or later, they were; and it is quite obvious that very few of them did like it: witness the persistent passive resistance of the left-bank Germans to their new French masters throughout the 1790s; or the great (though often overlooked) Belgian peasant uprising of 1798. These peoples certainly wished to recover their freedom: but what that meant in practice was freedom from French oppression. Similar things could be said of territories not annexed but occupied, looted and subject to puppet regimes that were brusquely changed whenever they resisted whatever Paris wanted. On the other hand the beleaguered Poles, appealing for French help in 1794 against predatory neighbours preparing to partition their country out of existence, received fine words but almost no practical help from the self-styled liberators of Europe.

One could go on with such examples: but I hope the point is sufficiently made. There was scarcely a principle with which the French Revolution was identified, at the time or in later perceptions, that the French did not violate, flout, reverse or brush aside during the Revolution's course. In other words, the Revolution appears to have stood for nothing constant at all.

But perhaps that is precisely the point. As I began by observing, people got excited about the French Revolution before they knew what it was going to stand for. Frenchmen or foreigners, all they knew before August 1789 was that France was to be regenerated by the movement gripping it. Clearly what really appealed to that generation was the idea of regeneration itself, and only very secondarily what that process was meant to achieve. The world could be *changed*; fresh starts *could* be made. That was the real message of the French Revolution, whether it thrilled or appalled hearers and onlookers. What by 1790 everybody was calling the *ancien régime* had been a time when things changed slowly, if at all. There seemed no prospect of making fundamental alterations to government, to society, or to any human institutions or habits. It was not that ideas were lacking. The Enlightenment had produced an outburst of criticism, theorising and system-building unprecedented in human history; and thanks to the equally unprecedented enrichment of west European society since the sixteenth century more educated readers than ever before were in a position to share in the intellectual feast. But at the same time everyday experience taught them that to expect comprehensive or radical change was utopian. Yet only if the existing order of things were changed utterly could human beings be improved: that was the message of Rousseau, which appealed so powerfully to the educated men of the later eighteenth century. Society, existing institutions, had corrupted men's natural goodness. This analysis did not incite men to revolution; but it certainly made them welcome it when it happened. It offered them an unexpected, hitherto inconceivable opportunity to change whatever they wanted to change; even for those so inclined, to change everything, rebuild everything, from the ground up. Suddenly everybody was able, or seemed able, to participate in making changes, as Wordsworth put it,

> Not in Utopia, subterranean fields,
> Or some secreted island, Heaven knows where!
> But in the very world, which is the world
> Of all of us . . .

That in the end the opportunity was squandered was beside the point. Most of those who thrilled to the news in 1789 sooner or later became disillusioned with what it had led to. It is as well to remember that even Burke was moderately excited in early 1789, and Gentz, his German equivalent, was quite as euphoric as Georg Forster or all those other Germans proclaiming that a new age was dawning. They all recognised, whether they continued to support the Revolution, or increasingly regretted the direction it was taking, or finally held it in abomination, that it represented a *principle of change*; and change on a scale never before deemed conceivable. It was this that unlocked men's minds and opened up European consciousness, in a permanent and quite irrevocable way. Of course the Revolution stood for nothing constant: after it had taken place, nothing was, and nothing would be, ever again. If, from now on, you did not like the world, you no longer sat around deploring its inadequacy, or wondering how by cultivating your garden you could at least marginally improve your bit of it. You turned to Revolution to change it. The French Revolution, therefore, not only introduced the possibility of comprehensive change; it also offered a different way of achieving that change, by violent revolt and tumult; reasoned, planned rebellion; and it offered a pattern over which future revolutionaries would brood and debate down the generations.

It was not only those who wished to make changes whose outlook the Revolution changed forever. It also transformed the perceptions of those established authorities against whom they were ranged. Under the *ancien régime* the established authorities had not feared change. They had, indeed, in most countries, been its most persistent promoters for their own purposes, thereby attracting the charges of despotism that the men of 1789 and their foreign admirers hurled so readily against governments. But the French Revolution changed all that, too. It showed, in the very way it developed, which I have analysed above, that one change could lead all too readily to another, and before you know where you were to the overthrow of everything. Such a gospel, which soon enough came to be known in all ruling circles as Jacobinism, had to be resisted, both intellectually and practically. So Conservatism was born, as much a product of the Revolution as the Rights of Man and the challenge to nobility and privilege. Ultimately it triumphed, in the sense that a generation after the Revolution began France and her upstart Emperor were at least defeated, the Bourbons were restored and calm returned to the Continent. But the *ancien régime* was not restored, and never could be; and the triumphant allies of 1815 owed more of their success to what they had copied and borrowed from the French than to a refusal to learn from them. Nobody, not even those who rejected it most vehemently, escaped the influence of the French Revolution, whether at the time or afterwards.

9

Reflections on the Classic Interpretation of the French Revolution

The last time I debated the origins of the French Revolution with the Professor of the History of the Revolution at the Sorbonne was in Ottawa in 1982. On that occasion my opponent was Albert Soboul.[1] Though charming and convivial in private, in public – and certainly in our debate – Soboul was firm and inflexible. In what proved to be his last statement on the origins of the Revolution he proudly stood by 'notre bonne vieille orthodoxie', if orthodoxy was what 'revisionists' wanted to call it. He himself, however, preferred another description for the interpretation he favoured: he called it classic. No doubt his aim in adopting this term was to invest his interpretation with the authority he certainly believed it deserved; but quite independently of that it seems to me that classic is a good and fair description of it. Soboul's version, inherited from a long tradition of formidable historians and fine scholars, had a coherence and a unity lending it great interpretative power. It had stood the test of time, which raised it above more ephemeral approaches to the Revolution and its history. Such qualities mark out a classic. But classics have another quality too, which perhaps Soboul did not think of when adopting this description. They do not need to be true: you can admire their qualities without accepting for a moment what they say. Some might even argue that the essence of a classic is that it is impressive,

---

[1] The text of our debate was published in *Annales historiques de la révolution française*, 54 (1982), at the suggestion of Soboul himself. After his death some of my more critical remarks were removed from my text by his successor as editor. The occasion of this paper was a debate with Michel Vovelle in 1989.

but dead. A classic is beyond dispute, but only because nobody any longer thinks it worth disputing.

In these senses, as well as Soboul's, the interpretation of which he was the most distinguished late twentieth-century exponent deserves the description 'classic'. It is an interpretation now in ruins, and over the last forty years we have been watching it fall apart. I doubt if it will ever disappear entirely, levelled like the Bastille. Despite the paranoid apprehensions of some of its defenders, no malignant and politically motivated army of revisionists has set out on a systematic demolition such as we see in the famous Hubert Robert painting. Huge, ruined remnants will continue to stand more or less intact, but other parts will have gone forever, depriving the rest of much of its coherence. The aim of this essay is to attempt a brief assessment of what is gone, and what remains – and in what state.

First we should remind ourselves quickly of the classic interpretation's main features. Fundamental is the type of interpretation it is: a socioeconomic one. The Revolution was the culmination of a long social evolution, itself economically driven. It marked a turning-point in economic history, too: the transition from feudalism to capitalism. The social manifestation of this transition was the defeat of a declining feudal aristocracy living off the surplus extracted from the peasantry by a rising bourgeoisie enriched by capitalism and characterised by moneyed rather than proprietary wealth. The Revolution was thus the decisive engagement in a class struggle in which, at a crucial moment, the bourgeoisie was able to mobilise the support of the masses in order to achieve victory. This is inevitably a very bald summary of complex matters, and the sources of the classic interpretation are complex in themselves. One source is obviously Marx, as Soboul and others were proud to acknowledge. But Marx himself derived much of his model for this stage in historical development from the French Revolutionaries' own version of what had brought about the great cataclysm. The classic version was thus a sort of self-confirming hypothesis which only empirical research not undertaken within its parameters was likely to challenge.

That is largely what has happened. So-called 'revisionism' has been mainly a matter of questioning the empirical basis of the main features in the classic interpretation. There is no space in a brief essay to trace the process by which it happened, and in any case it has often been done before. Much more important and interesting is to assess what has been destroyed by revisionism, and what, if anything can be salvaged from the ruins. The central casualty, I think, has been class conflict. By any reasonable definition of class, a generation of research has shown that the nobility and the bourgeoisie before 1789 (and indeed afterwards too) were part of a single elite rather than two conflicting and naturally antagonistic ones. Nobles and bourgeoisie shared the same wealth patterns, the same social aspirations, the same education and values, the same attitude to the lower orders. Economically speaking, the nobility's wealth, though mostly landed, cannot usefully be described as feudal – or declining; and in any case, the bourgeoisie held much land in identical ways. Equally, increasing numbers of nobles were involved in capitalism, whereas one basic characteristic of the bourgeoisie was to turn its back on the production of wealth as soon as enough capital was accumulated. None of this offers any basis for rooting the clashes between nobles and bourgeoisie during the Revolution in class struggle. Indeed, the economic developments that are supposed to have underlain the class struggle have also been reappraised. It no longer seems credible to think that sudden political convulsion, however massive, could have reoriented economic development as decisively as used to be claimed. Those who have studied long-term French economic development across the Revolution have emphasised the continuities beneath the temporary upheaval, arguing that the real economic turning-point came in the mid nineteenth century. Others add a subtext: how could an episode that brought such spectacular economic disruption be said to have advanced, or been intended to advance, capitalism? In many spheres such as overseas trade, it set French progress back by at least a generation.

What are the implications of all this? I would be the first to admit that it raises as many problems as it resolves. The greatest of all, of course, is this: if class conflict between bourgeoisie and aristocracy does not explain the Revolution, what does? At the heart of the problem there is an empirical fact to confront: nobles and bourgeoisie *were* in conflict from September 1788 onwards, and elements of this antagonism persisted throughout the Revolution. The revisionist response has been that this was a conflict within a class rather than between classes, and that it arose not from any long-perceived conflict of interests but from a specific political situation compounded of accidents, miscalculations and misunderstandings. If the Estates-General had not been traditionally divided into three numerically equal orders voting by order, the questions posed by their convocation might have been very different. That was an accident – one of several crucial ones that determined the course of things in 1788-89. As to miscalculations and misunderstandings, a detailed account of the politics of France during these momentous years is essential if we are to grasp what they were. Another theme of revisionist writing has been renewed attention to political detail and abandonment of the assumption that if the socioeconomic or class position of those involved is known, the politics will speak for themselves. That assumption led to questionable versions of the role of the parlements in the pre-revolutionary crisis and to over-ready acceptance of concepts like the 'aristocratic reaction' or the 'noble revolt'. These minor outworks of the classic interpretation now scarcely survive, either. The origins of the Revolution are now being sought in a political crisis culminating in the breakdown of the state, a vacuum of power; and this crisis was not the result of social conflict, it was its cause.

The origins of the political crisis, at least, are something about which there is no disagreement. They lay in the excessive cost of an overambitious foreign policy. How was the monarchy to pay its debts and avoid such burdens in the future? There were a number of way in which it might have been done. The problem was that none of them was thought politically acceptable because they would be rejected by public opinion. In other words, the government was restricted by cultural constraints. Culture was the area most neglected in the classic interpretation, which was based on the premise that human behaviour is dictated by material interests. In any case, the most outstanding feature of eighteenth-century culture, the Enlightenment, seemed easily explicable as the articulation of bourgeois values, and so posed no problems. In fact, it has become increasingly clear that the Enlightenment appealed to nobles quite as much as to (if not even more than) bourgeois. These findings have reinforced the picture of an elite transcending the demarcation between nobles and bourgeois, giving it a cultural dimension in addition to its economic one. Because class conflict no longer seems a credible explanation for the Revolution, more and more scholars are seeking one in the area of cultural transformations. Nobody has done more to promote this approach, of course, than Michel Vovelle with his pioneering studies of changing religious attitudes over the eighteenth century; although I suspect that he would not accept the autonomous role assigned to cultural developments by some of what I prefer to call the post-revisionists.

Nor indeed would I, because cultural developments do not happen in a vacuum: they occur in a market and we have to bear that constantly in mind. The artefacts of culture – works of art or literature, newspapers, the multifarious means by which people communicate with one another, are all intended for certain consumers. The institutions of culture – salons, academies, literary societies, public libraries, clubs, masonic lodges – must also appeal to certain sociable inclinations and values if they are to flourish. They presuppose a certain level of education and a certain amount of leisure. What we see in the eighteenth century is a huge expansion in all these things. A widening market for, and interest in, the visual and decorative arts; an insatiable demand for new books and new literature; the birth of modern newspapers, weeklies and dailies; a multiplication of academies and literary societies at an ever-increasing rate; the invention and rapid institutionalisation of circulating libraries; the runaway popularity of freemasonry. One could go on. What these things all add up to is the birth of a powerful and well-informed public opinion over the course of the eighteenth century which, as already noticed, was extremely influential in limiting the state's freedom of action.

Who were the people involved in these developments; and how were they paid for? It has to be admitted that in *ancien régime* descriptive terms these people were overwhelmingly, indeed increasingly, bourgeois. The nobility participated in these trends, and massively. That seems established now beyond doubt. But the nobility does not seem to have grown in numbers, so the social expansion of the cultural market cannot be attributed to them. The main participants in the cultural expansion of the eighteenth century must, therefore, have been the bourgeoisie. It is ironic that we still do not know for certain how large the bourgeoisie was, even after more than a generation's debate about them. One might have expected adherents of the classic interpretation to address themselves to this problem. But it seems beyond dispute that the numbers of the bourgeoisie expanded enormously over the century. Guesses that they tripled do not seem improbable. All this seems compatible, therefore, with the cultural expansion I have been describing. Such studies as have been done of participation in higher education, book and newspaper buying, joining of libraries, literary societies and masonic lodges underline and substantiate a growing role for the bourgeoisie. They were spending increasing amounts of their wealth on cultural activity. Where did this wealth come from? Some came from land, no doubt, because the bourgeoisie owned at least 20 per cent of the land of France, and rents soared over the eighteenth century. Even more, however, must have come from the traditional motor of the bourgeoisie: from capitalism, in all its manifestations, but in particular from the surging commercial expansion that marked the eighteenth century in France.

Have we, then, come full circle? Are we back with the classic interpretation in all its purity, with an *ancien régime* destroyed by a bourgeoisie of rising capitalists? I don't think so. The most salient feature, in social terms, of the eighteenth-century bourgeoisie was the traditional character of its behaviour. It may have been created by capitalism and liquid wealth, but throughout its history it showed a constant and vigorous tendency to transform that wealth at the first opportunity into status and real estate; and in the eighteenth century there was little sign of this character changing. So there *was* a rising bourgeoisie, as there always had been, but it was part of the ruling class – or at least constantly in the process of becoming part – rather than a rival, antagonistic class. Although it was propelled by capitalism, it was constantly seeking to abandon capitalism rather than push it to a position of dominance. Its cultural ambitions were one sign of that. Bourgeoisie and nobility together were different elements in one ruling class rather than two antagonistic ones, and one of the things that united them was a common culture. Another was an ability and a determination to extract surplus from other classes – and this bred a resentment in the latter that was briefly released by the Revolution. If we are looking for class conflict, there is the place to find it.

So the rise of the bourgeoisie and the rise of capitalism still have a role to play in our thinking about the Revolution – but it is a much longer-term and more distant perspective in which the Revolution no longer enjoys its old pivotal importance. Some Marxists (though not, I think, French ones) have stated that they find this picture acceptable. It was not Marx's own view, but it is not contrary to Marxism.[2] Whether or not that is so is for Marxists, not me, to say. It is certainly, however, a long way from the classic interpretation which they, and almost everybody else, accepted without much question until a generation ago.

[2] E.g. G.C. Comninel, *Rethinking the French Revolution: Marxism and the Revisionist Challenge* (London, 1987).

10

The Political Thought of Mounier

Mounier is often depicted as an impractical dreamer, whose visionary schemes for a balanced constitution took no account of the political and social realities of France in 1789. Accordingly, he and his fellow *monarchiens* were doomed to failure. Doomed to failure they may have been, in the circumstances of 1789; but it could be argued that it was not Mounier who was visionary, but rather those who defeated him. Mounier's ideas for a viable French constitution were eminently practical and shrewdly thought out. What defeated him was the refusal of most of his fellow deputies to face the political realities to which he drew persistent attention. That refusal, in turn, led to precisely the problems and disorder he had sought to avoid. Like Burke, he came later to enjoy the status of a prophet; unlike Burke, he lived long enough to be able to say, 'I told you so'.

Mounier's whole political outlook was a response to realities. Although widely read in the political and historical thought of his century – in Locke, in Montesquieu, in Rousseau (whom he often evoked in his writings) in Robertson and in Delolme – he was no provincial schematiser, elaborating ideal plans of government that only an unexpected revolution would bring the opportunity to try out. He was certainly an avid student of public affairs in the 1780s, and not only those of France. He had a detailed knowledge of the political conflicts in the Dutch Republic and in Sweden, of the constitutional debates currently going on in the United States, and (of course) of the issues preoccupying parliament in the England of Pitt and Fox, which in 1788 were the celebration of the centenary of the 'glorious' revolution, and the delicate problem of replacing the authority of a mad king.

Few of those who would sit beside him on the benches of the National Assembly were so well informed. Nevertheless, all this knowledge seems to have produced no vision of an alternative political order for France, until the political crisis of 1787-88 forced him, like all thinking Frenchmen, to confront the problem of despotism and the legitimacy of resistance to authority. Even then, the basis of Mounier's response was traditional enough, rooted in the doctrines and practices of French eighteenth-century public life.[1] A world of remonstrances, of *très humbles représentations* – and of ultimate obedience, if the king remained deaf to such protests owing to the wicked deceptions of his despotic advisers. This was the traditional outlook of the parlements; and the protest movement which first brought to prominence the *juge royal* of Grenoble began in support of the sovereign courts struck down by Lamoignon in May 1788. But by then even the parlements had begun to advance new claims; by then, they were demanding the estates-general, and Mounier echoed this demand enthusiastically.

From the start it preoccupied him as a practical problem. What was the best way to achieve a meeting of the estates-general? By unity; by not allowing the multifarious divisions of French society to fracture the solidarity of the nation in the face of despotic authority. The first great political achievement of Mounier – some might say his only great achievement – was to persuade the three orders, first of Grenoble and then of the whole province of Dauphiné, to unite in demanding the return of the parlements, the estates-general, and the resurrection of the Estates of Dauphiné on a basis of common deliberation and double representation for the third estate. At first sight, certainly, a call for the resurrection of provincial estates which had not met since 1628 hardly seems like a recipe for unity. Nor was it, if it were to lead to a strengthening of provincial particularism. But that was never Mounier's intention. The provinces were merely a convenient way of mobilising national opinion on national issues; but nothing would be achieved if the French 'ne parviennent pas à dissiper ce chaos où chaque Ordre, chaque Province, chaque Corps, chaque individu invoque des privilèges et des titres; où la liberté est sans cesse froissée dans le choc des prétentions diverses'.[2] ['cannot manage to dissipate that chaos in which each Order, each Province, each Group (*Corps*), each individual invokes privileges and entitlements, where liberty is constantly bruised in the clash of

[1] See Jean Joseph Mounier, *Très respectueuses représentations des trois ordres de la province de Dauphiné*, written by Mounier for the Assemblée des Trois Ordres de la Province de Dauphiné on 21 July 1788.
[2] Idem, *Nouvelles Observations sur les états-généraux de France* (n.p., 1789), p. v.

divergent claims'.] A prerequisite for any worthwhile political achievement was that orders and provinces should remain united, 'misérables
préjugés de profession [et] petits intérêts de corps ou de lieux particu-
liers' ['miserable professional prejudices [and] petty corporate or local
interests'] be avoided, and that 'l'ensemble de la Monarchie' should work
together like one great family.[3]

That metaphor was perhaps unfortunate: we all know what quarrels
can take place within a family. And certainly the French national family
was subject to plenty of arguments and disagreements over the winter
and spring of 1788-9. In the event, it was not the resistance of provinces
like Dauphiné which brought about the return of the parlements and
the granting of the estates-general. Yet the example of the estates of
Dauphiné, with their vote by head and doubled third estate, proved a
major inspiration to the 'patriotic' side in the debates over the composition of the estates-general which dominated that period. In the
abundant pamphlet literature of the spring of 1789, Mounier made a
contribution second only, perhaps, to that of Sieyès, with his *Nouvelles
observations sur les Etats Généraux de France.*

On the surface this pamphlet hardly seems a remarkable contribution
to political thought. One hundred and seventy-four of its 282 pages are
given over to a historical survey of previous estates-general – or as
Mounier terms most of them, so-called estates-general. For his argument is that only bodies which deliberated in common really deserved
the name. By the spring of 1789 that was now the key issue, since in
December 1788 Necker had already conceded the doubling of the third.
But by Mounier's criteria, not even the estates-general of 1614,
arguments over whose forms had inaugurated the great constitutional
debate of that winter, truly deserved the title. Only that of 1483 really
qualified. All this was special-pleading masquerading as scholarship,
based though it obviously was on a good deal of genuine historical
research. The real point was the overall purpose of the argument, which
was twofold. First, Mounier wished to establish that the 'forms of 1614'
enjoyed no more authority than any others, if precedent was to be
decisive; and that in fact there were better precedents for different
forms. Secondly, and even more importantly, Mounier's aim was to show
that none of these precedents amounted to a constitution. Repeating
what by this time was a commonplace, Mounier asserted that France had
no constitution. The very purpose of the estates-general was to give her
one. 'J'entends par constitution' he declared,[4]

---

[3] Ibid., p. 6.
[4] Ibid., p. 182.

un corps de règles fondamentales, sur lesquelles sont appuyées tous les ressorts du Gouvernement, qui laisse au Corps social le moyen d'obtenir les loix nécessaires au maintien de l'ordre public, mais de véritables loix, signes de la volonté générale; qui indiquent au Peuple ce qui doit lier son obéissance, qui retiennent tous les agens du pouvoir dans des justes limites, qui fassent que les Loix ne soient jamais vainement invoquées, qu'on ne puisse leur substituer les décisions arbitraires, et qu'en se conformant à ce qu'elles ordonnent le plus obscur des Citoyens puisse jouir d'ailleurs de toute l'indépendance de la nature.

[By constitution . . . I understand a body of fundamental rules on which all the powers of Government rest, which leaves to the social body the means of obtaining laws necessary to the maintenance of public order, but true laws, signifying the general will; which indicate to the People what should command their obedience, which keep all the agents of power within just limits, which ensure that the Laws are never invoked in vain, that arbitrary decisions cannot take their place, and that in obeying what they lay down, the most obscure Citizen may also enjoy all the independence of nature.]

A constitution, then, is more than any mere set of political ground-rules; it is also a set of guarantees of liberty. In fact, 'La Monarchie, l'Aristocratie, et la Démocratie peuvent exister sans constitution, sans aucune Loi positive.'[5] ['Monarchy, Aristocracy and Democracy can exist without a constitution, without any positive Law.'] But the essence of a constitution is the rule of law, a state of affairs where there is a generally accepted law governing every eventuality, and where arbitrary power is reduced to a minimum. By these standards France has no constitution, although it has a monarchy which recognises certain fundamental laws. What some people call the French constitution, he said (prefiguring Tocqueville) is merely 'les débris de la féodalité . . . des ruines gothiques'.[6] It was true that the breakdown of feudalism *could* lead to some sort of constitution – as it had for, example, in England. Here was Mounier's first mention of his favourite model. But in France the power of provincial institutions, and their shortsightedness, had prevented such an evolution at an early stage. So France merely had *usages*, not *loix*; the foundations, perhaps, of a monarchical constitution, but not the thing itself; and the monarchy of Montesquieu, relying for the mainte-nance of the laws on aristocratic intermediary bodies and institutions like venality, was 'un détestable Gouvernement'[7] unworthy of the French nation.

---

[5] Ibid.
[6] Ibid, p. 184.
[7] Ibid., p. 214.

How then was the nation to acquire something better and more desirable? How was a true constitution to be achieved? Here Mounier begins to go beyond the immediate political circumstances of the spring of 1789, to enunciate principles with which he would be identified until he joined the Bonapartist regime in 1802. First of all the constitution must be elaborated by a representative assembly. The nation is the source of all sovereignty, but 24,000,000 people cannot exercise sovereignty. It must be done through representatives. But even if it were practical for all members of the nation to assemble, as it had been for example in the ancient world, it would still be undesirable, for that would create a 'démocratie tumultueuse, sous laquelle il n'existe ni repos, ni sûreté, ni véritable liberté, où la loi est sans force, et ne sauroit enchaîner la volonté du grand nombre, dont rien ne peut modifier le despotisme'.[8] ['tumultuous democracy, under which there can exist neither quiet, nor security, nor true liberty, where the law is powerless, incapable of binding the will of the greater number, whose despotism nothing can modify'.] These perspectives were fundamental to Mounier's thought. He did not trust the populace, never had and never would. All his subsequent experience, whether in June and July or September and (above all) October 1789 only confirmed this outlook; and during all that time he never ceased to reiterate it. 'J'abhorre' he wrote in August,[9] 'l'abus de la force, la tyrannie ou la licence de la multitude, autant que le pouvoir arbitraire d'un seul'; because if 'la véritable liberté n'est que la sûreté des biens et des personnes; cette sûreté n'a d'autres fondemens que le respect des Loix. La licence ou l'anarchie est donc la plus cruelle ennemi de la liberté . . . l'anarchie est la licence de la multitude.'[10] ['I abhor . . . the abuse of force, the tyranny and the licence of the multitude, as much as the arbitrary power of one' . . .] ['true liberty being the security of goods and persons, this security can only be based upon respect for Law. Licence or anarchy is therefore liberty's cruellest enemy . . . anarchy is the licence of the multitude.'] Constitutional questions, he argued in a retrospective justification, are ones 'que la plupart des citoyens ne sont en état ni de traiter, ni d'ententre'.[11] ['that most citizens are in no state to consider, or understand.'] So even if the nation is sovereign, the people are not.

---

[8] Ibid., pp. 218-19.
[9] Idem, *Considérations sur les gouvernemens, et principalement sur celui qui convient à la France* (Paris, 1789), p. 2.
[10] Ibid., p. 7.
[11] Idem, *Exposé de la conduite de M. Mounier dans l'Assemblée Nationale* (Paris, 1789), p. 39.

'Vouloir', he was still reflecting in 1795, 'qu'une immense multitude se gouverne elle-même ou qu'elle dispose de tous les genres d'autorité, c'est prétendre qu'elle n'a pas besoin d'être gouvernée, qu'elle pourroit se passer de règlemens et de magistrats.'[12] ['To want . . . an immense multitude to govern itself or to deploy any sort of authority, is to claim that it has no need of government, that it may do without rules and magistrates.'] These were brave sentiments to profess in the midst of a movement which arguably owed its very survival to popular power, and in which, at least until 1795, the populace of Paris was a factor of constant importance, repeatedly claiming to incarnate the sovereign people. It is scarcely surprising that Mounier renounced the Revolution as soon as he did. The point to remember is that these convictions antedated his actual experience of popular power, unless we count the *journée des tuiles* in Grenoble on 7 June 1788. His departure in October represented no dramatic conversion. Popular power in action merely confirmed all that he had always believed.

This being the case, it is hardly surprising to learn that Mounier did not believe in the mandation of representatives.[13] They must have the right to make any dispositions they think fit, so long as they are freely elected, represent all elements in the nation, and vote by head. To bind them by their *cahiers* would be to introduce the paralysis of the Polish system; indeed, it was hard to see why deputies thus bound needed to meet at all. Their only mandate should be to ensure that they were a true national assembly by accepting only voting by head. Beyond that, they should be allowed to draft a constitution as their wisdom dictated, since, as he put it later in the summer, 'les électeurs ne choisissent pas un représentant pour leur seul intérét; c'est pour celui de la Nation entière'.[14] ['electors do not choose a representative for their interests alone; it is for those of the entire nation.'] The revolution of 1789 could not have occurred without the renunciation of mandates, for too many deputies came to Versailles bound by their *cahiers* to oppose much of what actually came about. In that sense, the renunciation of mandates was one of the most revolutionary steps of all. Mounier knew this; the

---

[12] Idem, *Adolphe, ou principes élémentaires de politique et résultats de la plus cruelle des expériences* (London, n.d.), p. 41.

[13] Idem, *Nouvelles observations*, ch. 26.

[14] Idem, *Considérations sur les gouvernemens*, p. 22. This principle is close to that enunciated by Burke in his speech to the electors of Bristol of 3 November 1774. It is not clear, however, that Mounier was familiar with Burke's doctrines before his enthusiastic reading of the *Reflexions on the Revolution in France* in 1790.

experience of the Dauphiné estates had made him conscious of it, and he exulted in the freedom it gave constitution makers – at least at first. Later on there are some signs of disquiet. When things do not go his way we rather surprisingly find Mounier invoking his mandate – as when he opposed the abolition of the right of *mainmorte* without compensation on 6 August.[15] Later still, looking back from exile in 1792, he openly condemned the fact that the National Assembly 'ne permit pas d'invoquer leurs cahiers, quoique la plupart de ses membres eussent promis, avec serment, de se conformer aux volontés de ceux qui les avoient élus'.[16] ['did not allow the cahiers to be invoked, although the greater part of its members had promised, under oath, to abide by the wishes of those who had elected them'.] Too late, he saw that mandates could restrain an assembly otherwise only too prone to go to extremes.

Given that before events got beyond what Mounier could applaud or approve, he favoured the renunciation of mandates and *carte blanche* for constitution makers; what did he consider the essential elements to be incorporated in a sound constitution? This question brings us to the features of Mounier's thought that made him most famous – or infamous. They emerged clearly even before the initial goal of a single assembly voting by head was secured. The key to any properly working constitution, he argued in the spring of 1789, was the principle of three mutually balancing powers.[17] A single assembly was no doubt competent to draw up a constitution; but for public and individual liberty to be guaranteed for future generations, 'la sagesse commande la balance des pouvoirs'. ['wisdom dictates a balance of powers'] It was an idea that he clearly derived from his study of the British constitution;[18] but what he had in mind was not the classic trio of executive, legislative and judiciary extolled by Montesquieu and established at just this time in America. The model for Mounier was clearly the trio of king, lords and commons.

The legislature should therefore be bicameral. The lower house would be the National Assembly, or *Assemblée des Représentants* with particular authority over finance and taxation. Although it would represent the whole nation, it should not be directly elected. That would

[15] Mounier, *Exposé de la conduite*, p. 32.

[16] Idem, *Recherches sur les causes qui ont empêché les François de devenir libres*, 2 vols (Geneva, 1792), ii, p. 45.

[17] Idem, *Nouvelles observations*, p. 248.

[18] It is central to the analysis of Delolme, *De la constitution de l'Angleterre*, which was clearly one of Mounier's main sources for British constitutional practice.

be, once more, to give too much power to the dreaded multitude. The people should merely elect the electors, who themselves should be confined to those with 'un revenu suffisant pour intéresser au repos public'.[19] ['a sufficient income to give an interest in public tranquillity'] This principle in itself proved uncontroversial enough. It was adopted (after Mounier's departure) by the Constituent Assembly in the form of the category of active citizens, and the eligibility requirement of the *marc d'argent*. It formed the basis of electoral law far into the nineteenth century. On the other hand it took six turbulent years before the idea of a second chamber, an upper house, became acceptable in the constitution of 1795.

Mounier saw what the objection would be right from the start. If the central struggle of the spring of 1789 was to destroy the division of the Estates-General into three chambers, why recreate division by adopting two? Especially when the obvious model for an upper house, the British House of Lords, was made up entirely of nobles and prelates, just the categories who in France sustained the division of the estates-general into orders. So even before the uniting of the orders had been achieved, he had begun to argue that the British House of Lords was a house of peers, not the representative body of an order of nobility.[20] These peers were 'Magistrats créés par le Roi, indépendans néâmoins de la Couronne, par l'hérédité de leurs places que la Loi transmet à l'aîné mâle de leurs enfans'. ['Magistrates created by the King, yet still independent of the Crown, by the heredity of their seats which the Law passes on to the eldest of their male children.'] All others had to stand for election to the Commons. In France such an upper house might be composed of the Princes of the Blood, the existing peers of France, great officers of state and a number of royal nominees; not all of whom need be nobles or prelates.[21] They would never outnumber the lower house and (as in England) they would have no power to originate or amend money bills. But their consent would be required for any measure to become law; and they would also constitute a supreme tribunal before which public men could be impeached, 'une Magistrature suprême, que la Nation elle-même auroit établie'.[22] ['a supreme Magistracy, established by the Nation itself.']

---

[19] Mounier, *Adolphe*, p. 72; idem, *Considérations sur les gouvernemens*, pp. 12, 22, 40-1. See, too, Mounier's speech in the Assembly, 4 Sept. 1789, *Moniteur*, 1, p. 421.

[20] Mounier, *Nouvelles observations*, p. 245.

[21] Ibid., pp. 270-3.

[22] Ibid., p. 268.

He returned to this theme in the great constitutional debates of early September, when he advocated what might be called a *Sénat*, a *Conseil National*, or (more tellingly) a *Chambre des Conservateurs*.[23] A few weeks beforehand he had argued that its members should be over thirty-five and in possession of a capital of at least 10,000 *livres*, an extreme extension of the eligibility principle for the lower house, that 'un riche propriétaire a plus d'intérêt au maintien de la trainquilité publique, il a plus de motifs pour redouter les innovations'.[24] ['a rich property owner has more interest in the maintenance of public tranquillity, he has more to fear from change'.] Such a chamber would also prevent the over-hasty adoption of any laws, good or bad; since the process of lawmaking demanded a 'marche lente et majestueuse dont [on] ne doit jamais s'écarter'.[25] There was realism and good sense in all these points, as later constitution-makers recognised. But in September 1789 there was no realism in expecting any sort of second chamber to be adopted by the National Assembly. Quite apart from hostile popular pressure, and the seeming irrationality of redividing a legislature so recently unified after a long struggle, even those who might have seemed the natural supporters of a second chamber, the deputies of the nobility, disliked the idea of a house of peers where most of them would never sit. The vote of 849 against and only 89 for was the most crushing of all the defeats sustained by Mounier and his friends, the party of the *monarchiens*.[26]

That very name, indicates the central doctrine with which they were associated, and of which Mounier was the leading theorist. Far more important than the second chamber in his thinking was the role of the king. Here again he was unequivocal right from the start. Any constitution must first establish 'des règles fondamentales pour assurer les droits et l'indépendance de la Couronne',[27] because

l'ordre et la paix ne peuvent exister dans un vaste royaume, si le Prince ne jouit pas d'une grande puissance pour faire exécuter les Loix. Le pouvoir exécutif doit donc être entièrement dans les mains du Monarque: mais le pouvoir ne suffiroit pas pour assurer l'independance de la couronne et le maintien de ses prerogatives. Quand la constitution sera formée, il faut, pour rendre imposs-ible tous les changemens préjudiciables aux droits du Trône qu'aucune loi ne

[23] *Moniteur*, 1, p. 421.
[24] Mounier, *Considérations sur les gouvernemens*, p. 41.
[25] *Moniteur*, 1, p. 421.
[26] See J. Egret, *La révolution des notables, Mounier et les monarchiens, 1789* (Paris, 1950), pp. 152-3.
[27] Mounier, *Nouvelles observations*, p. 250.

soit établie sans le libre concours de l'autorité Royale, et que le refus du Prince anéantisse toutes les résolutions.[28]

['fundamental rules to guarantee the rights and the independence of the Crown . . . order and peace cannot exist in a vast kingdom, if the Prince does not enjoy great power to have the laws applied. Executive power must then be entirely in the hands of the Monarch: but power would not suffice to guarantee the independence of the crown and the maintenance of its prerogatives. When the constitution is made, it is essential, to render impossible any change prejudicial to the rights of the Throne, that no law should be passed without the free consent of royal authority, and that the Prince's refusal may annul any resolution'.]

In other words, the king must have the power to veto proposed legislation. Later this would become the central issue. In the early stages of the Revolution Mounier concentrated his efforts on emphasising the general importance of a strong executive arm personified in a king. 'Depuis quatorze siècles' he declared to the Assembly on 9 July, in the name of the *comité de constitution*,[29] 'nous avons un roi. Le sceptre n'a pas été crée par la force, mais par la volonté de la nation . . . les François ont toujours senti qu'ils avaient besoin d'un roi.' ['For fourteen centuries . . . we have had a king. The sceptre was created not by force, but by the will of the nation . . . the French have always felt that they needed a king.'] In the constitution to come, royal authority must no doubt be clearly delimited, but not compromised. Even when, on 13 July, news of the dismissal of Necker suggested that a royal *coup de force* was imminent, Mounier, while recognising the necessity of resistance, urged his fellow deputies:[30] 'N'oublions jamais que l'autorité royale est essentielle au bonheur de nos concitoyens, à quelque point que puissent en abuser aujourd'hui ceux qui ont surpris la religion du roi;[31] n'oublions jamais que nous aimons la monarchie pour la France, et non la France pour la monarchie.' ['Let us never forget that royal authority is essential to the happiness of our fellow citizens, however much it has been abused in our day by those who have surprised the king's religion;[31] let us never forget that we love the monarchy for the sake of France, and not France for the sake of monarchy.'] Three days later, when the Assembly debated a proposal to petition the king for the removal of ministers, he declared

---

[28] Ibid., pp. 267-8.
[29] *Moniteur*, 1, p. 141.
[30] Ibid., pp. 150-1.
[31] The traditional formula used by the parlements to exculpate the king from blame for governmental actions.

that such matters should be none of the assembly's business. 'Refuser sa confiance à un ministre à qui le roi donne la sienne, serait de la part de l'Assemblée nationale une manière indirecte d'obliger le roi à le renvoyer, et un tel droit dans l'Assemblée y ferait naître une multitude d'intrigues'.[32] ['For the National Assembly to withhold its confidence from a minister to whom the king has given his, would be an indirect way of forcing the king to dismiss him, and such a right vested in the Assembly would raise in it a multitude of intrigues.'] In one of his rare criticisms of England, he went on to deplore how such manoeuvres were possible there. By the time the Assembly came to debate the question of ministers in the legislature, in November, Mounier had abandoned his seat and returned to Dauphiné. He was never, therefore, called up to deliver a direct opinion on this principle. But his earlier attitudes suggest that here he would have abandoned the British model for that favoured by the Americans, where the executive's choice of ministers is entirely uninfluenced by the legislature.[33] The Constituent Assembly adopted this model, too, but the subsequent history of successive revolutionary assemblies showed that the French were never prepared to accept the principle in its entirety. Repeated clashes occurred in which the legislature claimed the right to influence the composition of ministries.[34]

It was only late in August that the issue of the future extent of royal power became central to political debate: it was unfortunate for Mounier that the theoretical question was entangled throughout with that of whether or not Louis XVI would accept the decree of 11 August and the Declaration of the Rights of Man and the Citizen. His equivocations sowed deep doubts, not only about his own motivation but also about the dangers of allowing any king a legislative veto. But Mounier was well aware that the question could not be postponed, and in mid August he launched his campaign with the pamphlet, *Considérations sur les gouvernements, et principalement sur celui qui convient à la France*. 'Je

---

[32] *Moniteur*, 1, p. 166.

[33] Later, however, he seemed to recognise the disadvantages in having no link at all. In *Recherches sur les causes* (1792), p. 61, seemingly as a result of reading Hume's *Essays* in his exile, he concluded that the only way to place permanent restraints on the power of the legislative branch, was to ensure that 'les intérêts d'une partie des membres soient liés au maintien des droits du monarque'. ['The interests of a part of the members should be linked to the maintenance of the monarch's rights'.] Yet he offered no practical suggestions for achieving this end.

[34] In the spring of 1792, for example, or the following autumn, or at various points during the Directory.

ne suis', he there declared,[35] 'l'ennemi de l'autorité, que lorsqu'elle veut opprimer le Peuple', but, 'j'ai hautement professé mon attachement extrême au Gouvernement monarchique . . . je n'ai jamais séparé la liberté du Peuple, de la puissance légitime du Monarque'. ['I am only . . . the enemy of authority when it wishes to oppress the people . . . I have loudly professed my extreme attachment to monarchical government . . . I have never separated the liberty of the people from the legitimate power of the monarch.'] What was that legitimate power? It was a power subject to law, as Montesquieu had taught, but also to the practical checks of a legislature having sole power to consent to taxation, a free press, and the answerability of all public officials for their actions.[36] Thus constrained, the monarch could safely be entrusted with other powers and prerogatives – and indeed must have them. The crown must be hereditary, to prevent the danger of contested successions. The person of the king should be inviolable; and he alone should have the power to enforce laws, since 'la Loi n'est qu'un vain mot, quand il n'existe aucun moyen pour la faire respecter'.[37] ['The law is but an empty word, when no means exist to compel respect for it.'] The king should also be able to restrain the excesses of elected deputies by the right to refuse royal sanction to legislation. Such arrangements were in any case clearly authorised by most of the *cahiers*, which had spoken of laws being concerted with the king.

To those who claimed that such a royal veto blocked the will of the nation as expressed through its representatives, Mounier countered that the king, too, was a representative: 'Il doit être considéré comme le chef de la Nation et le représentant de la Majesté du Peuple Français.'[38] ['He should be looked upon as the head of the nation and the representative of the majesty of the French people.'] This theme was not developed far in the *Considérations*, but it grew in importance for Mounier as time went on. Only a few weeks later, in a speech to the Assembly (14 September) in which he rehearsed many of the themes of this pamphlet almost word for word, he went much further on the subject of the king's status. The monarch should, in fact, be considered part of the legislature,[39] he is as

---

[35] Mounier, *Considérations sur les gouvernemens*, p. 2.
[36] Ibid., p. 20.
[37] Ibid., p. 25.
[38] Ibid., p. 21.
[39] *Moniteur*, 1, p. 424.

much a delegate of the people as the deputies, and they are charged jointly with the expression of the general will. Thus 'lorsque le roi ne donne pas sa sanction, il ne résiste pas à la volonté générale . . . elle n'est pas encore formée'.[40] ['when the king withholds his sanction, he is not resisting the general will . . . it has not yet taken shape'.] The king should be a 'portion intégrante du corps législatif'.[41] On 5 September he emphasised that this was 'un des principes les plus sacrés de la monarchie'.[42]

Later, from his self-imposed exile in Dauphiné, he went even further and declared the king 'le représentant perpétuel du peuple',[43] alongside deputies chosen for limited terms. What Mounier was expressing here was a version of the British doctrine of the sovereignty of the king in parliament.[44] The problem with adapting such a doctrine to the circumstances of revolutionary France was that everybody had already recognised that sovereignty lay elsewhere. Not in the king, not even in the legislature including or excluding the king, but in the nation. The most, then, that king or deputies could ever be was representatives of the sovereign.[45] The problem was to make them answerable to the sovereign. With deputies, it could be achieved by election for limited terms. With a king, the problem was far more difficult, especially if he enjoyed any degree of independent power.

Yet this was what Mounier was proposing. The king must be able to refuse his sanction – and to refuse it, moreover, without explaining himself, 'car s'il était obligé de . . . faire connaître [ses motifs] aux représentants, ceux-ci pourraient se croire en droit de les juger, et conséquemment de ne point y avoir égard'.[46] ['for if he were obliged to . . . declare [his reasons] to the representatives, the latter might think themselves entitled to judge them, and consequently to disregard

---

[40] Ibid., p. 427.
[41] Ibid., p. 429.
[42] Ibid., p. 437.
[43] Mounier, *Exposé de la conduite de M. Mounier*, pt 2, p. 14.
[44] Made clear to him, no doubt, in chs 3 and 4 of Delolme's *Constitution de l'Angleterre*.
[45] Mounier admitted as much: 'Je sais', he declared on 4 September, 'que le principe de la souveraineté réside dans la nation . . . Je ne dis pas qu'elle puisse l'aliéner, mais enfin elle le confie . . . Une partie de la souveraineté de la nation française a été confiée au monarque, et l'autre doit l'être aux représentants librement élus.' *Moniteur*, 1, p. 425. ['I know . . . that the principle of sovereignty resides in the nation . . . I do not say that it can be alienated, rather that it is entrusted . . . Part of the sovereignty of the French nation has been entrusted to the monarch, and the rest should be to freely elected representatives.'] This was as near as Mounier could get to the British doctrine in 1789.
[46] *Moniteur*, 1, p. 438.

them'.] Two ways of doing so were envisaged. One was by dissolving the legislature; but Mounier did not dwell on this question much.[47] The September debates were concentrated mostly, given that the question of the hour was the sanctioning of the August decrees, on the second means, the veto. Mounier believed that the king should enjoy an absolute and unconditional veto on all proposed legislation under the new constitution. This did not imply, he emphasised, a veto on the constitution itself or, by implication, the August decrees, which had constitutional status. A national constituent assembly could be subject to no veto.[48] The constitution it eventually produced must, however, allow a royal veto as a way of preventing excessive pretensions on the part of the nation's elected representatives, whose powers were in themselves so wide as to be quite easily abused. The fears currently being voiced about the veto were much exaggerated. It would seldom be used. No king would want or dare to veto a law which had real and widespread public support. For the same reason a *suspensive* veto seemed to Mounier superfluous. Besides, it was incompatible with the dignity of the throne, 'indiquant le terme où il est forcé d'obéir aux représentants',[49] ['making clear the point at which he is forced to obey the representatives,'] and in that sense not really a veto at all. A suspensive veto would demonstrate the king's humiliating lack of freedom and independence, reducing him to little more than an obedient army general.[50] The most Mounier would concede to arguments for less than absolute veto was the idea, put forward on 5 September in the name of the *comité de constitution*, that the king might employ a delaying formula 'Le roi examinera', as in England.[51]

These arguments, too, failed to carry the day when the vote came on 11 September. A big majority (730 to 143) accepted the necessity of a veto. A smaller one, though still substantial (673 to 325) accepted that it should only be suspensive, operative at most during two successive legislatures. With that, Mounier resigned from the *comité de constitution*. The Assembly had rejected the two key elements in his constitutional proposals, so it plainly had no confidence in his advice. He believed it had acted largely through fear of the Parisian mob, that multitude which he feared but whose influence he hoped a balanced constitution and a

---

[47] Later he gave it more emphasis: Mounier, *Exposé de la conduite*, p. 9.
[48] *Moniteur*, 1, p. 428.
[49] Ibid., p. 429.
[50] Mounier, *Considérations sur les gouvernemens*, p. 26.
[51] *Moniteur*, 1, p. 426.

strong monarchy might curb. Within three more weeks, all that he most dreaded came about. The Parisians marched to Versailles and forced the king to come with them back to the capital, a prisoner. Mounier, who was president of the Assembly at the time, was present at all the crucial events and so was able to confirm to himself that the reality of popular power was every bit as terrifying as he had always claimed. It was the end of his political career. Even before his term of office was complete, he abandoned the Assembly and returned to his native Dauphiné, hoping to make it a focus of resistance to the new, popular tyranny as it had been to the old, authoritarian one. He was soon disappointed. Grenoble no longer trusted him. Within six months,[52] he felt under such hostile pressure that he chose to escape from circumstances which 'ont anéanti la royauté, détruit la force publique, confondu tous les pouvoirs, et tout subordonné aux caprices de la multitude'. ['annihilated monarchy, destroyed public authority, confounded all powers and subjected all to the caprices of the multitudes.'][53]

These complaints summarised Mounier's political philosophy, which in his subsequent writings he elaborated on and amended somewhat, but never basically changed. 'Tous mes travaux', he claimed in 1792,[54] 'eurent constamment pour objet une monarchie tempérée, où la puissance du trône et les droits des citoyens se seroient prêté à un appui mutuel, et auroient été solidement garantis.' ['All my labours . . . had constantly in view a tempered monarchy, where the power of the throne and the rights of citizens might lend themselves mutual support, and be solidly guaranteed'.] But 'sous le joug de la populace' ['under the popular yoke'] the National Assembly had become 'l'instrument d'une faction ennemie de la royauté' ['the instrument of a faction inimical to monarchy'] and all France's subsequent misfortunes sprang from that. While we may doubt the existence of a strong republican faction in the Assembly much before the early Summer of 1791, there can be no doubt of the radicalising role played in the Revolution from the start by the populace of Paris. It was realistic of Mounier to face the problem, again from the start.

The object of the Revolution, and indeed of any proper constitution, was in Mounier's eyes to establish liberty. But liberty was inseparable from property, and security for that property. 'Les citoyens sont libres, lorsqu'ils ne peuvent être contraints ou empêchés dans leurs actions ou

[52] See Egret, *Révolution des notables*, pp. 197-222.
[53] Mounier, *Aux Dauphinois, par M. Mounier* (n.p., n.d.), p. 25.
[54] Mounier, *Recherches sur les causes*, p. xii.

dans la jouissance de leurs biens et de leur industrie, si ce n'est en vertu des loix antérieures, établies pour l'intérêt public, et jamais d'après l'autorité arbitraire d'aucun homme, quels que soient son rang et son pouvoir.'[55] SURETE, PROPRIETE disent les Anglois, quand ils veulent caractériser la liberté civile ou personnelle.'[56] ['Citizens are free, when they cannot be constrained or prevented in actions or in the enjoyment of their goods and their industry, except by virtue of prior laws, established for the public interest, and never under the arbitrary authority of a single man, whatever his rank or power. SECURITY, PROPERTY, say the English, when they wish to characterise civil or personal liberty.'] The greatest threat to such liberty was the untutored, despotic passion of the multitude, which only strong, constant and resolute authority could contain – clear, firm laws supported by sufficient practical means. That meant a strong executive; and since France had always been monarchical, it was obvious that this executive must be a king. Kings too, of course, could be enemies of liberty – but not if they were restrained by explicit laws and institutions designed to inhibit their arbitrary tendencies. That was the meaning of political (as opposed to civil and personal) liberty,[57] and the example of England showed how it could work.

The whole turbulent history of the 1790s was to demonstrate how much France needed the security, stability and authority preached by Mounier. Therein lies his realism. If it had been possible to draft a constitution in a vacuum, insulated from everyday political pressures, common sense would no doubt have dictated the establishment of much that he advocated. But, as he himself once declared, 'les Français ne sont pas un peuple nouveau, sorti récemment du fond des forêts pour former une association'.[58] [The French are not a new people, recently emerged from the depths of the forest to form an association.'] One had to act within the constraints of existing circumstances. With powerful recent memories of the struggle to destroy a divided legislature; a deep and in many ways justified mistrust of the king France happened to have; an awareness even among those who feared the multitude that without its help despotism might yet triumph; not to mention a widespread patriotic disdain for following English models: under

---

[55] Ibid., p. 1.
[56] Ibid., p. 3.
[57] Ibid., p. 4.
[58] *Moniteur*, 1, p. 142, 9 July 1789.

circumstances like these Mounier's prospects for getting his principles accepted were never bright. But we should not dismiss the realism of his solutions merely because he was unrealistic about the chances of achieving them.

11

Revolution and Counter-Revolution in France

It has long been a commonplace to say that the French Revolution changed the meaning of the word 'revolution' itself. Recent scholarly writing on this question has confirmed the commonplace in convincing new detail.[1] Before the 1790s, revolution meant political upheaval, public vicissitudes, change in the state. It could, of course, be applied to some fairly momentous developments, such as what happened in Great Britain between 1688 and 1690, or in America in the 1770s. It was also, however, applied to many events that we should call mere *coups d'état*, or even to simply dramatic and spectacular transfers of political power with no implication of undue violence or a break in the chain of the law. Thus, to stay in the 1770s, the term was readily applied to the reassertion of royal power in Sweden in 1772 by Gustavus III, or to the overthrow of Struensee the same year in neighbouring Denmark, while France was in the midst of what everybody down to 1789 called the 'Maupeou Revolution', the remodelling of the judiciary by a determined and ambitious chancellor. When Maupeou was dismissed in 1774, soon after the accession of Louis XVI, this was hailed as another revolution.

The events of the late 1780s seemed at first like yet another: but by the middle of 1789 men were becoming aware that something quite unprecedented was happening. This was a revolution quite unlike any other in scope, range and ambition. By the end of the century it would seem unprecedented in achievement, too. The result was, that for the two centuries since it happened, the *French* Revolution has been the

---

[1] K.M. Baker, 'Revolution', in Colin Lucas (ed.), *The French Revolution and the Creation of Modern Political Culture*, vol. ii of *The Political Culture of the French Revolution*, 3 vols (Oxford, 1988), pp. 41-62.

litmus by which all other candidates for the name have been judged – to the extent, even, that events before 1789, though called revolutions by those who lived through or witnessed them, have found themselves retrospectively denied the title. Deciding which upheavals in the past were or were not revolutionary has become one of the favourite games of historians. The criteria they adopt in order to decide can be very elaborate and sophisticated, but they all come back sooner or later to the French model. The process began almost immediately after the first shock. In 1790 Burke's great polemic, *Reflexions on the Revolution in France*, was built around his sense of outrage when English parliamentary reformers tried to claim that events in France were of the same kind as (only better than) those in England a century earlier. Burke insisted that 1689 and 1789 had nothing in common. By the new standard, the glory of England's 'Glorious Revolution' was that it was not a revolution at all.

Events in France in and after 1789 redefined the meaning of revolution. They also spawned new concepts in response to that redefinition. Among these concepts was counter-revolution. This time the very term had not been heard before. There is no record of its use in French before 1790; the first examples of its use in English came shortly after that, in a context of direct translation from the French. Nor could it have had any logical existence in any language before the great redefinition of its antithesis, because implicit in the pre-1789 definition of revolution was a cyclical idea. A revolution, in its earliest meaning, was a turn in the wheel. One revolution succeeded another, as sooner or later the wheel turned again. There was no sense of turning it back, or being able to, or needing to. Malcontents simply waited for the next revolution. But the sheer scale of the cataclysm after 1789 demanded wholly new responses from those who disliked or opposed what had happened. This time, nothing less than turning the wheel back could repair the damage. Revolution was now conceived of as an experience so total that any response must be commensurate. Revolutionaries themselves expected as much: the term 'counter-revolution' was coined by them.

In the beginning nobody proclaimed themselves counter-revolutionaries. Opponents were called that (and fairly indiscriminately) by those who saw themselves on the revolution's side. From an early stage the assumption was made that conservatives, critics or simple doubters about the great national regeneration were intent on overturning everything that had been achieved, and restoring the former order, the *ancien régime*. Such people did, of course, exist, and in growing numbers.

By 1791 they would be unashamedly calling themselves counter-revolutionaries. The problem is that perhaps the majority of those who resisted authority in France during the 1790s would *not* have considered themselves counter-revolutionaries. Many would have indignantly denied the charge. Until about a generation ago, most historians would have been as disinclined to believe their denials as were contemporary revolutionaries. The achievement of recent years has been to get behind such blanket categorisations, thereby revealing the true complexity and diversity of opposition and resistance to the Revolution.

This process may be described, perhaps, as the last act in the disintegration of what the late Albert Soboul used to call the classic interpretation of the French Revolution. Heavily influenced in the twentieth century by Marxism, and perhaps first damaged in the 1950s by demonstrations that its more overtly Marxist elements did not seem to fit in with much of the evidence, the classic interpretation had deep pre-Marxist roots. A lot of them, indeed, went back to the Revolution itself, and François Furet, the most devastating of the classic interpretation's French critics, has pointed out that a much more accurate description of it than Marxist would be 'neo-Jacobin'.[2] That is because this interpretation assumes that the Revolution was one, all of a piece – in Clemenceau's famous phrase a *bloc* – and that the essence of what is was about could be found in its most extreme phase, the Jacobin Republic of the Year II, 1793-4, which began with the purging of the Girondins from the Convention and ended with the fall of Robespierre.

That phase of the Revolution was republican, centralised, anti-clerical; it was also popular, in the sense that many of the policies pursued then had the support of, and often emanated from, the Parisian *sans-culottes*. This was also a period of terror – indeed *the* Terror, which in common memory since has also seemed to epitomise the Revolution. It was, of course, regrettable that so much blood had to flow, but what was the alternative? Those dispatched by the Terror were counter-revolutionaries. The vast majority of its victims were people who had been working, directly or indirectly, to turn back the Revolution's course – either by their own efforts or by aiding the enemies against whom the beleaguered Republic was now fighting. However bloody, therefore, the Terror was nevertheless understandable: an essential defence of the Revolution, an expedient to destroy the Revolution's would-be destroyers.

---

[2] F. Furet, *Interpreting the French Revolution* (Cambridge, 1981), pp. 82, 88.

When it ended, it was no surprise that those destroyers began to crawl back into prominence and were soon dismantling much of what had been achieved. The Revolution was over, and most histories of it written before about 1960 stop in 1794. In the classic interpretation, the Thermidorian period of 1794-5, and the Directory which followed it, were times of sordid compromise doomed to failure. Hence the ultimate takeover by a military despot. In the context of this interpretation counter-revolution was not just a matter of conspiring with aristocrats and foreigners to restore the monarchy, hearing Mass from non-juring priests, hoarding vital supplies, or working for the success of the armies of Pitt and Coburg – all capital crimes, sure enough, in the Year II. Counter-revolution was also anything that had appeared to be resisting or obstructing the Revolution's progress towards the Year II, right from the beginning. If the essence of the Revolution was the Jacobin republic, the essence of counter-revolution must be anything that might have prevented its emergence. In other words, it was teleologically defined. The most extreme version of this position is that adopted by one of the last great French defenders of the classic interpretation, Jacques Godechot, who in a much-used book on the Counter-Revolution[3] argues that counter-revolutionary thought actually predates the Revolution itself; apparently it existed even before there was a revolution to counter. 'It would be interesting', he says,[4] 'to study the counter-revolution from around 1770.' It would also, surely, be absurd. Even if we can readily admit that counter-revolutionary thought had distant sources, to call those sources themselves counter-revolutionary is meaningless and impedes, rather than promotes, our understanding of what was really going on in the 1790s.

So pervasive, however, are the assumptions of the classic interpretation that even the most radical revisionists find it hard to shake them off. The great theme of the best recent general survey of the revolutionary period in France,[5] for instance, is the clash between the revolutionary impetus and resistance to it. The argument is that counter-revolution was not simply the activity of *émigré* dreamers and crack-brained plotters, 'not so much aristocratic as massive, extensive, durable and popular'.[6] It is argued, in implicit rejection of the way classic historians

---

[3] J. Godechot, *The Counter-Revolution: Doctrine and Action, 1789-1804* (London, 1972).

[4] Ibid., p. x.

[5] D.M.G. Sutherland, *France, 1789-1815: Revolution and Counter-Revolution* (London, 1985).

[6] Ibid., p. 14.

tended to describe the activity of some thousands of Parisian *sans-culottes* as *the* popular movement, that counter-revolution was also a popular movement. Although not stated in so many words, the evidence piled up throughout the book leads the reader to no other conclusion: counter-revolution was a movement infinitely more popular in terms of sheer numbers than anything Paris threw up. The argument almost seems to be that if there was a popular movement, it was not for the Revolution, but against.

This is an important and stimulating idea, fatal though it must be to any lingering remnants of the classic interpretation. It constitutes a baseline from which we shall all be working for some years. Nor do I question the evidence on which it is based, or the scholarship that has brought it to light. It is no longer possible to maintain that the French Revolution brought much benefit to most of the population of France, or that, after an initial surge of soon-disappointed enthusiasm in 1789, its work had the active support of more than a relatively small minority. It is perfectly clear that the history of the revolutionary years is one of constant resistance to the impetus coming from the centre. Nor was this just a matter of the well-known revolts – the Vendée, the Breton and Norman *Chouannerie*,[7] the sectarian strife in Languedoc, or the great federalist revolt of 1793 when the country's three most important provincial cities, and several lesser ones including its second naval port, rose up against what they depicted as the tyranny of Paris. It is also a matter of innumerable lesser revolts and riots, some hitherto over-looked: the year 1790, for instance, once generally agreed to be the quietest of the Revolution, is now recognised as a time of endemic rural unrest and defiance of the National Assembly's decrees,[8] while the 'White Terror' of the spring of 1795 along the Rhône valley is increasingly being seen as only one facet of the wider phenomenon of lawlessness that marked the whole history of the Directory and indeed also the early years of Napoleon's rule.[9]

---

[7] D.M.G. Sutherland, *The Chouans: The Social Origins of Popular Counter-Revolution in Upper Brittany, 1770-1796* (Oxford, 1982).

[8] S.F. Scott, 'Problems during 1790, the "Peaceful" Year of the French Revolution', *American Historical Review*, 80 (1975), pp. 59-88.

[9] C. Lucas, 'The Problem of the Midi in the French Revolution', *Transactions of the Royal Historical Society*, 5th series, 28 (1978), pp. 1-25; idem, 'Themes in Southern Violence after 9 Thermidor', in G. Lewis and C. Lucas (eds), *Beyond the Terror: Essays in French Regional and Social History, 1794-1815* (Cambridge, 1983), pp. 152-95.

Much of it originated in that final spur which also provoked the Vendée and *Chouan* revolts: conscription. Here were ordinary peasant boys who did not wish to go off and fight the Revolution's foreign enemies, and who would go to almost any lengths to dodge the draft. Emigration itself can also be viewed in this light. The statistical studies of Donald Greer showed us long ago that a large proportion of those who left the country were not nobles embittered at their losses and driven out by social persecution, but ordinary people voting with their feet against the turmoil and disruption that the new order had brought.[10] Looking at matters this way also makes far more comprehensible Greer's other, even more spectacular, statistics: those for the victims of the Terror,[11] where the proportion of ordinary people is yet more crushing. It would be more crushing still if there was any reliable way of quantifying what Richard Cobb has taught us to recognise as the 'anarchic' terror of the autumn of 1793,[12] which probably accounted for as many victims again as those enumerated by Greer, almost all of them ordinary people. If all these instances are added together, what strikes one is the massive *un*popularity of the Revolution among those who had to live through it. The Terror looks like the desperate ploy of a beleaguered minority of ideologues to maintain their grip on power in the face of the hostility of most of their fellow citizens. When those who ran it justified it on the grounds that the Republic was beset with enemies, they were speaking nothing less than the truth.

But was it beset by *counter*-revolutionary enemies? That is the question I should like to turn to now. For as long as we describe resistance to the Revolution in these terms, we are in a sense still accepting much of the Jacobin or neo-Jacobin picture enshrined in the classic interpretation: all we have abandoned so far is the claim, made frequently enough by Jacobins, that the Revolution enjoyed widespread popular support in France, and that the aspirations of the *sans-culottes* were the authentic expression of popular sovereignty. Even if we accept that most of the French people were soon disappointed with the achievement of the

---

[10] D. Greer, *The Incidence of the Emigration during the French Revolution* (Cambridge, MA, 1951).

[11] Idem, *The Incidence of the Terror during the French Revolution: A Statistical Interpretation* (Cambridge, MA, 1935).

[12] R. Cobb, *Les armées révolutionnaires: instrument de la Terreur dans les départements, Avril 1793-Floréal An II*, 2 vols (Paris and The Hague, 1961-63).

Revolution, and that vast numbers were positively outraged and alienated, so long as we assume that counter-revolution, a desire to go back to 1789 or beyond, was their natural reflex, we are still allowing ourselves to be dominated to a remarkable degree by the classic interpretation.

Some of the resistance we are discussing *was* plainly counter-revolutionary. The plottings of the princely *émigrés* and their circles in Turin and subsequently in Koblenz or Verona were quite explicitly aimed at overthrowing and reversing everything that had been done since 23 June 1789, the date of the famous royal session at which Louis XVI repudiated the National Assembly's seizure of sovereignty six days previously and attempted to impose a programme of limited reform which would have left much of the *ancien régime* intact. Similarly, on a more local level, the Catholics in and around Nîmes, whose leaders were in regular contact from 1790 onwards with the *émigré* court, and who staged defiant rallies in the form of the camps at Jalès, had the clear objective of reversing the seizure of power by Protestants that had been the first and momentous consequence of the Revolution in their area.[13]

But what has struck the increasing number of scholars working on aspects of internal resistance in the 1790s, whether the Vendée, *Chouannerie* or the federalist revolt, has been the relative vagueness and incoherence of the rebels' ideas about what might come after successful resistance. They knew what they were against, but they were far less certain about what they were for. True, the rebels in the Vendée called themselves a Catholic and Royal Army, but even that was vague enough. They identified with church and king because the regime they opposed was against those things. The 'federalists' of 1793, of course, identified with neither, hotly proclaiming their republicanism and ostentatiously ignoring the religious question. To lump all these shades of attitude and opinion together under the one counter-revolutionary label might be acceptable in contemporary polemics, where anything obstructing the war effort might be construed as likely to contribute to the reinstatement of the *émigrés* with foreign support, and thereby to the achievement of their incontestably counter-revolutionary aims, but it does nothing to promote our understanding of what really motivated the bulk of the active resistance encountered by French governments in the 1790s.

---

[13] G. Lewis, *The Second Vendéee: The Continuity of Counter-Revolution in the Department of the Gard, 1789-1815* (Oxford, 1978).

Awareness of these difficulties, in the course of the 1980s, produced a new concept for understanding these movements of resistance. A distinction has been drawn between *counter*-revolution and *anti*-revolution. It is a notion originated by Colin Lucas, whose own researches have latterly been concentrated on popular movements of resistance in the south and south east of France. He first launched the term 'anti-revolution' in 1984, at a conference in Paris,[14] and in the light of what I have argued I hope that what it is meant to encompass will be obvious. Anti-revolutionaries did not want to turn the clock back to the *ancien régime*. They merely wanted the Revolution, which had succeeded that regime, to have done different things, or not to have done certain things.

What often drove them on was not so much a spirit of reaction as one of disappointment. In the spring of 1789 there was a movement of boundless hope, a feeling that all problems and all difficulties would be resolved by the great movement of national regeneration that was about to begin. It was only encouraged by the process of compiling *cahiers*, grievance lists in which the king's subjects were officially invited to set out their discontents, with the implicit hint that the estates-general would redress them all. Such a hope was never realistic, but it was no less powerful for that, and when it came to nothing the let-down was all the more bitter. Instead of resolving the economic crisis, the Revolution made it worse. Instead of diminishing taxes and rents, it made them more heavy. Instead of making society more harmonious, it increased divisions. Instead of reinforcing law and order and public morality, it boosted lawlessness, crime and racketeering. Most important, perhaps, instead of lightening the weight of government on the governed, it increased it in almost every sphere. In a word, the Revolution accelerated many of the trends which a careful reading of the *cahiers* suggested most of Louis XVI's subjects wanted to stop or reverse. It is scarcely surprising, therefore, that so many of those subjects, now officially transmuted into citizens, sooner or later vented their disappointment and frustration by becoming anti-revolutionaries.

Counter-revolutionaries naturally tried to capitalise on this disillusionment. One of the arguments they were soon putting about was that the *cahiers* had provided no mandate for what was subsequently done. It is striking how little this line succeeded. Counter-revolution failed, one might say, largely because it proved unable to take over anti-revolution.

[14] C. Lucas, 'Résistances populaires à la Révolution dans le sud-est', in J. Nicolas (ed.), *Mouvements populaires et conscience sociale* (Paris, 1985), pp. 473-85.

Yet one can see why this was the case, once one recognises that anti-revolution was above all a reflex of disappointment. Counter-revolutionaries wanted to restore, or all-but restore, the *ancien régime*. Anti-revolutionaries had already rejected that and did not want it back. It was simply that they did not want what the Revolution had put in its place, either.

In promoting explanations such as these, the notion of anti-revolution, as something quite distinct from counter-revolution, represents an important and fruitful refinement of our understanding of resistance to the French Revolution. In so far as the French Revolution is a paradigm, perhaps the notion could also prove conceptually useful in the study of others. Even so, it has its dangers, and I want to conclude by reflecting on two of them. The first relates to some of the purposes to which it has already been put. Ideas spawned in the English-speaking world about the Revolution have always been slow to win acceptance in France, although in recent years the speed of penetration has markedly picked up. But even by recent standards, anti-revolution has prospered with amazing speed, having been taken up within a year by no less a person than the most vigorous defender of the classic interpretation of the Revolution, Claude Mazauric.[15]

The best sort of Marxist, Mazauric is undaunted by empirical difficulties, and he is always prepared to defend the central tenets of the creed by reformulating the outworks so as to rebut empiricist criticism. We have to accept, he now argues, that most of those who resisted the Revolution were not counter-revolutionaries: they had no programme for de-revolutionising France, and in that sense were merely anti-revolutionaries. But then, says Mazauric, what would you expect? The bourgeois revolution was bound to run against popular interests. Although the bourgeoisie could not have achieved their Revolution without popular intervention and help, they never had any intention of promoting popular interests where they did not coincide with their own. The class interests of the bourgeoisie and the common people of France from whose ranks most anti-revolutionaries were drawn, were fundamentally opposed. Since the object of the Revolution was to promote the class interests of the bourgeoisie, it is scarcely surprising that other classes opposed it, the populace quite as much as the feudal nobility. In

---

[15] C. Mazauric, 'Autopsie d'un échec: la résistance à l'anti-révolution et la défaite de la contre-révolution', in F. Lebrun and R. Dupuy (eds), *Les résistance à la révolution* (Paris, 1987), pp. 237-44.

this way, new perceptions of resistance to the Revolution are made to fit in neatly with the traditional, classic, Marxist/Jacobin overview, and thereby reinforce a refusal to question any other of the basic assumptions which have been thoroughly undermined during the past thirty years or so of fervent debate about the fundamental nature of he Revolution. To save a Marxist view of the Revolution, in other words, Mazauric is quite happy to abandon the Jacobinical idea of *counter-revolution* to empiricist attack. Those persuaded of the value of the anti-revolutionary distinction should beware that it is not necessarily one more nail in the coffin of the classic interpretation: it can be made compatible with it – or at least with its Marxist refinements.

This suggests that a careful unpicking of the idea of counter-revolution will only take us so far, and might well prove less radical a breakthrough than it seems at first sight, unless we take the whole process a step further to a point that I think someone like Mazauric would find difficult to integrate with his convictions. What I am suggesting is that we rethink our use of the term 'the Revolution' itself.

I am not, of course, advocating anything so utopian as to try to abandon it altogether, even if that were desirable in some ideal world. We cannot abolish the French Revolution from history or histori-ography. What we can do is to use the term far more circumspectly than we have tended to do, and try to avoid personalising it or speaking of it as a single event – the Revolution did this or that, the Revolution demanded something or achieved something – as if it had some coherent, conscious, objective and unitary existence that can be separated from those involved in it and the circumstances they had to contend with. Many of those involved did speak of it in this way, all the time. But as I tried to suggest earlier on, this tendency lies at the very root of the problems we are confronting.

The classic interpretation derives directly from the Jacobin image of the Revolution as a single, logical and coherent event. Yet all the work of recent years has tended to suggest that the whole experience was the product of a series of accidents, chances and mischances, choices (unfortunate but real enough), and fateful miscalculations; and that, thanks to all these things, events moved in certain directions that nobody could have foreseen or, in many cases, even desired or dreamed of.[16] The Revolution never ever meant one thing or coherent set of things, but at different moments its payload, as it were, differed. How else can

---

[16] See N. Hampson, *Prelude to Terror* (Oxford, 1988).

we explain a movement (if we should even allow ourselves to call it that) which began with the triumphant storming of a state prison but within four years produced a regime that interned tens of thousands of suspects? Men who in 1790 proclaimed peace and non-aggression to all nations but who two years later launched a war that was to last the best part of a generation, and at one time or another involved hostilities against every state in Europe? Reformers who wished to purify the church and make it serve the faithful better, but who ended up closing down every church in France and sanctioning every sort of blasphemous outrage against religious observance? Subjects who wept in 1789 at the benevolence of the best of kings, but who, four years later, cut off his head in the name of a republic nobody had shown any sign of wanting when the Revolution began? One could go on with such glaring contrasts, which have done so much to invest the French Revolution with its terrible fascination for onlookers, both at the time and since. The sheer contrast between aspiration and achievement has never ceased to appal, and to pose a formidable challenge to explanation.

In order to take up that challenge, we surely need to go beyond the response of a small group of ideologues (and all recent studies of counter- or anti-revolutionaries are making increasingly clear just how small it was) who wove events into what they longed to believe was a pre-ordained and predictable pattern and then proclaimed, at whatever point they had reached, that the Revolution's course and meaning were clear, and that whoever opposed or resisted their interpretation was self-evidently counter-revolutionary. Anatomising resistance to the Revolution, in other words, involves anatomising the Revolution itself, and recognising that much of what happened during that turbulent decade had no necessary relationship with the ideology proclaimed in 1789 and modified by the great quarrels, first with the church and then with the monarchy – whatever Jacobins might proclaim.

It was not *necessary* for the purposes of securing the gains of 1789 that, say, paper money should be launched on the security of confiscated church lands, with all the inflationary consequences that followed. It was not *necessary* that such an uncompromising attitude to the church in general should have been taken, with all the divisive results that stemmed from that. Above all, it was not *necessary* that the Legislative Assembly should try to export France's self-imposed problems by inflicting them on her neighbours through launching a war against Europe – the most fateful of all choices made by those who inherited power from the defunct *ancien régime*. These were all occasions when men had real choices, and revolutionary commitment dictated no obvious course. The debates which preceded the actual decisions demonstrate that plainly enough. Those decisions, once taken, had fateful consequences for ordinary French people, consequences which, abundant studies have convincingly shown, pushed many of them in directions which would inexorably be called counter-revolutionary, as rebels protested at the economic hardship, the moral and spiritual disruption, and the unprecedented demands of organisation and manpower that these great decisions entailed.

It was not *the* Revolution that did all this, and made all these demands, whatever Jacobins might say to justify it all. It was certain groups of individuals entrusted with national power and authority at critical junctures. They were animated by certain principles and loyalties which they identified with the Revolution, sure enough, but for all that, made each choice as a thing in itself rather than as part of some obvious pattern or plan. If we look at matters in this way, the French Revolution, and resistance to it, whether we call it anti- or counter-revolutionary, inevitably will begin to appear less principled, less pre-ordained, less apocalyptic, though scarcely less tragic in its consequences.

12

Thomas Paine and the Girondins

The radicalism of Thomas Paine, Englishman, and Thomas Paine, United States Citizen, is well established and recognised. It is useful nevertheless at the outset to remind ourselves briefly of Paine's claim to radicalism in the English-speaking world; because my main purpose is to establish those claims in the French-speaking world, too. Paine established his credentials in 1776, when he advised the American rebels in *Common Sense* to renounce their allegiance to George III and proclaim themselves an independent republic. By 1778, in the pamphlet series, *The Crisis*, he was advising the people of Great Britain to get rid of monarchy too. He took this theme up more memorably in Part 2 of *Rights of Man*, published in the spring of 1792, where monarchy was denounced as 'the master-fraud, which shelters all others'; and where he put forward a comprehensive programme, not for *reforming* the British constitution, but for *giving* his native country a constitution for the first time; since he believed that until then all it had was 'merely a form of Government without a constitution' – a situation which obtains to this day. His prescriptions were radical indeed: redistributive taxation, an end to primogeniture, old age pensions, subsidised education, and of course a written constitution ensuring fair representation of the sovereign people and strict constraints on the abuse of power. By 1796 he was publicly castigating his old hero, George Washington, for just such abuses of power and monarchical tendencies. And just before that he had thrown down a challenge to Christians of all persuasions with *The Age of Reason*, that democratic denunciation of theology, revealed religion and those who lived well on the profits of such impostures – the clergy.

Throughout most of these writings the message of Thomas Paine is that there are better ways of conducting human affairs; that they can be

achieved if men recognise their own capacities, and their own autonomy; and that, for the first time in human history, a better way has been
attempted. It has been attempted in America, the example of which
suffuses the *Rights of Man* as much as if not more than that of France,
especially in Part 2; and of course, from 1789 it has been attempted in
France, when men seized control of their own destiny, not on the edge of
virgin forests, where it was relatively easy to begin afresh, but in the very
corrupt heart of old Europe, an 'Augean stable of parasites and
plunderers too abominably filthy to be cleansed, by anything short of a
complete and universal Revolution'. Apart from refuting Burke and his
'horrid principles', the avowed purpose of *Rights of Man* was to offer an
accessible translation into English of the founding manifesto of the
French Revolution, the *Declaration of the Rights of Man and the Citizen* of
August 1789, the destined preamble (as it still was when Part I of Paine's
book was published in the spring of 1791) of the new French
constitution.

All this is well known. What is perhaps less well known is that when he
wrote Part I of *Rights of Man* Paine scarcely knew France. He had spent
three months there in 1787. He had spent most of his time there in the
company of Americans, or Frenchmen like Lafayette who liked to speak
English. Although we have no reason to doubt that the translation of the
Declaration of the Rights of Man and the Citizen is his own, it is well attested
that he *spoke* no French. We all know what a world of difference there is
between using and understanding the written, as opposed to the spoken
word in a foreign language. Thus it was that when, in January 1793, as a
member of the French national Convention, he made his only attempt to
address his fellow deputies, he stood mute on the tribune while his
speech was read for him. Nor had he, in France in 1787, foreseen the
Revolution; much less that it would turn republican. Louis XVI at this
time was in fact a king he rather approved of, for had he not come to the
aid of the United States in its struggle for independence? Of *revolutionary*
France he knew nothing at first hand until the end of 1789; and the
account which he gives in *Rights of Man* of events there between the fall
of the Bastille and the October Days is entirely second-hand, even if the
source of his information was no less an observer than Thomas
Jefferson. But his first sojourn in regenerated Paris, during the first
three months of 1790, was at a time when the Revolution's initial
enthusiasms had not yet turned sour; and when he returned to England
to take up cudgels on its behalf, it was this euphoric phase that was his
only direct experience of it. By the time he returned once more to Paris,

in the spring of 1791, *Rights of Man* had been published, and he was now the best-known defender in the world of two revolutions.

By that time, however, the French Revolution had moved on; and the euphoric consensus of twelve months before had not survived. The costs of comprehensive revolution were becoming apparent, and bitter divisions and resentments were beginning to open up and fester, notably over the questions of religion, and of the monarchy. Always suspected but never proven, the king's hostility to the work of the Revolution was brought to the surface by the religious question in the spring of 1791. As that year opened, all beneficed clergy in France were required to take an oath of loyalty to the constitution. Those who refused to do so were to lose their benefices. Louis XVI had sanctioned this law, but he knew (as the world was to know some months later) that the pope disapproved of the oath. Accordingly the king refused to confess to or receive the sacraments from any priest who had taken it. This refusal could not be disguised, so that the spring saw mounting suspicion of the king and his intentions. This atmosphere in turn impelled the king to think of escaping the country; which he finally tried, with disastrous results, on 21 June: the ill-fated flight to Varennes. Paine was in Paris as this storm blew up, then broke; and as in 1776 his reaction was one of common-sense. The king had proved impossible to deal with, so the only solution was a republic.

What was Paine doing in France that spring? He was returning to where the action was; and perhaps keeping prudently out of England until the first storm over his book blew itself out. The company he kept there was that of his old, English-speaking friends. Jefferson had by now returned to America, but Lafayette was very much in the centre of things, as commander of the National Guard. Paine lodged with Condorcet, the last of the *philosophes*; was on familiar terms with Brissot, a leading journalist and enthusiast for all things American; and was closely associated with one of the leading intellectual centres of early revolutionary Paris, the *Cercle Social*.

The *Cercle Social* has long enjoyed a special reputation among historians. Among the men of the left who dominated historiography of the French Revolution for two thirds of this century, the *Cercle Social* was identified as a centre of progressive thought and radicalism. Karl Marx himself commended it, even if he thought much of its activity utopian. But in its concern for wider democracy and social justice, and the campaign it fought in its famous newspaper, the *Bouche de Fer*, against the electoral restrictions envisaged by the National Assembly, it was seen as forward-lookiong and a precursor of the popular values which were to triumph, however briefly, in 1793-94. It proudly proclaimed itself committed to the ideas of the Enlightenment; and particularly those of Rousseau; and it made no secret of the inspiration it derived from freemasonry. No wonder Paine was drawn into its circle. He was a democrat, he was a fervent disciple of the rational Enlightenment, and indeed a sympathiser with masonic ideals, on which late in life he wrote an essay. When the king fled, members of the *Cercle Social* were among the first to draw the obvious conclusion that now was the time to get rid of the monarchy entirely and establish a republic.

Having Paine among them at this moment seemed providential, and they turned to him, as the world's best known anti-monarchist, to put their views into words. When some of them formed themselves into a 'Society of Republicans' and launched a journal *The Republican* to propagate their cause, they had Paine write the leading articles and then translated them for him. They asked him, too, to write a republican manifesto which appeared all over Paris on 1 July, a clear attempt to re-enact the triumph of *Common Sense* in America fifteen years beforehand. This time it did not work; or at least it did not work in the same way. There is no doubt that French republicanism, which did not exist in 1789, was born in the weeks following the flight to Varennes, and that Paine played a key role in articulating it. But it was far from a movement that swept the nation overnight, as it had in America. Its immediate fate was to be crushed, when republican petitioners were shot down by the Paris national guard on 17 July in the massacre of the *Champ de Mars*. It took another year to get rid of Louis XVI, and for a lot of that time republicanism had gone underground. Paine himself returned to England on 13 July, just before the massacre, to write Part II of *Rights of Man*, and he remained there, in the thick of controversy, for the next fourteen months. He played no active and direct part in the final overthrow of the French monarchy, on 10 August 1792, but his republican credentials were acknowledged when he was proclaimed a French citizen and, the next month, elected by no less than three departments as a member of the Convention which was to endow France with a republican constitution.

But let me now briefly return to the *Cercle Social*. It used to be thought that it, and the *Bouche de Fer*, disappeared forever in the anti-republican repression that followed the Champ de Mars massacre. Historians therefore treated it as a curious but premature forerunner of more serious reform that was to come later; but with no direct connection with the Jacobin republic of the Year II, which was the real, if ill-fated, social and political experiment. In 1986, however, the American historian

Gary Kates devoted the first ever scholarly monograph to the *Cercle Social* and its history, and he discovered a number of remarkable surprises. He was able to show that the group behind the *Cercle* and the *Bouche de Fer* did not disperse or cease their activities after July 1791; they simply became less a club than a publishing house. As such, they remained an influential source of radicalism and republicanism. But those they supported and worked with were not, as you might expect, the Jacobins who were to triumph in 1793. The *Bouche de Fer* was in fact the mouthpiece of those who were to be the Jacobins' main opponents in 1793, and whom they and the *sans-culottes* of Paris were to purge from the Convention at the beginning of June that year – the Girondins. People like Brissot, Condorcet, Roland; and of course Paine.

Clearly this poses a major problem of interpretation and understanding. How could people who had been so radical in 1791 have become so moderate in 1792 and 1793? Historians of the Girondins have always wrestled to some extent with such difficulties, but Kates' research has made them even more acute. In their early days we now know their leaders were a lot more radical than we thought, so the contrast is even more glaring. This in turn highlights what has always been something of a problem in the interpretation of Thomas Paine. How was it that the great radical republican, once he was elected to the Convention and became an honorary French citizen, sat and voted with the Girondin moderates and – irony of ironies – even tried to spare Louis XVI's life? For the famous occasion mentioned earlier when he had a long speech read to the Convention was in fact during the voting on what penalty to impose on the now convicted king. Paine's solution was that he should not be executed, but kept in prison until the end of the war, then banished to the United States, where he should pass the rest of his life learning from the everyday example of a free and republican people what liberty really meant: 'There . . . far removed from the miseries and crimes of royalty, he may learn, from the constant aspect of public prosperity, that the true system of government consists not in kings, but in fair, equal and honourable representation.'

Paine's stated grounds for preferring this elaborate form of penalty were twofold. One was sentimental: that Louis XVI, though a despot, had been a patron of liberty at the time of the American Revolution, and in helping the Americans to free themselves, had performed 'a good, a great action'. The other was more principled: Paine was opposed to the death penalty. 'This cause', he declared, 'must find its advocates in every corner where enlightened politicians and lovers of humanity exist.' In a pointed though in no way rancorous reference to one of the leading advocates of killing the king, he noted that at an earlier stage in the Revolution Robespierre had actually moved, unsuccessfully, the abolition of capital punishment. What Paine is saying here, in effect, is that Robespierre had changed his principles but I have not changed mine. As far as he was concerned, principles were what the Age of Revolution was all about: 'I have no personal interest in any of these matters' he said to Danton some months later, just before the downfall of the Girondins, 'nor in party disputes. I attend only to general principles.'

So, it seems to me, did the Girondins. This is surely the key to the difficulties of interpretation thrown up by Kates' conclusions on the *Cercle Social*. For too long the Girondins have been depicted as social conservatives whose domination of the Convention had to be broken if the progressive and popular programme of the Jacobins and *sans-culottes* was to triumph. But in 1972, in what seems to me the most important book ever written about the politics of the Convention, the Australian historian Alison Patrick demonstrated conclusively that those called Girondins were far from the dominant or leading group in the Convention; and she noted, what detached observers ought surely to have remarked on long before, that they were on the losing side in most of the crucial votes. While accepting that none of the groups could be legitimately described, or would have been content to be described, as political parties, she was able to demonstrate clear voting patterns, which could only be made sense of by postulating that it was the Jacobins, not the Girondins, who were running the country in the winter of 1792-93. She also showed that those whose voting patterns could be described as Jacobin tended to be older and more politically experienced than their opponents. They were practical men; and they said that there was a war on, and that it was going badly, and that every effort had to be made to win it; or the Revolution would not survive. That was why the Convention had to co-operate with the *sans-culottes*, the people of Paris who had overthrown the monarchy. It was true that the *sans-culottes* had perpetrated the horrifying September massacres a few weeks earlier, but with the Convention sitting in Paris there was no alternative but to go along with what these people wanted, even if that went against many of the things that the Revolution of 1789 had been all about.

What came about in 1792-94, the period of the so-called Jacobin republic, was the complete reversal of all that the National Assembly had tried to establish in 1789 and 1790. Government was centralised, when the aim of the Revolution of 1789 was *de*-centralisation. Power at the centre was unified, when the aim in 1789 had been a separation of powers. Elections were suspended, when regular accountability had been the initial aspiration. Justice was politicised, when a dream of 1789 had been to make it independent. A controlled economy was introduced, when educated opinion had been unanimous that free trade was the natural economic order. I am not saying that the Jacobins necessarily believed in any of this, any more than they believed in some of the more utopian declarations made during their period of power but – significantly – never implemented. What they did believe was that, like it or not, it had to be done: just as most of them plainly did not believe in the purging of the Convention in June 1793, and agonised for weeks before acquiescing in the forcible removal of elected deputies from the national representation. Their reluctance to see this happen strikes me as perfectly genuine; but in the end they concluded it was necessary in order to remove a major obstacle in the way of saving France and its revolution from destruction.

What was that obstacle? In a word, Girondin intransigence. The Girondins did not believe that the republic should conduct its affairs according to the desires and dictates of the people of Paris; and they did not believe, either, that the issue could be postponed. That was perhaps the essential difference between them and the Jacobins, a difference between idealists and pragmatists; or if you like, between first principles and forced principles. Because, argued the Girondins (and you can distil this from their innumerable speeches), the Parisian issue goes right to the heart of what the Revolution is about. If the *sans-culottes* can dictate to the Convention, they do so by force and intimidation, rather than by law. They have shown in their September massacres what they are prepared to do to their opponents – massacre them in cold blood without trial or any semblance of legality. In 1789 the people of France set out to establish the rule of law and to guarantee the civil rights of all citizens. How could one run the country by taking orders from those who had shown nothing but contempt for those principles? Besides, the Convention was the representative body of the entire Nation, and not just Paris. The deputies of the capital, the core of the Jacobins, number only two dozen, and yet they are trying to force the priorities of their constituents down the throats of the representatives of the rest of the nation, much of which plainly does not want to be dictated to in this way. The power wielded by Paris was an affront to the electoral principle, an attempt to confiscate national sovereignty by a small section of the Nation, and because of that yet another clear contravention of the Revolution's original principles.

It was not even as if the *sans-culottes* spoke for the whole of Paris. Sensible, educated, enlightened people had gone to ground: the ignorant mob had taken over, the sort of people men of education had always thought should not be entrusted with power, and whom they tried to deprive of the vote in 1790. What would happen if such people got their way was seen in the case of the grain trade, on which the *sans-culottes* wanted strict controls, just as there had been during most of the old regime. Towards the end the royal ministers had toyed timidly with a freer market, and this was not the least of the reasons why ministers were so unpopular in 1789; but almost unanimously the men elected to the National Assembly in that year believed that the Revolution offered an opportunity to establish an enlightened freedom once and for all – the first unequivocal triumph for free market economics. The *sans-culottes* wanted to reverse that, and in 1793 they succeeded in doing so by forcing the Convention to decree the law of the Maximum, in the teeth of Girondin opposition initially, and then only finally and fully after they had been purged. In Girondin eyes this was the triumph of sheer ignorance and prejudice over enlightened principles – again the very antithesis of what the French Revolution was supposed to be. Ever since the days of the *Cercle Social* the Girondins had made plain their belief that the Revolution was the fruit of the Enlightenment, and an opportunity to put into practice enlightened principles in a way that would have been impossible under the old order. These opportunities would be lost if the ignorant were allowed to override with their prejudices the benevolent convictions of educated men.

All this, it seems to me, suggests that the conventional label of *moderates*, so often attached to the Girondins, is in fact profoundly inappropriate. Moderates make and live by compromises, steer a middle course, avoid extremes. Only the political overlay resulting from generations of left-wing adulation of Jacobin populism as the ancestor of later socialisms, only this has prevented historians from seeing that the moderates, in the sense of the compromisers, the realists, the deal-makers, were the Jacobins. The real revolutionaries, in the sense of the men who put principles before practicalities, were the Girondins. It was they who were the starry-eyed idealists, who believed that you could not defend the principles of the French Revolution by compromising them; and that if the Rights of Man were a universal code they could only be defended by being observed. Those who have written about them in our own time have all agreed that there was no sense in which they constituted a party, or anything like one, and that, indeed, they often indignantly rejected charges that they were one. But this is entirely what one would expect if they were idealists of the sort I am suggesting. Deputies were not there to pursue prearranged programmes or to make deals. They were there to vote according to their conscience and their principles about the public welfare. The party, if there was one, was the Parisian delegation with its regular block-voting and its outside headquarters at the Jacobin club, its systematic conciliation of the *sans-culottes* and compromising of the principles of 1789. The mere fact that only something like party organisations makes representative assemblies remotely manageable was of no consequence. What was right would be obvious, and opinion should not need to be dragooned in order that right triumphed.

This faith in the conquering power of true principles is also shown in the Girondins' attitude to foreign powers. It was they who launched the movement towards war in the autumn of 1791, not because they wanted the vast generation-long upheaval that resulted, but because they thought the conflict was bound to be short, sharp – and victorious. And that was because the French cause was so self-evidently right that subject peoples groaning to follow the French example would rise up at the approach of French arms and overthrow their despotic rulers; and because the enthusiasm and faith in liberty of the regenerated French nation would overthrow the paper-tiger armies of those same despots. After initial uncertainties, in the autumn of 1792 that is exactly what seemed to happen, and it was in these circumstances that Brissot declared that France must set all Europe alight, and that the Girondins induced the Convention to offer French fraternity and help to all nations seeking to recover their liberty. This was certainly no moderate policy; and it so alarmed the supposedly extreme Jacobins that in April 1793 they carried a vote rescinding the fraternity and help decree. They were right, of course. Such an open-ended offer was totally reckless and utopian. But what it is evidence of, once again, is the proposition that I have been arguing, that the true French revolutionaries were not the pragmatic, practical, compromising Jacobins, but the principled, *im*practical, intransigent Girondins. This conclusion makes their ancestry in the utopian *Cercle Social* no longer surprising, but on the contrary entirely consistent and to be expected. It also makes them obvious soulmates for Thomas Paine.

This brings us back to Paine. I hope that this lengthy detour about the nature of the Girondins does not seem irrelevant. It ought no longer to seem the least surprising that during his time as a deputy to the Convention he should have been identified as a Girondin. All his previous links with France (with the exception of Lafayette, who had by then defected to the Austrians) were with those who now constituted the Girondin leadership. All his radical, republican instincts were also with men who believed that, even in wartime, the French nation could be governed in accordance with the rights of man and the rule of law rather than the demands of metropolitan pressure groups and threats of force. The true revolutionaries were those who wanted to make the Revolution and its principles work, rather than postpone their implementation until emergencies were over. If the principles of 1789 were sound, and valid, they should be workable, and proof against transient circumstances. Paine's writings, too, are steeped in the conviction that rational, radical republicanism works. In revolutions that aim at positive good, he wrote in Part II of *Rights of Man*,

> Reason and discussion, persuasion and conviction, become the weapons in the contest, and it is only when those are attempted to be suppressed that recourse is had to violence. When men unite in agreeing that a *thing is good*, could it be obtained . . . the object is more than half accomplished. What they approve as the end they will promote in the means.

Now we may say that such an approach to public affairs is impossibly naïve and utopian, and doomed to disappointment. In Paine's case it certainly was. In June 1793 his Girondin friends were expelled from the Convention and arrested; in October, under pressure from their *sans-culotte* enemies, they were executed; at the end of the year Paine himself was arrested, and remained in prison for nine months, seven of them under real threat of being guillotined. When he turned to his beloved United States to secure his release, as one of their most eminent citizens, they made no great efforts on his behalf. Although the second-rank Girondins who remained alive were restored, like him, to their seats in the Convention in the autumn of 1794, and were influential in producing the directorial constitution of the Year III, that attempt to get back to the first principles of 1789 was no more successful than the first revolutionary constitution, and within four years had been overthrown by a military coup, just as Burke had predicted would happen, much to Paine's scorn, in 1790.

Despairing of France, Paine returned in 1802 to America, only to find that his popularity had vanished there too as a result of the anti-Christian polemics of *The Age of Reason*. At the time of the French Revolution's bicentenary in 1989, it was fashionable to sneer at the attempt made 200 years ago to build a new, better, more humane and more rational world. Weighty volumes were written to prove that the whole enterprise was doomed from the start to end in blood, destruction and terror. As regimes collapsed across Europe the lesson was drawn that the only wise approach is to be practical, and sensible, and to accept things as they are rather than trying to build a better world. Thomas Paine and the Girondins thought otherwise and, though they failed to bring the world of their dreams into being, there is a genuine tragic heroism in their *naïveté* – which the Girondins who were executed carried through to the end, singing the *Marseillaise* as they went to the guillotine. This was not empty swagger. Between the inertia and absurdities of the old order, and the butchery perpetrated by the practical, reality-facing Jacobins, these true revolutionaries offered not a moderate middle course, but an extreme commitment to the improvement of human affairs by reason, argument and example. We can surely applaud their ambition, and lament their failures, even as we shake our heads at their sad overconfidence that these pure ends could be achieved by means just as pure.

13

Avoiding Revolution in the Revolutionary Age

How many people now remember Mrs Thatcher's unseemly intervention in the French Revolutionary bicentenary celebrations in July 1989?
It was not a creditable episode. Why were the French making such a fuss
about the Rights of Man, she said. They didn't invent them, the British
did; or if not the British, then the ancient Greeks. Not only was this rude;
it was also rich, coming from the head of a government which had spent
much of 1988 trying to play down the *tercentenary* of a revolution which
finally established representative government in Great Britain. Characteristically, the British government's ambivalence towards its own
revolutionary heritage was motivated by contemporary political concerns: the effect which too much exulting in the thwarting of popish
tyranny might have in Ireland. Equally characteristically, the government of France takes a loftier view of its own heritage, or does so long as
a socialist sits in the Elysée. The French Revolution, after all, was a far
greater upheaval than that of 1688. It led, indeed, to a redefinition of
the very name and concept of Revolution so fundamental that by this
new criterion the bloodless expulsion of James II has often been denied
any claim to be called revolutionary at all. And it stood for the rights, not
just of the members of one nation, as that of 1688 did, but those of all
mankind. No wonder President Mitterand chose human rights as the
theme for the bicentenary. The French Revolution, unlike the English
(if it even was one) was an event of universal significance for the whole of
mankind.

There is a long tradition behind this approach. It goes back to 1789
itself, when right from the start the French identified their cause with
universal principles, valid for all nations. In practice we know that the
Declaration of the Rights of Man and the Citizen promulgated on 26
August 1789 strongly reflected overwhelmingly French circumstances

and preoccupations, and took the final form it did as a result of a very particular process of discussion, debate and refinement, carried on in a uniquely charged atmosphere. But once the declaration was proclaimed, all that was forgotten. It became the founding manifesto of a movement of universal significance and validity, and it was at once recognised as such all over Europe. The ideals espoused by the French revolutionaries in August 1789, which meant the declaration plus the abolition of feudalism and privilege effected on the night of 4th, three weeks beforehand, became the heart of a revolutionary ideology which explicitly rejected a political and social *ancien régime* in the name of universal principles. Doing so, it invited people everywhere to emulate the French example and overthrow their own *anciens régimes* – at first by implication, but by 1792 quite explicitly as France declared war on German monarchs and promised fraternity and help to all peoples seeking to recover their liberty. By then the example, and the ideology, of the French Revolution were both intended and seen as a challenge to established orders all over Europe, an invitation to Revolution everywhere.

What actually happened? The answer is, next to nothing. Nowhere else in Europe witnessed anything comparable to what occurred in France. It is all too easy to be dazzled by the enthusiastic effusions of poets, philosophers and literary onlookers when they heard in 1789 of the fall of the Bastille; and to forget that by 1792 most of these early friends had fallen away. If we go from there to look for revolutionary outbreaks, rather than mere expressions of enthusiasm and sympathy, in the Europe of the 1790s, we emerge with a pretty thin haul. In Russia, largest of European states, we find a renewal of peasant unrest, in which vague rumours of upheavals further west may have played some part, but nothing more. In Austria and Spain, minor conspiracies mouthing French-inspired slogans, but involving no more than a few dozen intellectuals. In Germany there was some peasant unrest which again, as in Russia, may have taken some comfort from what was reputed to be going on in France; but German Jacobins were never more than a tiny minority anywhere, and only moved into action when invading French armies had already done the real work for them by removing their old rulers and the apparatus of their states. The same can be said of Italy. There seem to have been more genuine Jacobins there, although even then I suspect a count would not reveal more than a few thousand. None of them lifted a finger before the French arrived, and when their protectors withdrew temporarily in 1798 they were swamped by massive popular hostility to the invaders, their legacy, and to those who had collaborated with them.

As to the Low Countries, what happened there owed little to the French example, although invasion forced a French clamp upon it. Upheavals in the Dutch Republic antedated the French Revolution by almost a decade. The French invasion of 1795 was most significant for internal Dutch affairs as a reversal of the Prussian-backed regime of Orange repression which had brought to an end the previous unrest in 1787. And the Brabant revolution, too, which plunged Belgium into turmoil three years before the fall of the Bastille, had its own objectives and preoccupations which were very different from those of the French, hard though Europe's self-styled regenerators found it to believe. Although a minority of the Belgian revolutionaries, the Vonckists, derived some inspiration from the French example, the vast majority of Belgians wanted nothing to do with the French or their ideas: three years after they found themselves forced to be French citizens, the peasantry showed what they thought of their new status in the great peasant war of 1798.

Resistance to foreign domination also largely explains the Polish uprising of 1794. Although Catherine II called it Jacobinical, although some Poles formed clubs and sang the *Marseillaise*, and although approving noises were made in France, Kosciuscko's great struggle was in reality one more round in the endless Polish quarrel with geography – and like previous and subsequent ones it was soon snuffed out, with the French offering nothing but words to help sustain it.

Finally, there is Great Britain. Most British historians seem to agree that there was no danger of revolution there. Whereas it is probably true that there were more sympathisers with revolutionary France and its aspirations in Great Britain than in any other state in Europe (with the possible exception of the Dutch Republic), most of that sympathy was channelled into a characteristically native form: agitation for parliamentary reform – the great pathetic fallacy of British history. British democrats were obsessed with means rather than ends. It is, of course, true that the British realms witnessed the only major pro-French uprisings of the revolutionary decade: the great Irish rebellion of 1798. It was bloodier, proportionately, than the Terror, and fought with a savagery unmatched except perhaps in Poland or the Vendée.

But the parallels with Poland do not end there. Even for the United Irishmen who planned it, it was really more anti-British in intent than pro-French. Its aims were national rather than revolutionary, and no social programme was seriously envisaged in the event of the rebellion succeeding. In fact the rebellion that actually took place was not the one planned. Most of those involved spent more time seeking to butcher their sectarian enemies than to propagate liberty and the rights of man; and the few French troops who did arrive in Ireland, a couple of months after the main outbreak was over, were greeted as soldiers of the Blessed Virgin. Irish historians, therefore, agree that their revolution, too, was in no danger of succeeding; or at least not without French help – which although it did materialise, did so either too early or too late.

The whole of Europe, therefore, avoided revolution in this so-called revolutionary age, with the exception of France itself and of those territories invaded or overrun by French armies. Even the latter sought to restore the old order the minute the French were gone – although of course Humpty-Dumpty could never be put together again. Can it be, then, that the message of the Revolution was not so universal after all, and the example of France by no means so obvious in its appeal as the participants in her revolution assumed? And if that is true, how did so many contemporaries, not to mention historians since, get it wrong?

For get it wrong they did. There can be no doubt that kings, nobles, churchmen and property-owners in general throughout Europe looked on what was happening in France with unalloyed horror, and regarded the example as thoroughly pernicious and dangerous. They really thought that they *were* threatened with revolution. How else do we explain the vigorous measures that governments took, and most nobles, clerics and property-owners supported, to repress all signs of subversion, opposition or even independent thought within their own countries? Far more obviously than a decade of liberty, the 1790s were a decade of repression, on both sides of the revolutionary divide. All over Europe secret policemen proliferated, books were banned, newspapers closed down or totally controlled, meetings heavily circumscribed or forbidden, suspects rounded up. Even in Great Britain, the freedoms so recently vaunted in 1788 at the *first* centenary of the Glorious Revolution were systematically circumscribed or limited. Public meetings were all but banned, newspapers licensed or prohibitively taxed, habeas corpus suspended. When trial by jury failed in 1794 to produce the convictions Pitt's government wanted, laws were enacted to strike at the same subversives by other routes. In order to fight the Rights of Man, the rights of Englishmen were set on one side.

All these measures, whether in England or on the Continent, were driven on by two convictions about the French Revolution. One was that it had unlocked the forces of popular savagery – whether called anarchy, tumultuous democracy, the swinish multitude, or any number of other epithets – and that this force threatened property and the social order with the envy and bestial appetites of the lower orders, who had nothing to lose. The populace of Paris could perhaps be pardoned for their role in the overthrow of the Bastille, which few could find it in their hearts to condemn; but by the time of the October Days, when the royal family was dragged back to Paris by a mob of raucous fishwives, the dangers were clear. The emergence of the *sans-culottes* three years later, amid scenes of massacre and terror, vividly underlined them. With such monstrous forces let loose, nothing less than mob rule, the folly of any change was vividly demonstrated. The principles of the French Revolution led straight to the destruction of social and political stability, a war against the haves on the part of the have nots. Nobody with anything to lose could possibly condone such an example, or wish news of it to be widely disseminated in a Europe where the numbers of the poor were perceived to be expanding at an already alarming rate. That was the first conviction. The second concerned what had brought this dangerous chaos and insubordination about. It had, of course, been the Enlightenment. Whether it was a deliberate conspiracy to subvert established governments, society or religion, or merely an ill-advised outburst of wild theorising unconnected with any possible consequences, the Enlightenment was what had sapped the fabric of the *ancien régime*, destroyed men's confidence in it, and instilled utopian aspirations into the lower orders. Free thought had driven out good sense. It would do the same in other countries if not stopped by decisive action. So what the repression of the 1790s was, above all, was an attempt to destroy the machinery of the Enlightenment – books, newspapers, clubs, meetings, intellectual networks. Revolution, the inference was, would have been avoided in France if all these things had not been allowed to get out of hand, corrode faith in the established order, and filter doctrines of insubordination down to the lower orders, filling them with dreams and desires that could only end in anarchy, chaos, and mayhem.

How well grounded were these driving convictions? That is the question I want to address in the rest of this essay. Recent work, I will argue, has cast important new light on the validity of both, which makes Europe's relative failure to respond to the appeal of the French revolutionary ideology less problematical that it might at first appear.

First, then, the question of the 'lower orders'. The whole drift of modern research on the popular movements of the later eighteenth century has emphasised that whoever those involved were, they were *not* the poor, and they were not people with nothing to lose. Whether we are talking about the Parisian *sans-culottes*, or the English artisans who joined the corresponding societies, or the Irish defenders sucked into the maelstrom of 1798, what we are dealing with is not the shiftless poor, who had nothing. The poor, as we have come to know them through the work of people like Olwen Hufton, Alan Forrest and Colin Jones, played no part in the age of revolution except as helpless victims of the well-intentioned but utopian theorising of the educated. The propertied classes had nothing to fear from the poor except petty crime – a persistent and very visible threat it is true, but no danger to the basic social order, because the poor were illiterate and above all unorganised. They lived below the level of public life, even in revolutionary Paris, as we know from George Rudé's analyses of those involved in the various revolutionary *journées*. The dreaded *gens sans aveu* are conspicuous by their absence. They even failed to respond to the way the revolutionary assemblies swept away the *ancien-régime* structure of charity and relief on which they relied, putting nothing in its place. The poor were passive victims of the revolutionary age, their numbers swelled, their resources considerably diminished, but with no chance of being able to affect anything that was done to them.

Professor Christie has recently argued (and he is by no means the first) that the existence of a poor law in Great Britain was one reason why that country avoided revolution in the 1790s. If what I have just suggested is right, the poor law was probably quite irrelevant, because the threat, if threat it was, came from elsewhere. The lower orders to be feared were those with something to lose. The activists in popular movements at the end of the eighteenth century were people in work, with jobs, with common interests that they clearly perceived, and with habits and traditions of combining and associating that they were easily able to adapt to political and public purposes. In other words they knew what they wanted (or rather what they did not want) and they knew how to organise themselves to achieve it.

There is nothing new about these observations. They have been made by a generation of social historians who have dissected popular movements and preoccupations with meticulous care and demonstrated their economic substructure and their mental preoccupation with economic morality. What mobilised them was the need to defend established values and practices: in that sense the Irish defenders were well named. They were, in fact, fundamentally movements against exploitation by the rich and the propertied, against economic innovations which threatened their livelihoods; against free trade in basic commodities which eroded their disposable incomes in a time of inflation by pushing up prices; against economic and social competition from intruders from outside their communities; and against those perceived as (though not necessarily objectively responsible for) perpetrating all these things.

From the moment when Albert Soboul recognised that his *sans-culottes* were not the first exemplars of the revolutionary proletariat in action, but were in fact pursuing a whole range of traditional aspirations behind their revolutionary and democratic rhetoric, the whole drift of modern research on the popular movements of the 1790s seems to me to have demonstrated their fundamental conservatism. Parliamentary reform itself in Great Britain, as I have already implied, was basically a conservative panacea: parliament is all right – it's just the people who get into it and what they are doing, or rather not doing, that need to be changed. What the people of Paris demanded from the revolution was above all what, since the 1760s, the *ancien régime* had increasingly tried to deny them – the moral economy of guaranteed supplies of basic commodities at affordable prices, what they eventually achieved by the Maximum of 1793-4.

Another thing recent research – in this case even more recent research – has revealed, is how much all this had in common with counter-revolutionary popular movements. They too were basically protests against change, although in this case the accelerated change brought about by the revolution itself – the economic disruption; the sundering of local communities brought about by the exponentially expanding ambitions of government and the new local elites drafted into its service and profiting handsomely from it at the expense of other less well-off groups; above all the moral upheaval caused by the anti-clericalism that soon became a central feature of the French revolutionary ideology. These features have been most deeply explored, of course, in studies of the anti-revolutionary outbreaks in the French west by Paul Bois, Charles Tilly, Don Sutherland and Roger Dupuy. But quite clearly much the same considerations were operative in anti-revolutionary outbreaks elsewhere in Europe, particularly those of 1798, which occurred all the way from Flanders to Calabria. In all of them the arrival of the French brought a sudden acceleration in the pace of change – economic , social, institutional, and above all perhaps religious – which first disoriented and then disgusted a populace with a tenuous but nonetheless tenacious stake in stability and established patterns of behaviour. The result was a massive rejection of the French Revolution and all it stood for, a popular movement or series of movements whose size completely dwarfed that of the Parisian *sans-culottes* and their embattled friends and sympathisers in other places inside France or abroad. As Don Sutherland has suggested for France, and Tim Blanning for Europe as a whole, the true popular, in the sense of most widely-supported, movement of the 1790s was not that for, but that *against* the French Revolution and its ideology. Here again, incidentally, we are not dealing with the poor, but rather echelons of society (although this time rural society) with things to lose – stable rents, common lands, local property unexpectedly thrown onto the market by the new order; local autonomy threatened by the urban outsiders entrusted with enforcing the legislation of new regimes; the reassuring moral framework given to rural communities by established religion; the security of able-bodied sons now taken from the family economy by conscription.

If, then, the *sans-culottes* and hundreds of thousands of rebels against the Revolution and its message throughout western Europe were both characterised by hostility to change, how was it that they ended up on different sides of the revolutionary divide: the one group at the cutting edge (quite literally) of revolutionary radicalism; the other espousing churches, kings, routine, superstition and the rule of aristocracy? One reason, of course, is that conservatism does not preclude conflicting interests. Quite obviously urban *sans-culottes* and peasants were on different sides of the eternal conflict between consumers and producers, where one man's moral economy may be another man's pauperisation. One of the greatest, and by now best-explored dramas, of the French revolution is the way these town-country antagonisms worked themselves out. But there is another and surely at the time even more important factor. Operating in Europe's intellectual capital, enjoying a level of literacy far beyond that of most peasants, the *sans-culottes* had their conservatism catalysed into a democratic ideology by the language of the articulate, educated politicians operating from October 1789 in their midst. They were, in other words, infected by the Enlightenment, just as the men of order and government all over Europe believed. The Enlightenment in general passed the lower classes by – but not in a Paris dominated by an Assembly full of its self-professed adherents, an Assembly which owed its very survival to popular action, and with which, therefore, the active Parisian populace had umbilical links between 1789 and 1795. The experience of the Revolution educated the city's working elites, remoulding their traditional concerns into a new democratic ideology. This could not have happened if the language of those making the Revolution in its successive ruling assemblies had not been steeped in the concepts of the Enlightenment. Which brings me to the second element in the analysis of those seeking to avoid revolution in the 1790s by action against its vectors.

The anti-revolutionary actions that governments took in the 1790s, and which I discussed earlier, were based upon a historical perception about what had caused the Revolution in France: it had been the Enlightenment. It was an analysis with a long future ahead of it, and one can see why. It had an attractive and comprehensive simplicity, and it was particularly useful in explaining the Revolution's attack on the church – which of course, the Enlightenment had also attacked. What's more, there was no need, with this explanation, to think about more painful and complex possibilities – that there might have been something seriously wrong with the *ancien régime*, and that what had been or gone wrong might be very difficult, not to say painful, to analyse. Far simpler and more comfortable to jump straight to the conclusion that a perfectly viable order had been subverted by a millenarian intellectual conspiracy. Above all, perhaps, there was the obvious fact, to which I have already referred, that the revolutionaries of France themselves, and their friends in other countries, gloried in being the heirs and executors of the Enlightenment, claimed it for their own, appropriated its language, and openly revered its leading exponents as their prophets and inspiration. Their enemies saw no reason to challenge the attribution. This interpretation of what brought the Revolution about remained, and remains, influential in conservative, and above all Catholic circles. But by the mid twentieth century most serious historians had abandoned it in favour of grittier, more materialistic, social and economic explanations – which in their turn heavily influenced attempts to explain why other countries avoided revolution. The problem is that all these social and economic analyses seem in recent years to have run into the sand. The old Marxist or at least *Marxisant* orthodoxies are now long discredited. Alfred Cobban's attempts to forge something to put in their place have also led nowhere. Many, accordingly, have felt pushed towards the conclusion that the Revolution had no socio-economic *causes* (although of course it must have had socio-economic *origins*, rather a different thing). Perhaps, then, we need to turn back to intellectual causes after all; and to the Enlightenment?

I think we do, but by no means in the traditional way. Nothing, I think, did more to undermine the old regime, and prepare the way for its collapse than a general failure of confidence in it among a wide range of the king's subjects over its last thirty years or so – and rational, utilitarian criticism of the way it worked played an important role in this erosion. On the other hand, the Enlightenment was not confined to France; elites espoused it in other countries, and there is little evidence that a similar erosion of confidence occurred there – with the possible exception of the Dutch Republic. The really dangerous role played by the Enlightenment, in fact, was in its effects not on subjects, but on governments. They were far quicker to espouse 'enlightened' values of rationality and utilitarianism than those over whom they ruled; but when they tried to act according to such precepts, they ran into trouble – whether we are talking about anti-free trade riots in Spain in 1766, or France in 1775, or resistance to the innovations of Joseph II in Belgium and Hungary during the last years of his reign, or universal rejection of the headlong attempts of Struensee to recast the whole of Danish society and the Danish economy along physiocratic lines in the early 1770s. In these cases Enlightenment certainly could lead, as in Denmark or Belgium, to the overthrow of established authority; but the impetus came from resistance to it, not inspiration by it. In this perspective, it was governments that were led astray by the Enlightenment and seduced from their duty, not subjects.

In this France was no exception. The influence of enlightened principles can be found throughout French public and administrative life during the closing decades of the *ancien régime*: but in the context of the government's other failures – international, political, financial – it only contributed to the draining away of confidence which culminated in the collapse of August 1788. The men who picked up the abandoned reins of power the following year believed that too little Enlightenment had underlain the *ancien régime*'s failure. The populace whose intervention saved the Revolution during its first great crisis in July 1789, however, believed that there had been too much. What they expected from the new dawn was a return to a pre-enlightened world of imagined security and stability, underpinned by a controlled economy. Once the National Assembly moved to Paris, they were in a position to insist on it for a number of years – and it was the need to justify this role which sparked the elaboration of the democratic *sans-culotte* ideology which came to be seen as the founding experience of modern popular politics. No other ordinary people, however, were in this unique position of being able to dictate to a national government, and accordingly their experience of the 1790s, wherever they were, was very different.

In other places, when the French Revolution or its fellow-travellers took power, the populace was exposed to the full glare of Enlightenment; or rather Enlightenment radicalised by the political experience of the summer of 1789 in France, and schematised into the anti-feudal, anti-privileged rights of man ideology proclaimed then, and subsequently amplified with anti-Catholicism and republicanism. It proved deeply unpopular, especially when carried abroad on the points of French bayonets. How could it not? To be put into effect, it required the overthrow of most of the major landmarks of institutional, social, economic and spiritual life. The only people to welcome it, where it was welcomed at all, were a small minority of intellectuals; most of them long identified before 1789 with enlightened ideas. I am not claiming that this had made them plot or dream of revolution, any more than the men who came to prominence in 1789 had in France. But once revolution came about they embraced it as a totally unexpected opportunity to make Enlightenment a practical reality – again so much like the men of 1789 in France. Should we not, in fact, see the revolutionary age as an attempt to seize control all over Europe by an intelligentsia, *l'élite des lumières*, convinced of the moral superiority of their own ideas and, because of that, determined now the opportunity offered, to enforce them on everybody else? In that sense the great bogey of contemporary monarchs, international Jacobinism, perhaps had more to it than historians are normally prepared to admit. By that I do not mean that there was some sort of quasi-masonic, concerted conspiracy, of the sort discerned by Barruel in 1797, and in which so many people plainly believed. I mean that certain types of men, everywhere, instantly recognised the value of what like-minded fellows were doing, and derived encouragement, inspiration, and incentive from the news. In that sense the ideology of the Rights of Man, the Enlightenment radicalised and schematised, really was a programme of universal application and relevance.

Everywhere – and this is my final but crucial point – everywhere its appeal was not felt by the generality of mankind, but only by a small, well-educated minority. It varied enormously in size, both geographically and temporally, shrinking steadily as the 1790s went on. But having been handed power – whether in France in 1789 as a result of a comprehensive state breakdown, or elsewhere later in the nineties as a result of French invasion and support – it was quite understandably determined both to use that power to implement more enlightened policies, and to hang on to it when opposed or challenged. The problem it faced was that its vision of the world as it should be was opposed or challenged by most of the rest of society – and by none more so than the lower orders. The only ones really on the enlightened elites' side were the *sans-culottes* of Paris, and even they were determined to prevent the elite from pursuing the economic policies in which they believed. But this unsteady alliance gave the Jacobinical cause a popular allure which completely misled and distracted the established authorities of other countries, watching with horror what was happening. They thought Jacobinism enjoyed popular support. Therefore the one thing they hardly ever did, in their attempts to avoid revolution, was try to enlist popular support and try to mobilise it against Jacobinism.

There were some isolated instances of it being tried. There was Cardinal Ruffo's Sanfedist army raised in Calabria in 1798, and above all there were Pitt's attempts to rally loyalist opinion in the British Isles, either in the encouragement he gave to patriotic associations, or the concessions he made to the Irish Catholics down to 1793. The record of success in these cases was to say the least mixed. Ruffo's forces soon got out of control. By 1795 and 1796 unrest was more widespread in England than before the patriotic associations were launched; and concessions to the Irish Catholics arguably exacerbated rather than assuaged the lethal sectarian antagonisms of Ireland. These experiences seemed to underline the wisdom of not playing with fire. If what I have been arguing is right, the measures which established authorities did adopt to prevent or avoid revolution in the 1790s were not, as they are too often portrayed, misguided attempts to dam a mighty and irresistible flood. Their attacks on the machinery of the Enlightenment were sensible and even effective measures to strike at, and shut up, people who fostered revolution, and among whom the idea and attractions of it flourished. Persecuting a few Jacobins, and trying to destroy the machinery and networks through which their ideology circulated, would not in themselves have avoided revolution. The odds in any case against a repeat of the French experience in any other country were simply too great. In that sense the danger was much exaggerated. But for those who believed it greater than it was, and wanted to avoid it, to attack the intelligentsia and its institutions was probably the right place to start.

Index